What people are saying
about the new paradigm;
Uniqueness is a Red Striped Zebra©

Here it is folks! The secret recipe for doing business in the 21st Century!

Francis X. Maguire
Former Senior VP; Federal Express and KFC
CEO Hearth Communications Group
Internationally acclaimed speaker

The Middle East

In today's competitive marketplace, you must constantly strive to keep your edge. You need to be ahead of everyone else. We at Arpal Gulf have achieved this because we are evolving into a Red Striped Zebra company. We are *miles* ahead of the competition ... and still don't have all the stripes. It works because we see and do things differently from everyone else; we learned and are still learning to do that through the Zebra process.

Red Striped Zebra not only changed our business ... it changed my life! That's easy to say, but not easy to say when it comes from the heart! Neill Newton and John Gilbody are special people, but don't take my word for it, meet them for yourself and find out why.

John Gavigan - General Manager
Arpal Gulf LLC - Dubai, United Arab Emirates

United Kingdom

I've been involved in this firm in a senior capacity for thirty years. I can quite honestly say that in this period, this represents the best business development programme - indeed the best mind-opening programme, that we've *ever* experienced. Expert attitude-adjusters, or mind-shifters! Your Zebra programme is exceptional and you're a credit to the World of Enterprise!

Geoff Adam, MBE.
Chairman, R.P. Adam Ltd., Selkirk, Scotland, (U.K.)
(Winner of the Queen's Award for Export Excellence)

Our business here is going absolutely crazy. Busy all the time. Your Red Striped Zebra strategies have made a difference to our brochures, e-mails and marketing. It really works! Especially in our highly competitive travel industry!

George Glen - Owner
World Direct Travel, Glasgow. (U.K.)

United States

Neill Newton's Red Striped Zebra strategy is enormously appealing and valuable for any type of business. It will help you to break free from the herd, differentiate yourself from the competition and be a leader rather than a follower.

Robert Kriegel Ph.D. ... Best selling author of:
If it Ain't Broke ... Break It! - Sacred Cows Make the Best Burgers,
... Internationally known speaker

If you are *starting* a business, *growing* a business or wanting to *transform* your business this is a MUST READ! This is *not* a flavor of the month, here today, gone tomorrow work. If you follow the strategies and steps that are outlined, your opportunities for long-term success will be greatly enhanced.

Howard D. Putnam
Former CEO Southwest Airlines and Braniff International
Speaker, Author, Advisor to Business
Chairman - Aircraft Interior Resources

Neill's message of embracing change with applied creativity generates excitement to reach for high performance and financial goals.

Jane Pierotti - Nationally acclaimed speaker.
Former National Product Marketing Director; IBM
and VP Marketing; Holiday Inns

I enjoyed your Red Striped Zebra seminar and brought back several new concepts and ideas that I presented to our marketing committee. They were very well received and we actually were able to use them for our new marketing directive. Very thought provoking!

Belvia Bourland
Vice President - Senatobia Bank

I wasn't sure if I could relinquish six hours of valuable time to another 'marketing' seminar. But after 30 minutes I was hanging on Neill's every word. The Red Striped Zebra program is not just for independent marketers, like myself ... but about any business desiring to rise above the din. No more 'me too' thinking. Original. Mind-bending. Fun. That's how I describe this dynamic program. Trash your next newspaper ad and spend your money on a Zebra seminar instead.

Robyn S. Farber - President
Farber Marketing and Public Relations - MS

Uniqueness is a Red Striped Zebra is so appropriate, because of all the acquisitions and mergers taking place. This program is packed full of useful tools to build upon and stand out from the crowd. A most dynamic approach. Not only educational, but entertaining. Your ability to capture your audience is exceptional.

Kathy B. Smiley - First Vice President
Planters Bank & Trust Company

Thank you for the wonderful presentation of the Uniqueness is a Red Striped Zebra program. As you can see from the enclosed evaluation summary, the effectiveness of your strategies was highly rated.

Cheryl Forbes - Director - Small Business
Chamber of Commerce, Memphis

You've significantly energized the marketing staff with the Zebra program, making a real difference in our ability to serve our clients.

Joseph Schifano - CEO
Regional Blood Center - Jackson TN

Australia
You're obviously the leader of the pack in teaching people how to be successful!

Harvey Baden - Group Training Manager
Pfizer Pharmaceuticals - Sydney, Australia

Just a sample of the exciting results being gained in Scotland, England, the Middle East, Australia and the United States.

Your business can be next!

Also by Neill Newton

The Magic of Metamorphosis (audio)
PlanetZebra (audio)
ZebraWrite (manual with audio)
The Good Guys Wear White Hats (audio)
Standing on the Shoulders of Giants

Uniqueness is a Red Striped Zebra (13 part television program)

Neill Newton is available for a limited number of speaking engagements an d consulting assignments, time permitting.

Also available: A selection of audio cassette and video programs, newsletter s and reports encompassing the Uniqueness is a Red Striped Zebra coaching .

For further information, contact Newton World Training Inc.
Post Office Box 242023, Memphis 38124 TN.

Phone: (901) 683 4244 or Toll-Free: 1-888-683 4244.

WWW.PlanetZebra.com

Uniqueness is a Red Striped Zebra

Dare to Break Free ...
Like a Red Striped Zebra

Neill Newton

Published by:
FALKIRK HOUSE
Memphis TN

Library of Congress Card Number: 00-100513

ISBN: 0-9673381-0-7

Publisher's - Cataloging In Publication
(Prepared by Quality Books, Inc.)

Newton, Neill.
    Uniqueness is a red striped zebra : dare to
break free-- like a red striped zebra / Neill
Newton. -- 1st ed.
    p. cm
    Includes index
    ISBN: 0-9673381-0-7

    1. Marketing--Management. 2. Success in
business. 3. Creative thinking. I. Title.

HF5415.13.N49 2000   658.8
                QB199-1905

Zebra herd logo created by: *Jeff Lewis*
Book cover design: *Foster & Foster*

.

Dedication and Acknowledgments

To Georjean, my wife, for 30 years of support and encouragement.

To my son Adam, for inspiration and perseverance.

To Anita Chandler, for backing and belief.

To these legends who freely offered their support:

- Jane Pierotti, celebrated speaker, former National Product Marketing Director; IBM.
- Francis X. Maguire, international speaker, former Senior VP FedEx and KFC.
- Dr. Robert Kriegel Ph.D., best selling author of: *If It Ain't Broke ... Break It!* and *Sacred Cows Make the Best Burgers*.
- Howard Putnam, acclaimed former CEO of Southwest Airlines.
- Jon Spoelstra, former President of the New Jersey Nets and author of *Ice to Eskimos*.
- Jeff Slutsky, author of *Street Fighter Marketing*.

To Sir Tom Farmer, founder of the *Kwik-Fit* auto repair chain in the United Kingdom, who offered his timeless wisdom on our audio tape programs.

And a special dedication to John Gilbody, the acclaimed
British business consultant, who joined me in developing
and spreading the Red Striped Zebra message.

---

*If I have seen further,
it's by standing on the shoulders of giants*
Sir Isaac Newton

To every business owner and manager who has the foresight to read this book, to invest in the concept of breaking free and standing apart ... and for desiring to make their business as

Unique ... as a Red Striped Zebra

CONTENTS

Foreword

When I was President and CEO of Southwest Airlines in Dallas, TX, our first priority was to develop a clear and concise *vision* for the fledgling company. My role (I was the second CEO) was to position Southwest for the future in a *unique* way. We wanted to be *different* from all the others in the industry and to lay a foundation for long-term profitability and success. This meant building an infrastructure and processes that could accommodate growth. It meant developing a marketing approach that was different. It meant developing a culture and attracting the right kinds of people. It meant *hiring attitudes* and *teaching them skills*. Bottom line improvement comes through people; people that think cross functionally, have a passion for their work, and have fun!

If you want to be a *Red Striped Zebra*, you have to start with the vision and establish your uniqueness. Until you figure out who you are, *understand what business* or *businesses you are in* and establish your uniqueness, success will be difficult to attain. In the case of Southwest, we determined we were not an airline. We were in the business of *mass transportation*. That is a totally different mind set and business than being an airline. We focussed on growing our own markets from the automobile and the living room. We doubled the size of a market within twelve months when we entered it. We didn't steal from the competitors. We developed a value proposition based on frequency of service, simplicity, high productivity, safety, price and *a great spirit in our people* that fliers come to love again and again. Southwest has been a profit sharing company with its people and a profitable company for its stakeholders every year for twenty five years. No other air carrier can match that performance!

Neill Newton called me three years ago from Memphis, TN and introduced himself. He told me of his upbringing in Australia, and of his successes and frustrations with traditional ways of doing business in his earlier days in insurance. He had done much research and experimentation over many years in management and marketing looking for the keys to unlock old mind-sets, and to get people to think in a fresh and forward looking way. He had found solutions and brought them to the USA in 1991, to further develop them through speaking, training, consulting, writing, etc.

He explained some of the *Red Striped Zebra* concepts and beliefs to me on the telephone that day. I then asked him why he called me and he replied that he understood that I had practiced many of the concepts and had written about our experiences at Southwest and at Braniff International, in "The Winds of Turbulence." We stayed in touch and eventually got together in Memphis for a long and satisfying recording session matching concepts and experiences together on a unique audio tape program of four tapes, called *The Magic of Metamorphosis; Transforming your business for success.*

Since then, he has launched his work globally, assisting grateful clients in not just the U.S., but in Scotland, England, Australia, Europe and the United Arab Emirates.

The concepts and strategies outlined by Neill in this book do work! Neill shares himself as a person as he weaves ideas, specific how to's, and interesting case studies throughout the chapters.

If you are *starting* a business, *growing* a business or wanting to *transform* your business this is a MUST READ! This is *not* a flavor of the month, here today, gone tomorrow work. If you follow the strategies and steps that are outlined, your opportunities for long-term success will be greatly enhanced.

Howard D. Putnam
Speaker, Author, Advisor to Business
Chairman - Aircraft Interior Resources
Former CEO Southwest Airlines and
Braniff International

Reno, NV   June 1999

Giddyup!

Meet the Red Striped Zebra

Imagine! ... In your 'mind's eye' imagine a herd of Zebra feeding on a wide, dusty African plain. Hundreds of Zebra with that familiar bold black and white pattern. See how all those Zebra blend together and create an impregnable wall of stripes ... and see how difficult it is to tell where one Zebra stops and the other ends? That's because they were all created to be 'indistinguishable' from each other!

Now, imagine one of those Zebra with bold, red stripes. See how that Zebra stands apart from all the others. In fact, it is hard to 'not' notice this peculiar animal. Bold red stripes that set it apart and causes it to *get noticed*.

The Lions of competition also notice this Zebra, so he must perform 'differently' to all others. He must zig when they zag, out-perform, out-maneuver, out-wit and out-do every other Zebra in the herd ... or get eaten!

Today's Businesses

In business today, there exists fierce competition, the likes of which we've never experienced. Mounting and unrelenting. The Zebra herd has grown so large it is difficult to compete with. It's become a global herd!

Too many business animals ... all doing the very same thing. And many of these businesses that make up the herd are doing things *exactly* the same as all others. It is difficult for customers to see where one business differs from the other ... and even to distinguish between services and products. Same-ol'-same-o'. One hotel is like another, one airline is very similar to all others, one dry cleaner, dentist, doctor or lawyer ... much like another. Black and white Zebra ... all trying to attract the same customers with the same tired offerings!

The Red
Striper

Not so the Red Striped Zebra! His difference is by being *different.* He does not try to be 'better than' all the others ... he is simply 'different to' the black and whites. He gets noticed and attracts attention because he stands apart.

The Red Striped Zebra business does things differently. Performs differently. Treats customers differently. Offers different guarantees, sales offers and services. Promotes differently ... even packages products differently! And customers love it! Why? Because people (customers) are confused by change. They are confused by the overwhelming variety and offering. They have become cynical and mistrusting of businesses which promise and don't deliver. They are inundated and saturated with thousands of sales messages daily which have become a blur. A blur of black and white Zebra!

Now, they are seeking the Red Striped Zebra business
which stands apart from the crowd ... and
offers them something different.

That's what this book is all about. Being *different to* ... not *better than*. It's all about creativity, innovation and uniqueness in business ... it's about getting 'noticed' ... and it's about seeing your business through the eyes of customers ... not your eyes!

And it's about 'daring' to break free from the crowd

... like a Red Striped Zebra

Newton's Law

17 Success Laws for Business-Breakthrough

I. Creating the PERCEPTION in the customer's minds that your business is their _preferred_ and _only_ choice to buy from is vital for success.

II. Breaking free from the crowd will eradicate the INVISIBILITY that your business may suffer from, and will help the business to _get noticed_ and _attract_ more customers.

III. Creating more _value_ and ADVANTAGES will make you far more _valuable_ to customers.

IV. Providing customers with an AWESOME customer service philosophy that _inspires_, and _spoils_, will guarantee their _continuous return_ and loyalty.

V. Creating potent, _results-expected_ advertising copy, rather than "corporate" advertising, will increase the Magnetic Value (MV) of your adverts, resulting in spectacular sales increases.

VI. Marketing strategies that work well in other industries, can be _borrowed_ and _employed_ in yours. In many instances, these borrowed strategies will produce far more stunning results than what they do in their host industries. Adding a number of these borrowed strategies will give you _exponential_ growth.

VII. TRANSFERRING the "risk of buying" from customers and back onto you will dramatically increase their buying decisions ... and your sales.

VIII. Providing customers with a Perception of Value Education (POVE) about your product or service will increase sales, and position that product or service as the _only_ one to buy.

IX. *PERSONALIZING the business so that customers relate on an emotional level and human relationship level will boost sales.*

X. *Developing a SYNERGISTIC partnering relationships with complimentary, (or even competitor's businesses) spectacularly multiplies your available customer base, sales and income.*

XI. *MAXIMIZING the 3 areas of business growth; (More customers, price, repeat sales) gives a percentage increase in each. Combining the three, gives <u>exponentially</u> large percentage increases.*

XII. *Discovering and implementing the <u>hidden assets</u> in your business, will help you increase new sales and profit resources.*

XIII. *Exercising the Customer's Long-Term Value (CLTV) will give you <u>absolute control</u> of your business, increase sales, and secure your future.*

XIV. *Developing and growing Customer's Perpetual Buying Habits (CPBH) guarantees <u>continuous sales</u> and profit.*

XV. *Learning how to sell more products and services to <u>existing</u> and <u>inactive</u> customers will give new sales and revitalization to your business.*

XVI. *Adding <u>innovation</u>, <u>uniqueness</u> and <u>creativity</u> will place your business ahead of both change .... and competitors.*

XVII. *Installing quality, either in a formal process, or as a philosophy, is paramount for success in this fiercely competitive world. Undergirding quality products or service with a succinct UMP will give you an <u>unfair marketing advantage.</u>*

Uniqueness
is a
Red Striped
Zebra

Dare to break free from the crowd, get noticed and attract more customers to your business ... time and time again!

I received an excited call from Australia. It was John Gilbody, the acclaimed British business consultant who has worked in all points of the globe for some of the world's most recognizable corporations. He had just finished a grueling session with a group of academics, leading business people, scientists and government personnel. The mission was to lead this oftentimes polemic group through a maze of decision making, in order to reach a new direction for some of Australia's natural resource problems.

John told me it was very tough going, possibly the worst in his career, with people 'at each other's throats' ... but the only thing that saved the day was to forget about the 'old' ways of thinking about business consulting ... and to apply the creative effulgence of the Red Striped Zebra program. To introduce a totally new philosophy that comprised idea generation, creative strategies, innovative ways at looking at things ... and a fresh, new approach to problems.

He said it was like a magic wand. No longer were participants focussing on problems, point scoring with each other, promoting their hidden agendas and demonstrating outright hostility. The Red Striped Zebra thinking caught them off guard, got them excited and took them through a *perceptive-mind shift*. It worked!

New Paradigm
for a Chaotic World

John then told me that through his four decades in academia, plus consulting worldwide with leading corporations, and now with this group of professors and business leaders, he was totally convinced that the *Uniqueness is a Red Striped Zebra©* program is the solution for doing business in the new Millennium. The new model for business success ... in fact, he called it;

The new 'paradigm' for a world in chaos

John had worked with me for a few years in presenting the Zebra program to client firms, from Scotland to the United Arab Emirates, England to the United States, and knew first hand the potency of the program in helping businesses break free from the crowd, getting noticed and growing exceedingly. But until he stood by himself in a group such as this, he didn't realize the excitement it could engender and the *fire of enthusiasm* that could sweep through a group.

Perceptive
Mind-Shift

Some time back, I received a letter from Geoff Adam, MBE, the Chairman of *R.P.Adam Ltd.*, a chemical manufacturer in Scotland. John and I had completed an in-house seminar for this firm and Geoff was responding. All their management team had joined us in seminar on a cool September weekend at the magnificent Duke of Roxburgh's 'Sunlaws House' estate in Kelso, Scotland.

In this spectacular setting we presented the Red Striped Zebra program to 'kick start' this 107 year old firm into a brand new direction. In part, the letter reads:

> *"I have been involved in this firm for over thirty years. In this period of time this represented the best business development seminar - indeed the best mind opening seminar - that I and my colleagues have ever experienced. We view you as expert attitude adjusters and mind shifters!"*

Wow! Bloody Brilliant! That said it all for us. We had labored for years in business transformation work ... and in developing the Zebra program. But here was an eminent business leader who had put his century old firm into our hands and was saying things like mind-opening, attitude adjusters and mind shifters.

The Penny
Drops

We had never thought of the Red Striped Zebra program as mind-shifting. We had labored long and hard over the years to develop strategies and formulas for business success. And yet, when we noticed the *perceptive mind-shift* in people it started to dawn on us. The penny started to drop. We started to realize that if people are exposed to the Red Striped Zebra thinking and strategies, they do undergo a change, simply because they have been 'locked in' to a system for years that taught them the 'correct' way of doing business.

The Zebra thinking released them from all that and showed that there is a better way, an easier way to attract more customers and make more sales.

There Has to
Be a Better Way

In the late 70's, just prior to my entering the business consultancy and education field, I labored long and hard as a Regional Sales Manager in New South Wales, for an insurance firm. I found this position to be frustrating, to say the least. My work involved constant recruitment of potential insurance agents, then training them for their new careers. At best, after recruiting a number of people, we would manage to grow the agency by only one person per year. Endless time, money and training went on people that would simply drop out after a period, some as long as two years.

I was constantly saying to the firm's management that there *must* be a *better* way to grow a business. And there must be a better way for these frustrated new agents to grow their businesses. There was something missing, something we were not focussing on.

The two missing factors for business success

1: The People
Factor

It became apparent after a number of years searching for these answers. In fact, it became crystal clear! This frustrating period became the catalyst for my headlong pursuit into finding ways to make businesses work better. I was constantly asking; *"What must one do to win more business?" "How do we make 'more' sales, attract more customers, make our businesses irresistible?"*

What became apparent was the *focus*. I started to notice that businesses were 'out of focus' with what was really important. Their focus was from *their* viewpoint. Certainly not the customer's viewpoint. They had forgotten that customers are people. In forgetting this businesses had changed the word *people* into *customers, clients* or *guests* - depending on the profession, and further expanded names to *prospects, sales, targets, goals*. They were not seen as living, thinking, feeling, caring and educated people with needs and desires. They were simply seen as the next target for a sale ... and dollars.

Back in the insurance years, I was training agents to look at people as prospects. Their mission was to convert those *prospects* into *appointments*, then into *sales*. We even had a name for old, cold prospects. They were called *china eggs*. They were not taught to see people as human beings and work at becoming a *valuable asset* in their lives. It was a numbers game, both in sifting through prospects and in training and recruiting agents.

A sophisticated 'foot-in-the-door' selling system that replaced people with cold names. And this system was not related to just the insurance trade. It covered the broad spectrum of business, from the small firms to the large. It was the 'us only' thinking. We (the business people) thought of our desires, needs, goals and businesses as 'more important' than customer's needs. We had forgotten that our *greatest asset* was customers!

2: The Conformity Factor

In losing the focus on the customer, businesses did not need to *please, delight* or *thrill* customers. They simply had to *sell* them something. And because they didn't have to try hard, they didn't have to try to be too much *different* from all others. They simply conformed to a business 'standard'.

In my insurance days, most of the firms looked similar. (And still do!). There were no firms doing anything *different*. No firms trying to stand apart from the crowd. They were as *indistinguishable* from each other as any Zebra would in a herd of black and whites.

Today, the field has not changed much. There are a few firms doing things differently. Computer firms like *Gateway* sell their goods via a toll-free number rather than by retail stores. Car dealers such as *Saturn* sell with a no-haggle atmosphere, but by and large the majority of businesses still conform to the norm. Not too many have 'dared to break free' like a Red Striped Zebra would in that herd of black and whites. They haven't yet realized that customers are on the prowl for those firms which stand apart and perform *differently*. These 'new Millennium' customers are seeking firms that are innovative ... and firms which can *make their lives better!*

The new era of fierce competition and overwhelming change

Back in the early years of the development of the Red Striped Zebra program, businesses did not want to know us. Why change? Things were going well. Business was booming. Today, the story is very different! There is so much more at stake now. The world has changed so much and so quickly. And to thrive in business the two aforementioned mistakes need to be corrected immediately. Businesses must learn to *stand apart* and customers need to be *put first!*

Three Characteristics of Chaos

"Are We There Yet?" Many would like the answer to be a resounding yes, for the headlong rush at warp speed that has overtaken our fragile planet has become almost too much to handle.

The operative word now being heard worldwide is *chaos*. A world in *chaotic change*. Some see change as exciting and exhilarating, but for most it is fraught with the three characteristics of chaos;

- **Uncertainty.** *Uncertainty for the future floods our minds daily. We simply do not know what is in store - good or bad. There is nothing rock solid in business to rely on.*

- **Confusion.** *Just trying to fathom what to do for the best, what new idea, strategy, information system or machinery to install in our businesses, is perplexing.*

- **Upheaval.** *This world is certainly in upheaval, for never before on this planet has mankind experienced so much rapid, mind-numbing change.*

> *Never before on this planet has mankind experienced so much rapid, mind-numbing CHANGE!*

It's a sort of 'controlled' chaos ... we seem to be in control - to a point, but nevertheless, it's definitely chaos! ... A tiger by the tale!

The Chaotic Twins - Change and Competition

It is this *change* and rising *competition* that fuels this chaos. They are the chaotic twins. But, business people in particular are the most troubled, for they are the *life-blood* of a nation. They are troubled because with chaotic change comes higher demands for investment in information technology, systems, marketing ... and in training people to simply keep up to the rapid advances being made.

Coupled to this is the overwhelming competition, domestically and abroad, causing available markets and dollars to shrink.

- *As down-sizing increase, hordes of new businesses are rapidly emerging as laid-off workers spread their wings into their own ventures*
- *Adding fuel to the fire is the fierce and growing competition from overseas products and firms*
- *And reductions in available foreign export markets as emerging countries rise to compete with ours.*

It is time for YOUR business to break free ...
and become as Unique as a Red Striped Zebra

The New Paradigm for a World in Chaos: Uniqueness is a Red Striped Zebra

That's a bold statement to make isn't it? Saying that this program is the new paradigm, the new model, the answer to chaos and the formula for outrageous business success.

Believe me, I was not always this bold. All I was ever trying to do was find a better way to make more sales for businesses. I found it, simple as that! (More precisely, I developed it, over twenty years of constructive research and plain hard work!). I named it Red Striped Zebra because that is exactly what it is. A program that helps businesses to *get noticed*.

What our clients say though is a different matter. If they see it as the answer, the new paradigm ... and the perceptive mind-shifter, then we will gladly accept their endorsements. Because the more people who get *excited* about it the more opportunity we will have to fulfill my life's mission; that of taking the Zebra program throughout the world.

Our clients now extend to three continents, but we have only scratched the surface in coaching businesses in how to break free ... and to thrive in business, like a Red Striped Zebra.

Let's now look at what happens to a business which dares to break free ... Red Striped Zebra style

Putting on the Stripes

The Red Striped Zebra program and philosophy is not defined in just treating people right. Nor is it in understanding the *psychology of buying* (antithetical to the *psychology of selling*). Neither will you understand it in thinking it is just a 'spit and polish' job ... or a fresh coat of paint for your business. It is too complex for that!

No, the Zebra program cannot be defined so tightly, because we have found that every one of our clients alters, adjusts and modifies its strategies, formulas and concepts to suit their business' varying needs. It is always emerging. It is always discovering 'new' ways to grow businesses. The questions I asked twenty years ago are still ringing in my ears. More answers are found daily. This book will become obsolete soon, (hopefully) because we will have expanded the program light-years in all directions as clients relate newly discovered Zebra methods that have increased their businesses. The Red Striped Zebra program is a work in progress. It will give runaway success now ... but will continue to enlarge and offer far more than what this book outlines.

But for the sake of brevity, here's a six-fold approach to form a framework for you ... and in the ensuing chapters you will come to understand more.

Six-Fold Success
Foundation

To adopt the Red Striped Zebra program, your business must have a six-fold success foundation. These six form the foundation to build upon and to take the business to new heights.

The six-fold foundation for the Red Striped Zebra business

1. *Create a positive 'perception'*
2. *Remove the 'invisibility' your business may suffer from*
3. *Personalize your business*
4. *Individualize your business*
5. *Increase the 'Magnetic Value' of your advertising*
6. *Incorporate 'Awesome Customer Service'*

Although these are covered in detail in the following chapters, we will expand on them a here. Let's look at perception first.

1. You must create the PERCEPTION in customer's minds that YOUR business is their 'preferred' choice and the 'only' one worth considering buying from. This will be covered in detail in *The Good Guys Wear White Hats.*

   Just imagine ... customers thinking that your business is their *preferred choice*. If you can do that, they will be coming to you in their thousands. If you can somehow manage to change their thinking, their perception they have of your business, you will have runaway success.

   Strategies you will need to implement:
   Unique Marketing Perception (UMP)
   Perception of Value Education (POVE)

2. You must remove any INVISIBILITY your businesses suffers from, and make it highly visible, so that it 'stands apart' from the crowd.

Many people think their businesses are highly visible, when in fact they are as hidden as any number of black and white Zebra that stand in a herd, unnoticed. To truly remove any invisibility, you must become highly visible by being 'different to' ... rather than being 'better than' ... and it's to do with the color of your stripes!

Strategies you will need to implement:
Marketing Pillars, Customer's Long Term Value (CLTV), Synergy, Customer's Perpetual Buying Habits (CPBH).

3. You must PERSONALIZE your business so that customers relate on an emotional and human relationship level.

In a very crowded marketplace, people are far more apt to want to buy from someone, or some business, they know. The old principles of *trust, confidence* and *reliance* are far more important now than ever before. It's like recognizing a reassuring face in a crowded room.

Strategies you will need to implement:
Pro-Active Service, not re-active, Brochure Personalizing, Business Cards and Letterhead Personalizing, Advertisement Personalizing, Newsletter Personalizing, etc.

Before we move onto No. 4, let's expand more on *personalizing,* to show how potent any one of these six foundations can be.

(Un)familiarity Breeds Contempt

Why do we prefer to have a *personal* hairdresser, dentist, doctor, accountant or lawyer? Because we, as humans, want to feel a sense of *importance.* We want to feel that we can go to some professional who knows our situation and can *personally attend* to every need. We go to the same hairdresser because they *know* our hair, and exactly what result we desire. The accountant has our records, knows our business and tax situation and can solve *our* problems. It's called: *personal attention.*

But, when we, as customers, go and buy a car, shop for shoes, clothes or eat at a restaurant, many times over we do not know a single soul in the businesses. Those businesses which sell the cars, shoes, clothes or meals, most always promote *only the business and products,* and simply fail to promote the people who staff them.

They fail to *personalize* their business, and as a result, fail to *maximize* customer attraction.

Our world is now flooding with unrelenting competition. To survive, (and thrive) both now and beyond, means to think like a Red Striped Zebra ... to be very different to the the black and whites. *Personalizing* your business will do just that, for two reasons;

1. It makes a business break free from the crowd and *get noticed*

2. It taps into a number of basic human psychological needs; The need to *feel safe* and on *secure ground,* the need to be *wanted,* and the need to *feel important.*

Ever walked into a crowded nightclub, or into a party, or attended a business seminar or luncheon? Any place where a large crowd is gathered? And during that time did you ever feel like all eyes were on you ... a feeling of self-consciousness?

Do you remember when at last, you see some person whom you *instantly recognize,* causing you to finally feel at ease and in *familiar* territory?

To a lessor scale, the same feelings of *familiarity* are stirred when you personalize your business and make potential customers feel at ease. It removes subconscious sales resistance *barriers* ... and opens the door to your business, for customers to readily enter.

Here's an example ...

The Personalized
Roofing Firm

The U.S. roofing business is rampant with competition. It also has a reputation of harboring many types of people, some of whom you would prefer not to be on your property.

One firm decided to change all that by becoming a Red Striper. They simply used the business-boosting strategy of *personal.zing.*

Naas Ferreira runs a Norwalk Connecticut roofing firm· *Flat Roof Doctor.* In a five-mile radius of his business, 70-80% of homes have additions, or flat roof sun rooms. And these $400,000 homes are owned by upscale discriminating people.

In targeting these owners, Ferreira has chosen to not only personalize his brochures and business, but to incorporate a number of zebra style strategies. As opposed to other black and white roofing businesses, he has chosen gloss, heavy card stock that shouted *high quality* and the brochures start off with a sharp, effective headline: *All Leaks ..... Fixed!*

He uses the Zebra strategy; *Perception of Value Education (POVE)* in the brochure, explaining in great detail about the awesome service he provides, and no mention of price. (Bravo Ferreira - and price slashers beware!).

He explains in detail common roof problems, illustrated by full color photographs and diagrams and then gives solid, usable advice to home owners so they know exactly what they must do to look for these conditions in their own homes. (That's providing an *advantage* for the customer. It's the Zebra strategy called: *Customer Advantaging.).*

Then, he incorporates the gem that has skyrocketed his business. He personalizes by including four full color photographs of himself and his staff, and a short, interesting bio of each person.

This addresses the two very important psychological needs of the homeowners.
1. It shows the owner *who* they should expect to see working on their home. (Familiarity factor). Highly reputable people whom they can *trust* to work on the roof of their expensive home.
2. It shows the level of *expertise* and *experience*, demonstrating that this firm is truly professional. They are there to guarantee

their work, not be fly-by-nighters ... or people who 'case' the home for future activities.

These two needs are answered, thereby building confidence in the customer ... and helps in removing the 'risk' of buying.

Ferreira sent 1,000 of these brochures out for 10 weeks, which resulted in up to 30 calls per week, of which 99% bought. Obviously, with these proven results, the strategy of *personalizing* his business works ... and using this brochure format has caused his sales to boom! If he follows suit, with a newsletter, business cards and letterheads, all in a personalized style, he will experience even more increase.

Personalizing his brochure and business has caused his sales and income to BOOM!

I even have one client who has personalized his *invoices*, with photographs of the accounts department people and a specially crafted script outlining the benefits for customers who pay their bills on time.

That has worked well and reduced the *Customer's Perpetual Paying Habits (CPPH)* ... you know, those 60, 90 and 120 day payers who have been *educated* into paying late. Personalizing can help you 're-educate' them ... if you do it right!

The Scottish Chemical Manufacturer

R.P. Adam Ltd in Selkirk, Scotland has used this Zebra strategy to gain a boost. They manufacture cleaning chemicals for the health and hygiene industry ... and like many black and white Zebras, they were struggling with competition. But, in taking on a plethora of Red Striped Zebra strategies, they have leap-frogged over the competitors and captured choice business accounts, such as major airlines and hotel chains. They used *personalizing* in a very unique way. They've used it to bring the factory to the customers.

Research Chemists - Personalized and On Call

We discovered that they had these research chemists with many years of expertise, locked away in laboratories. (Untapped hidden assets - *Newton's Law X11*). What a brilliant asset to have and to *tell* customers about. We advised them to bring these guys *into the open.*

On their new (once again, full color, high impact brochures) they featured these chemists, with photographs of them holding test tubes up to the light and going about their business ... with a bio on each. This bio explained their immense experience ... and *how* that experience *benefits* customers. They were portrayed as the 'customer's' problem solvers - *not* the firms!

A toll free number was installed, so that customers with complex cleaning problems in their businesses (hospitals, nursing homes, hotels, airlines, health clubs etc.) could simply pick up the phone and immediately get through to the chemists ... and receive invaluable 'how to' advice. They advise on the products, on the specific cleaning problem, formulations ... and even how to reduce cleaning costs.

Customers love this 'personalizing' - which in this instance goes even further than just the factory floor.

Even
the Chairman

The corporate brochure also contains photographs of the Chairman and the Managing Director, in friendly, warm poses, with personal messages of promise and guarantees for the reader. The whole effect has created a very approachable, 'visible' business ... one to which customers *warm* to and *prefer* to buy from. And this is a far cry to the 'formal' competitors who hide behind titles and departments.

In effect, the company has turned itself 'inside-out' by featuring the inners of the factory. Demonstrating what goes on in the research laboratory, on the factory floor, in the ordering dept., showing who's who and who does what. They explain exactly *how* the customer is *advantaged* with this personalized approach and the results substantiate that this strategy works exceedingly well. They've become giant slayers as they capture more and more clients throughout the U.K., from under the very noses of the black and white competitors.

Turn Personalizing
Into an Advantage

It is easy to get carried away with personalizing a business,

34

featuring the management and staff and creating that 'human' touch, but more importantly is to *turn* personalizing into *advantages*.

For instance:
- If you tell how 'Bill Smith' in the shipping dept. has 17 years expertise and experience, it then allows you to also explain 'how' that expertise will *benefit* the buyer. He could also have a personal note that invites customers to call him if anything is wrong with the order or shipping methods ... and he will personally fix it! (That's an advantage!)
- If you mention the President's or the Marketing Director's experience in your personalizing, you could feature the corporate guarantee or promise of quality also, i.e. because the President has many years of commitment to the firm and to its clients, the new client can also feel secure in buying the products or service, knowing they too will be assured of the very best. (That's an advantage!)

Points to Ponder

Personalizing will make your business *familiar* to customers ... and they will be *assured* of professionalism, competence, honesty.

Everybody prefers dealing with a *friend* rather than a stranger. Your business can become a *friend* to customers by simply personalizing every brochure and advertisement.

A simple foundation ... but one that can
make a huge difference to your business

Let's now move back and explore the next three:

4. You must INDIVIDUALIZE your business to *break it free* from the crowd and help it become the most 'unique' and 'innovative' choice available. (Throughout this book you will learn of many businesses that have created and adopted individuality.).

In a herd of black and whites, the Red Striped Zebra must out-perform, out-maneuver, out-run all others simply to keep from being eaten by the prowling Lions of competition. Once your camouflage is broken, it's time to act. Only innovation and creativity can do this. The customer will fall in love with the firm that knows this ... and demonstrates how.

The business which can *stay ahead* and add *real value* to their lives, with the latest cutting-edge service, products and offers, will win!

Strategies you will need to implement:
> *Risk Transfers, Package Selling Offers, Perpetual Re-selling, Data-Base Building and Selling, Added Bonuses, Irresistible Sales Offers (ISO's).*

5. Increase the MAGNETIC VALUE (MV) © of advertising to attract customers - and make the cash registers ring continuously. This success foundation is vital, for it is the customer's *door* to your business. It must be inviting for them ... otherwise they simply will not enter! Following, is perhaps one of the most profound statements in this entire book. Please read it a number of times.

> ***Millions of dollars are simply wasted on advertising every year because what customers 'want' to hear has absolutely 'nothing' to do with what businesses want to tell them.***

The advertisement, promotion and marketing campaign are the life-blood of a business. Does it not then stand to reason that a Red Striped Zebra business must be seen to perform very differently in this area?

The trick is in minimizing the cost of advertising and maximizing the results, while making sure that 'every' advertisement makes customers 'act' immediately! Learn much more results-producing advertising in the chapter; *ZebraWrite.*

Strategies you will need to implement:

Hot Headlines, Perception of Value Education (POVE), Motivating Factors (MF's), Perception of Desire Education (PODE), Bonusing (LAC/HPV), Actionizing, etc.

6. Incorporate AWESOME Customer Service - over and above what customers expect - to *spoil* them and create fierce loyalty! You will learn all about this exciting service in the chapter; *ZebraServe.*

   This is the area that *re-installs* caring and customer focus. It's the *Psychology of Buying.* Knowing *exactly* what motivates customers to buy from 'you' ... rather than your competitors.
   Understanding the customer will change forever the way you write advertisements, the guarantees you give, the offers you make, the pricing of your products or services, the quality you provide and if you make buying from you fun ... or a miserable experience.

Strategies you will need to implement:
> *The Philosophy of Awesome Customer Service, Extra Mile Thinking (XMT), Customer Conversion Offers (CCO's), Customer Advantaging (CA), etc.*

Working on the six-fold success foundation for your Red Striped Zebra business will ready it for unlimited growth. Change can be driven, or it can drive you. It's your choice. Better to be in control and transform your business exactly the way you want it to be.

It means working ON your business, not just IN it!

The three ways to grow a business

Now, in fleshing out the Red Striped Zebra program, we need to add to the six-fold foundation an understanding of the only sure-fire way to gain substantial growth in a business.

For years, business people have focussed on the front-end of every customer. Selling them a product or service and then promptly forgetting about them. What a stupid waste! It cost big money to 'buy' a customer through advertising or other means. Then, to simply sell them something and then watch them walk away, *not knowing* if they will 'ever' come back - is paramount to business suicide! Years back, I was always asking the question; *"How do you get customers to come back and buy again and again and again - even forty times more?"* This is what I learned:

Not having in place a formula for gaining repeat sales ... and for creating a long-term relationship with customers is business suicide!

There are three ways, not just one, to grow a business

A business grows by: ....
1. Making sales to customers
2. Getting more for products or service
3. Gaining repeat sales from customers

Many businesses concentrate on No.1. They sell to a customer, then 'hope' they may return. Even worse, some couldn't care less if they returned or not. Many do not create customer data-bases, they do not 'lock' customers in to long-term sales offers, nor do they actively promote offers or demonstrate any good reasons for customers to return and buy again. However, *quantum growth* will occur by increasing *each* area individually, i.e. more sales, more for your product or service and more repeat sales. Lets see how the combined results *far exceed* the initial increase of each area.

Here is a business that makes 2,000 sales at an average of $100 per sale, with 2 repeat sales per year from customers. Total is $400,000.

Customers	Average Sale	Repeat Sales	Total
2,000	$100	2	$400,000

The best that business could do if it only focussed on the front end, i.e. the 2,000 sales, is probably around 10% growth. It is difficult to keep gaining more and more sales just to grow the business. It costs money to buy every customer that comes in the door. A big part of that $400,000 would go towards this cost.

Let's see what would happen if the business focussed on the three areas, instead of just the one and increased each by just 10%.

2,200	$110	2.2	$532,400

Sales increased by 10%. So did the repeat sales and the price for the products. But the end result is not a 10% increase. It's a 33% increase at $532,400 ... That's weird isn't it?

Quantum Growth

What would happen if we applied our formula differently, by increasing the sales/new customers by 50%, packaging our product or service so we could charge 33% more, and did all the right things to get the customers back by 60% more ...

3,000	$133	3.2 repeat sales	$1,276,800

Wow! We end up with a 320% increase in our business revenue at $1,276,800. We're talking about real *quantum growth* here, not simple 10% growth each year ... but an expansion in a number of directions, all caused by simple increases in 'each' area.

You only get this type growth when you learn to break free from the crowd a ... nd start to focus on:

1: The front-end.
2: The product/service value. (packaging, combo deals etc.).
3: Having your customer buy from you over and over and over.

This is the area where you will need the strategies called; *Customer's Long-Term Value (CLTV), Customer's Perpetual Buying Habits (CPBH), Customer's Conversion Offers, (CCO's), Customer Advantaging (CA), Irresistible Sales Offers (ISO's), Data-Base building* ... and a host of other Zebra strategies that lock customers in and breaks a business free.

Through the Roof

Let's push the envelope here and see what else would happen if this business did a massive marketing campaign (Red Striped Zebra style) to achieve a 75% increase in new customers/sales, then packaged the service and products in such a way as to gain that 33% increase, and created 100% more repeat sales by furnishing reasons for the customers to keep returning and buying again.

3,500	$133	4	$1,862,000

Through the roof!

To save you calculating that final result into a percentage, it figures at 465% increase over the first effort. $1,862,000 simply by increasing the repeat sales from 2 to 4, lifting the product/service price by 33% (and that can be done in the way they are packaged - to 'add' real and perceived value for the customer) ... and by increasing customers from 2,000 to 3,500.

Zebra Eye View

That's how a Red Striped Zebra business has to perform, think and act. By not focussing on just getting sales and new customers through the door, but by seeing the 'whole' ... or the 'bird's eye view' of growing a business. The 1, 2, 3 view of growing a business and achieving overwhelming sales

Maybe it should just be called; the Zebra's eye view!

The Zebra success triplets

Near the beginning of this chapter, I mentioned perceptive mind-shift and attitude adjusters. Perhaps the very first requirement in adopting the Red Striped Zebra philosophy and program is in doing a 'check-up-from-the-neck-up' of every person in a business.

We have found that in many firms there always exists a small number of people who simply do not get it! They find it very difficult to change, to adopt new ideas or to think outside of their 'box' ... and so they cause havoc by resisting anything new.

This could be because of:

- *An inability to perform any better than what they now do*
- *A fear of losing points or runs on the ladder, or control of their part of the business, because what is being introduced is too difficult for them to handle.*
- *An inability to think or act creatively*

On occasions, clients have asked us if we consider that certain people with these characteristics should remain with the business, or should they be 'moved' on. We've been reluctant to make any judgements, because people can and do change. I've seen people who have 'bad mouthed' our program, yet one year later they are the firm's best supporter. Others simply have not lasted the distance and exited.

Nevertheless, for the Zebra thinking to take place there is a major necessity for creative, no-limit people to drive the program forward. Also, there is a real need to demand the existence, installation and usage of the *Zebra success triplets*. Without them, the program simply will not work for you.

Those triples are:

1. *Creativity*
2. *Innovation*
3. *Uniqueness*

And it's all to do with people. That perceptive mind-shift we spoke about, is in discovering a new way to do business ... and in actually 'allowing' the people in your business to adopt the Zebra triplets. Here's why ...

To perform like a Red Striped Zebra business,
the people in your firm must:

Innovation
Innovate
EVERYTHING
- product, packaging, service,
marketing, administration, sales,
shipping, accounting etc.

Uniqueness
Engineer your firm
into one that is to be 'seen' by
customers as very
UNIQUE
... and 'different' to all others

Creativity
The 'ethos' of the firm, or the
'mind-think' must be
openly creative.
EVERY person applying their
'creative' thinking ability to solve
problems and generate ideas.
An unstoppable, no-limit,
can-do team.

These are the ingredients and foundations for your new Red Striped Zebra business. Now, there remains just one question to ask:

Will YOU dare to break free like
a Red Striped Zebra ...

... and break the success barrier?

The Magic of Metamorphosis

*How to transform your business into
a customer attracting success*

Q: In a rapidly changing world, how can a business cope with change, handle fierce competition and still make profit?

A: By pro-actively undergoing a corporate transformation ... or metamorphosis.

Francis X. Maguire is a man of much corporate wisdom, gleaned over many fascinating years of business building. As one of the key players in the founding of *Federal Express* and *KFC*, he worked side by side with the founding legends; Fred Smith and Colonel Harlan Sanders. Frank once showed me a unique and rare photograph of himself and the Colonel, surveying the 'business venture' scene in Red Square, Moscow. What a head turner, these two Americans, with one dressed in his pure white suit, white goatee beard and silver cane.

Who would have thought you could sell chicken in a box all over this planet, or send packages to Memphis on one plane, reload them onto another, then get them to their destinations, absolutely, positively overnight? Frank was one of those who believed it could be done!

This former Senior VP of Industrial Relations for Fedex, and a senior manager in the KFC early days, is now a renowned speaker at conferences nationwide. His message focusses on being different, breaking free from the crowd, and standing apart. Fedex has certainly done that, and it's ironic that the color scheme for the *KFC* brand is red and white stripes ... symbolic of a Red Striped Zebra business, perhaps?

Frank makes a profound statement in his keynote addresses that sums up the immediate and dire need for transforming businesses.

He says:

*"The best way to predict
your future, is to INVENT it!"*

Many times people get bogged down, stressed out, overworked and frustrated just trying to make their businesses work. And unfortunately, out of ignorance of better methods, or an unwillingness to try other strategies, they continue to use old thinking, old practices and woefully inadequate systems that simply fail to excite, motivate, energize ... or simply get RESULTS.

Time to Change?

If this is the case in your business, then it's time to change. Are customers or clients beating a path to your door? No? Then it's time to change! Are your sales or revenue falling behind this year's projections? It's time to change! Are your competitors beating you with superior service, products or quality? It's time to change!

And are you enjoying the success in your business that you initially set out to achieve? If NOT, then it's certainly time to change!

Here are examples of Red Striped Zebra businesses that have undertaken change and are now positioned as leaders in their fields.

Scotland's Other Cherished Liquid Asset

The Scottish firm of *R.P. Adam Ltd.* wanted change. Here was a firm that had survived for 107 years. They manufactured superb health and hygiene cleaning products and generated fifty million pounds yearly. They had gone through the TQM and ISO processes ... and had even won the *Queen's Award for Export Excellence*, but they were finding it tough to make headway against their competitors. The 'Goliaths' in their industry were causing them grief.

It was time for change!

As mentioned in the previous chapter, we started in September 1996 at a stunning location; the conference room at the Duke of Roxburgh's estate in Scotland. We presented the *Uniqueness is a Red Striped Zebra* program to all their managers, flown in from far afield as Dubai and Malaysia.

And now, the years of 'adding the stripes' have given them real, and measurable results. They have truly broken free from the crowd and have become 'giant slayers'. Every time they secure a new major client, (such as the prestigious *Savoy Hotel* in London, or the *Millennium Group*, or supplying of military bases all over the United Kingdom), it is little wonder that the competitors emerge with bloodied noses ... and refer to them as *"that shitty little firm in the Borders"* ... A reference to Selkirk, the firm's headquarters in the English/Scottish Borders region.

To me, that just sounds like the familiar whining cry of black and white zebra businesses. They don't know how to do anything unique or innovative, nor compete with a fast moving red striped model!

R.P. Adam Ltd. learned how to apply all the stripes. I learned this first hand at my last visit to their plant. Stacked to the roof were hundreds of pallets of boxes, not the old brown cardboard of old, but bright blue with white print. These were the national colors of Scotland, adopted as the firm's corporate colors. And on the side of these boxes, just underneath their logo, was the slogan we originally developed years back. It states: *Scotland's Other Cherished Liquid Asset.* A reference to the 300 Scottish whiskey distillers who produce the world's finest Scotch. They see their cleaning chemicals as the finest and highest quality in their industry - so they tell the world.

This sea of blue and white delivery boxes was the result of their concept of the Red Striped Zebra philosophy. It means transforming the 'whole' corporation, from front office to back door, from products to service, from marketing to 'blue and white' boxes. They caught the vision. A vision of winning by being different, being individualized and distinctive from all others. Daring to break free and standing apart. Even if it means changing something as basic as brown cardboard into an eye-catching color scheme, so be it.

There is nothing more determined than a determined Scot, or a determined Scottish firm, and perhaps it's in the very nature of the Scots that they enjoy being different ... demonstrated in this firm's embracing of the Red Striped Zebra program.

When those boxes of product are shipped to customers throughout the United Kingdom, Europe or to their branches in Dubai or Abu Dhabi in the Middle East, an immediate impact is made.

An impact that states in bold blue and white;
here's another box of R.P.Adam's products.

'Different to'
... not 'Better than'

Gateway Computers does the same with their's. Black and white cow designs set them apart and builds a *perception* in the mind of the customer that somehow, this firm is 'different to' ... not 'better than'.

It is simply not necessary to be 'better than' the competition. To try is folly and results in price cutting wars. Being 'different to' is the essence of a Red Striped Zebra firm. It allows you to be innovative, unique, creative and in tune with what the customer really wants.

R.P. Adam Ltd. learned step-by-step how to Zebraize 'every' aspect of their business, as they went through their metamorphosis (and are still going through - for it is a continuing process) from a black and white zebra firm, to a red striper. The colored boxes however, caught me by surprise, and demonstrated that they were teaching me how to suck eggs!

Bravo *R.P. Adam Ltd.*

From Then
to Now

R.P. Adam Ltd. had been in business for over 107 years before taking on the Red Striped Zebra program. Many things were 'set' in concrete - especially the 'mindset' of people. The initial in-house seminar helped to break that thinking. *"It's always been done this way"* ... to a new perceptive-mind shift that said; *"What we've done before isn't working, let's give this a go and see what happens."*

That became the spark that ignited the firm ... and if I were to offer the key that starts the initial change in any firm, (or the 'lock' that holds it back) it has to be the one of an 'open' (or 'closed') mind ... and the willingness (or unwillingness) to try new strategies.

It ALL starts with that perceptive-mind shift!

Next, came the hard work. We had very constructive meetings with management where we labored over and drafted a brand new *Unique Marketing Perception* (see the chapter: *The Good Guys Wear*

White Hats). We conducted our *MindStorm Seat* © with managers from every aspect of the business, from shipping to research, from the customer service dept. to sales. This session allowed people, and 'expected' people, to offer ideas, concepts and formulas that were undergirded by creativity. It literally helped send the firm off in new and exciting directions.

Management
Profiles

Over the ensuing months we interviewed every manager and created profiles and monitoring tools to guide their professional development. Red Striped Zebra strategies in copywriting, advertising and promotions were added, which built into the strategic marketing plan. Excess product lines that were slow sellers were eradicated and new, more effective formulas were added. Labels and packaging were redesigned to 'break them free' from the competitors. And even a new computer network was installed to cut down wasteful practices of old.

When a business becomes a Red Striped Zebra firm it sends a new message to customers and creates a new 'perception' in their minds. They soon reach the 'inescapable conclusion' that this firm is the ONLY one to buy from - their preferred choice. This makes the sales person's job much easier. It increases sales ... and more importantly; PROFITS!

I recently asked Robin Leith, Managing Director, if they would have secured the military bases throughout the United Kingdom as clients, if it was not for the Red Striped Zebra process. His comment? *"No way, they wouldn't touch us before!"*

Red Stripes in Texas

Glen Hinckley had a vision! The status quo did not satisfy this Texas cattleman. For years he had played the game of cattle producer and rancher, competing with every other cattleman in the country in producing the fattest cattle, and taking the most show awards. But still, he wasn't content. He wanted to break tradition, and stand his business apart as a Red Striped Zebra.

Was it possible to undergo a metamorphosis in business ... especially the cattle business, with its deeply entrenched culture of ranching, cattle breeds, cowboys and Stetsons? Hinckley believed so, and his vision was strong enough to pull it off.

His vision was to produce an end product that was totally opposite to the American requirements of beef; low fat! Specifically; four to seven percent fat content, compared to ordinary prime beef of up to eighteen percent.

Having an end result in mind for your business starts with a vision.
A vision undergirded by driving passion to excel ...
... and to break free from the crowd.

Hinckley states that it all started with a <u>vision</u>, which brings to mind the wise statement of old;

> *Without a vision, the people perish*
> (and so does a business).

What Business Am I In?

Hinckley then asked some profound questions, questions that tore at the very heart of his cattle business. He asked himself;

- *"What business am I in?"*
- *"Am I a cattle rancher, or a beef producer?"*
- *"If I am a beef producer, then why do I produce an end product that is so high in fat?"*
- *"Do I really care about my customer, the American public, if I give them an end product that is loaded with deadly health-destroying fat?"*
- *"If I am becoming aware of the rapid change in food nutrition choices, surely my customer is also becoming very aware, and now making demanding new choices?"*

With these probing and boat-rocking questions answered, Hinckley was now on the launching pad for his business to undergo a metamorphosis, and hopefully; to eventually position the business as a leader in his field.

With the help and input from his daughter, a Texas Christian University nutrition major, and a computer, this hardened 55-year old rancher embarked on an electrifying journey to transform his ranch into a low-fat beef producing industry leader.

Going against all the ingrained culture of what cattle breeds a *respectable* Texas rancher raises, Hinckley analyzed carcasses of cattle from all over the state. He then identified the genetic bloodlines that match up with the desirable traits, eventually coming up with eight that consistently produce very high-quality, low-fat, tender meat.

The Vision
Materializes

Hinckley then moved closer to the realization of his vision by purchasing the descendants of his now identified bloodlines. He had no interest in looks, or if indeed his chosen cattle would even win show awards. It was the final product, *his vision of low-fat meat* that drove him. And that vision took six years of breeding and raising his herd of Simbrah - a mix of Simmental and Brahman.

The Metamorphosis Completed

His cattle look nothing like the big heavy duty monoliths that are considered the 'norm'. They are robust and handsome, and Hinckley defines them as the *athlete* of the cattle world. And they are healthy too, seldom requiring antibiotics and never needing growth hormones.

Glen Hinckley *forged his own industry breakthroughs* and wrote his own rule book. His *Cody Beef*, (his product's trading name), will lead the way in America not just as a fine, low-fat and sumptuous beef product, but as a Red Striped Zebra product!

Hindering Old Habits

Hinckley's biggest problem he had to overcome was to 'break' old habits. Old habits of doing business the way they had been done for over a hundred years.

In any business, prior to undergoing a metamorphosis, there are old habits that need to be broken ... and old habits are a hindrance that

MUST be broken, before any progress can be made.

Hinckley's example in having a strong vision, and an end result, is the answer for any business, and for your business, prior to undergoing a metamorphosis, or corporate transformation.

You may be asking:

> *"Why is it necessary to undergo a metamorphosis in business. Why change, why transform?" "Wouldn't it be much easier just to modify, adjust, fine tune by small degrees?"*

To answer that, I ask you:

> *"Are YOU the leader in your field, and do you stand apart from the crowd, making huge gains in your business?"*

In today's world, we have to lead, take charge, and get out in front. The customer is a more sophisticated and demanding individual than in times past. There are a myriad of choices and opportunities available to them. The global marketplace has added another dimension of fierce competition, and like it or not, if we stay as we always have done, we will be left behind in the rush.

Another of Frank Maguire's favorite statements, is; *"If you're NOT the lead dog, the view NEVER changes!"*

It makes me laugh when I hear him say it, with his emphasis on 'not' and 'never'. The very thought of being strapped into a harness behind the lead dog of a snow sled, and watching that rear view for endless hours is certainly not a pleasurable thought. And yet, in business, how many are running their race, forever looking at their competitor's butt?

If you're NOT the lead dog, the view NEVER changes!

It must be so refreshing being that lead dog. Every new bend in the trail brings a fresh view, a fresh breeze. You're out there in front, leading the pack. What an emotional boost and pleasure that must be, not to mention the new business you gain, and the untouched ground you cover every inch of the way.

That's exactly why it's necessary to undergo the *Magic of Metamorphosis*, so you can leap over the competition and claim your rightful position as market leader!

Caterpillars into Butterflies

We are all very aware of what takes place in nature, especially with caterpillars. Perhaps this is where the word 'metamorphosis' comes from, and possibly it's the best way to describe the process.

The caterpillar positions itself in a suitable environment and starts spinning a silken home, enclosing itself in a protective barrier while it awaits its transformation. Through some magical process it eventually emerges as an apparently different insect, a beautiful butterfly.

It does not particularly concern us how all this happens ... more importantly is the *final result* of the metamorphosis. A breathtakingly beautiful butterfly emerges, and not just a transformation in size, color, shape and attributes, but this insect can literally take to the sky. It flies! A far removed wonder from the caterpillar crawling stage.

In business, this same principle applies.
It's not just change, or modifications, or fine tuning that is the goal ... but a complete and wondrous transformation.
A business that flies!

And because this metamorphosis is undertaken, the business is then in a position to overwhelm competition, and step into the rightful position as leader in the field ...

... Becoming Maguire's lead dog!

The House of Oxford

(A Store With NO Customers)

George Bakarnis has a men's clothing store, and he has NO customers. He's doing great! He is a merchant who knows exactly what it means to be a Red Striped Zebra, and to undergo a metamorphosis in business, simply because he did it.

And the transformation of his business caused an immediate four hundred percent increase in sales ... but with no customers.

Unsatisfied

Bakarnis, just like Hinckley, was not happy with the status quo. He owned his retail men's wear store in St. Kilda, a suburb of Melbourne, Australia, and business was fine. However, it was not what he really wanted to achieve in business. Bakarnis yearned to focus on a segment of the market that pleased and rewarded him more, the corporate executive market.

That was his vision, his end product, his goal ... but to reach this he realized he would also have to undergo a metamorphosis and break free from the crowd. *"And would the final result be worth the effort?"* He wondered!

Reassuring
Research

Just as Hinckley researched, so did Bakarnis. He discovered that executives do not buy clothing, they buy *image*. This was his secret to his store's metamorphosis. He would sell them an image.

He asked the same question; *"What business am I in?"* and came up with the answer; the providing of a powerful image to his executive clients.

And then his journey, just like the caterpillar, began in earnest. He closed his doors and put the store into a

It meant, horror of horrors; losing all of his existing client base, clearing out all of his extensive clothing stock ... then decorating, repositioning, advertising ... and a whole lot more undiscovered problems associated with transforming a business.

55

'cocoon' of papered up windows. He then rented a local hall, advertised and wrote to all his customers, explaining how he was changing the image of the store, and all remaining clothing is up for grabs at considerably reduced 'never to be offered again' prices.

The results of this sale were outstanding. He experienced wall to wall people who flooded the hall leaving him with no stock, but he was all cashed up.

The Power of a
Name Change

He then changed the name from *'The Male Man'* to *'House of Oxford'*, instantly positioning the business with 'class' in the mind's of future customers. Then he renovated the store with image and style in mind, and even installed beautiful cabinets and tables to display his new, incoming stock. He hand-picked reasonable priced, high quality suits, shirts, ties and products to complete the transformation, then embarked on a totally radical marketing plan.

Re-inventing the Mind-Set
... From Customer to Member

The next step was to ban the word 'customer' from being used, replacing it with *member!*

Mind sets are remarkable. They are walled mind processes, and some of those walls are as rigid as concrete, yet they can be toppled with something simple as a name change.

One simple name change, from customer to member, instantly removes that mind-set and energizes us with a new thought process. The word member conjures up someone who is *special*, someone who *belongs*, someone who needs to be *looked after*.

Bakarnis recognized this and now all his customers are called *members*. He will be the first to tell you he has NO customers, only members.

He then went about attracting these new members to his business. He wrote letters, asked for referrals from existing members, and advertised, eventually growing his member base from 200 to 950.

*Many business folk have an entrenched 'mind set' of customer service, with all the attached 'names' and opinions of what customer service is, how to apply it, how to improve it ... Check out the chapter called **ZebraServe** - a refreshingly new approach!*

A Buying "Experience"

At The House of Oxford, the metamorphosis is complete. You do not walk in and buy a suit from a pushy sales person, then take it home to find it doesn't look so great afterwards. You undergo a buying *experience*.

There are beautiful dining tables and seats for you to drink coffee or tea, or a bar for drinks while you are being served. The clothing is shown hanging in special display wardrobes, where you can see a fully coordinated display of your choice. The serving team is infused with integrity and professionalism, assisting you to develop a total 'look', swapping and changing accessories until the final image emerges.

Bakarnis wants every member to leave the business 'feeling like a million dollars' in the new clothing image, and to relay the shopping experience to their colleagues.

His underlying theme is anything less than perfect service is NOT good enough, and if any sales member slips up not only does a verbal apology follow, but a gift, such as flowers or a shirt would be sent to the member.

The members must be treated like guests in the house of a friend!

Finishing Touches

When undergoing a metamorphosis, a butterfly emerges with some very fine and beautiful finishing touches. So too, must a business!

The House of Oxford achieves this with a number of clever ideas and strategies. Inside the coat of every suit a member buys they sew in a label which states; *'Specially Tailored for "your name" by The House of Oxford'*.

The business also introduced outrageous service strategies, such as providing a *"Lifetime Perfect Fit Guarantee"*, which means when you lose or add weight, simply return the suit for free alteration. If you lose a button, return the suit and it will be fixed for free!

Bakarnis introduced a small fashion newsletter, keeping members abreast of changing fashion styles, so they may stay ahead of their business peers.

A *Porsche* for the Day!

However, one strategy really sets the business apart; the *"Porsche for a day, suit for a lifetime"* offer, which means every member who introduces a friend to The House of Oxford's buying experience receives a Porsche to drive for a day!

The list of service strategies and member's services seems endless ... but more importantly, what stands this business apart from most others is the fact that it has gone through a corporate transformation, or metamorphosis. It now operates as a Red Striped Zebra amongst a herd of black and white ... and has taken the Maguire *lead dog* role, an enviable position for any business!

When Times Look Tough ... TRANSFORM!

If you were the industry leader in your field, why would you contemplate a radical change in your business operations?

Lowe's Companies Inc. did! Back in 1981 they stood at the forefront in the home improvement and building supplies industry, but with a new vision they embarked on a corporate transformation that revolutionized their business in the ensuing decade.

This 49-year old giant currently stands as the 29th largest retailer as of this writing, according to *Forbes* magazine, and is second behind Home Depot. Two hundred and nine of its 334 stores are new, having being built since 1988, with selling space doubling within the last three years.

Once housed in drably functional small stores, business is now conducted in bright and colorful superstores, and their product range has grown from 14,000 to 40,000.

Motivated by
a Dull Future

The future did not look too bright for Lowe's. They had a strong commitment to market research, brought about by Robert Strickland, the chairman of the board in 1978, and Leonard Herring, President and CEO. This research showed that although they possessed a loyal contractor customer base, the building industry was cyclic at best, and the future for new housing starts looked poor.

They also found through further research that customers wanted one stop shopping, and surprisingly 50% of their customers were women, who contributed up to 70% of the buying decisions.

It's amazing how research explodes our preconceived beliefs of who our customers and clients are ... and what they want to buy.

It was time for radical change, to undergo a metamorphosis, and to invent the future. Lowe's did just that. They were doing very nicely indeed back in 1981, and could have maintained their position.

Many other businesses have carried on as before, resisting change, but Lowe's chose to become a Red Striped Zebra, and established a new vision to reach for and accomplish.

The results of this metamorphosis has been staggering. Presenting a 'supermarket' approach to their customer base, they have had consistent profits, a 15 percent compound growth over the last four years and a 64 percent rise in net earnings in some years alone!

Shopping at a Lowe's store nowadays is a different experience to ten years ago. Not only are the stores a delight to be in, but the choices are profound. If you go to buy paint, you most probably will leave the store with drop cloths, brushes, turpentine and sandpaper. That is the desire of Lowe's people, to provide 'awesome' service and to meet all your needs.

Their staff provide service that goes 'far beyond' the ordinary, with people who specialize in kitchen design, glass, interior design ... and many stores offer specialized gardening centers.

Training is considered paramount, with every store having training rooms and training coordinators to assist the staff to reach maximum performance levels.

Lowe's lesson is not so much the metamorphosis they put the corporation through, from top to bottom, but why they decided to undertake this journey.

It was because of the future, revealed via market research. There were problems and storm clouds on the horizon.

One doesn't decide to undergo a costly transformation on a whim. There must be a good reason. This could be to grow aggressively, or to out-pace the competition, and in Lowe's case it was to avoid the perceived downturn in the building industry, by moving from strong reliance on contractor's business to the home owner 'retailing supply' business.

The fact that they increased sales, customers, and profits was in essence, icing on the cake, and icing that they would no doubt be well pleased with!

The High Road to Scotland
... and Success!

To own and work a farm in the Scottish countryside, some 60 miles north of Edinburgh would seem like an idyllic situation to most. In fact, Jean and Rob Lewis had done that since 1982, farming sheep and cattle. But with three children to rear, life was tough in the beginning, and money wasn't exactly flowing profusely. The situation was glorious though, with the farm sitting on a rustic track that runs the length of Loch Voil, near Callander, right next to Rob Roy's first home. The farm, set on 2,000 acres, gives a commanding view of the snow capped 'Braes of Balquhidder' across the loch.

So, what has all this got to do with metamorphosis and a Red

Striped Zebra business? Simply put, Jean and Rob Lewis took their farm through a transformation, which resulted in one of the great success stories that you should know about.

The Journey Started

Reported in the *Scotsman* by journalist Nicola Barry, the story emerges how Jean had heard about a "farm diversification grant" which was the catalyst for transforming the farm into a hotel. The grant allowed them to build a conservatory onto the front of their house, to be used as a dining room, and to build en-suites in all bedrooms.

Step by step, they changed the business. They secured a liquor licence and grew to three people in the kitchen, as well as a barman, two waitresses and a chambermaid. The metamorphosis is now complete, from a struggling farm taking just a few thousand a year, to being a highly successful hotel business. To stay at "Monachyle Mhor" in a double room costs between £55 and £70 with breakfast. Dinner is £18 to £21, with dishes such as Roast Supreme of Duck and a mixed citrus jus ...... exquisitely cooked by the Chef; their son Tom.

From Farm to Hotel of the Year

The hotel has won several awards, and in the *Which* hotel guide, 1995, it was voted *hotel of the year* for central Scotland. No wonder, for Jean Lewis demands perfection in her metamorphosised business. She trains her staff to exude personality, in their smile, and in what to say, or how to say it.

And she drives herself with a passion for this Red Striped Zebra business. She's up at the crack of dawn, making the traditional Scottish 'scones' for breakfast. She bakes her own bread, orders fish from Mallaig, makes her own sauces, orders fresh fruit and vegetables from the supplier, cooks, cleans, prepares endless exotic ingredients and supervises her staff of seven.

This two story, 18th century hotel hums like a fair ... a place that makes the weary traveler feel like a million dollars! It's a real zebra success story, but what makes it really amazing is when you see the burn marks on Jean Lewis's arms, from her cooking ...

That's when you realize this lady changed her business into a Red Striped Zebra while being totally blind!

Bloody Marvelous!

Your Metamorphosis

In these case studies the results share a surprising similarity ... there are substantial increases in sales, customers, and profit! You can experience substantial results in your business too.

Throughout this book you will learn Zebra strategies to apply, success tips, formulas and concepts. How high your results will be will depend on how many of these strategies you use, and on how far you take your business through the Magic of Metamorphosis.

The Magic of Metamorphosis yields outstanding results for the brave hearted, those who will take the steps needed to move through the journey of radical change.

In today's rapid world, we simply do NOT have a choice, we cannot stand still, we cannot slow down, we cannot copy what the other guy is doing. We must invent our own future and position our business as the leader in its field, and we do that by pro-actively choosing to undergo a corporate transformation; a metamorphosis!

Establishing
Your Vision

At the start I quoted the Bible verse, *Without a vision the people perish.* If this is true, then the opposite also must be true;

WITH a vision, the people (or business) flourishes.

The logic of this is to first establish YOUR vision for your business. And you do this by asking yourself questions, such as ...

- *Where do I want my business to go?*
- *What do I want it to look like when it gets there?*
- *How long do I want that journey to take?*
- *What sort of results do I want? In sales per year?*

Many questions need to be asked in developing the vision, not just an ill conceived grasp at an idea, but some careful soul searching, researching and question asking. Creative genius is within us all. We all have the ability to tap our genius within, and we have the capacity to reach genius level, the recent research from leading neuroscientists shows us that. The only hindrance is our belief system. As Henry Ford stated; *"If we think we can, we CAN. If we think we can't, we're right again!"*

If you are going to make the effort to establish a vision, a dream, a goal for your business, then establish a BIG vision, a BIG dream, and a BIG goal!

If you can develop a vision of your business that places you leaps and bounds ahead of your competition, then the battle is half won. It only takes an 'open mind' that can visualize and see it happening.

Butcher Paper
Planning

The most exciting and profound methods for developing a vision, and sorting out the ideas, problems, and concepts is by the simple use of colored felt tipped pens and large sheets of whiteboard paper, (which I call Butcher's paper) fastened to a wall. In all my experience, no other method awakens the creative genius of the right hemisphere of the brain like this.

The brain responds to color, patterns, shapes and ideas. By *writing your vision and aspirations* on large sheets of paper you awaken your creative genius within. Usually six or more sheets will accomplish your task, and by writing the statement of your vision in the center of the first sheet you can trigger many other ideas that will flow from the central theme. Use many colors, many shapes like arrows, boxes, circles, and let it flow, like a skilled artist adding or subtracting thought until you arrive at the zenith; your final electrifying vision for your business.

Mind
Synergy

They say two minds are better than one. In this case that's so true. If you can use your staff, partners, friends, or some special customers, then do so. Spend a few hours of 'inventing' as you chart your way through a metamorphosis. And the great benefit of this method is that you can walk away from it. You can go have coffee, lunch, and even leave it for a day or two. Unlike meetings of endless talk, the ideas written on your wall sheets are still there when you return, refreshed and ready to proceed. You can add to them, modify them, adjust and fine tune the ideas, until the final vision is achieved.

In one exercise our team spent two days and four whole walls of paper planning our vision, and clarified our thinking for a five year period.

Across the
Street View

Have you ever walked away from your business, especially if you have retail or office space, to gain a different perspective? In your vision setting exercise it could be very beneficial to remove yourself, literally, and your team in synergy, away from your business and across the street for a different view. It would amaze you how others see your business.

Getting away from the business helps you gain crystal-clear focus .... and a totally different perspective.

By standing and looking from a different position you will see things that may never reveal themselves otherwise. And when you're looking, ask yourself if you see a Red Striped Zebra business ... or one that simply blends in with the herd.

Jane's
Way

A colleague of mine, Jane Pierotti, a leading professional speaker on establishing visions and communication skills, took her own advice and did just that. In her case though, she took two of the most creative people she could find to a hotel room for two long and intensive brainstorming days, away from her home city. They drank gallons of coffee, and invented, re-invented, and created her successful speaking business that she has today. It's vital to gain the input from other people.

Through the
Customer's Eyes

Wouldn't it be exciting to get into the mind's of our customers and clients, just for one day, and understand what they are thinking about our business? We can. All we need to do is ask them. In a vision setting exercise, especially one that is designed to metamorphosise the business, asking the customer is very important. Lowe's asked their customers what they wanted, they answered with 'one-stop' shopping.

If you are a small business you may have a few cherished clients or customers, who see things so very differently than you do. Why not ask them? Tell them what you're doing, invite some of them to an hour or so of planning. Get their input, find out their desires, their ideas, their wants, and their advice. They will think you're wonderful, asking them for advice, and they will give you concepts and ideas you never would have thought of.

Whatever they give you, add it to the vision planning paper, and see what finally filters out. It could be a seed or nucleus of brilliance that may energize your business.

Through the
Staff's Eyes

No person knows a business better than the staff. Many times the lowest paid, bottom rung person in a business has more insight and knows what pleases the customer more than the top rung. Why? Because they are at the 'coal face' of customer and client contact. In fact, it has been reported that the very people who are face to face with customers have an 80% better knowledge of customer's needs, with managers only knowing around 20%. (Makes it hard for managers to make any decisions whatsoever on customer service, if this is the case, don't you think?)

The people who serve tables in a restaurant are more in touch with what pleases a customer than the manager behind the scenes working on accounts. The switchboard operator takes the first brunt of a customer complaint long before the department manager. The sales person at a clothing retailer communicates with customers all day long, far removed from the buyer who deals with suppliers.

Tasmanian Hotel

In a vision setting exercise for a leading hotel in Tasmania, Australia, my coaching partner; John Gilbody and I gained permission from management to bring in to the session not only department heads, but *housemaids, porters, front desk, kitchen and dining room staff.* It took some strong handling and direction to guide such a mixed meeting, but three hours later we unearthed many problems ... developed many new ideas, and an energized vision was forged to establish the hotel at the very forefront in service and efficient operation.

In Gemba

What was a real eye-opener though, was the statement by the hotel's manager that he had no idea the staff had felt or thought negatively about many of the major issues we covered. He had remained locked away in his office and was not at the coal face ... or as the Japanese say; not in *Gemba* (not aware of the entire situation).

When a Japanese manager starts work for a firm, he is escorted to the factory floor. A chalk line is drawn around him in a circle and he is told to simply stand and observe. He is to stand in that circle and remain *in Gemba*. Becoming aware of everything that goes on. Perhaps this is a philosophy western firms need to introduce? (If you desire to know more about Gemba, contact our office.).

If you do not have staff to include in your session, go talk to staff in similar industries. Ask them what they would do to build a better business if they were allowed to take control ... then bring their ideas back home to your business.

Do Your Own S.W.O.T. Analysis

During the course of your vision setting, it would be a great benefit to place your existing business under the microscope, before the metamorphosis begins.

One method for this is called the S.W.O.T. Analysis, and many consultants will do this for a few thousand dollars or so for you. Save money, do it yourself!

The object is to gain an understanding of the *Strengths*, *Weaknesses*, *Opportunities*, and *Threats* to the business.

Once again, it is conducted using large sheets of whiteboard paper, and forms part of the vision setting exercise. Simplified, it means rounding up the staff, customers, partners, managers, or whoever you would like in the session.

(These first two are 'inside' the business, or *intrinsic*).

- On the first sheet of paper write the heading *Strengths*
- On the second; *Weaknesses*

(These next two are from 'outside' the business, or *extrinsic*).

- Third; *Opportunities*
- And fourth; *Threats*

Under each respective heading write down the answer to the following questions;

What are all the Strengths of the business?
What are all the Weaknesses of the business?
What are all the Opportunities for the business?
And what are all the Threats to the business?

Search in infinite detail for the answers, and get them clearly written and defined for all to see. Having this information then gives you strengths to build upon, weaknesses to address, opportunities to pursue and threats to overcome.

Plan Your
Metamorphosis

With your vision for the business finally arrived at, it is then time to make the changes, one by one. Some changes will be radical, others slight, but starting with the end in mind is the first major step.

It may require new staff, or specialized training for existing staff. It may mean a new fresh look to your office or building, or a move to a more stylish one. It may require a new range of stock, services or re-packaging the existing. It may, as in the House of Oxford, require a radical name change, or a radical change to end product as in Cody Beef, or even in customer focus as in Lowe's.

Only you know your business and its potential for exciting change, so proceed with your vision as your guide.

And as Zig Ziglar states;

**If you are going to change,
do it now ... and do it <u>flamboyantly</u>!**

The Business Butterfly

Why is it in nature that people generally take no notice of a caterpillar, but stand in awe at a beautiful flying butterfly? Simply because there is beauty there, combined with the awesomeness of flight!

You're in business to make profit. But while you're reading this your competitors are doing everything they can to steal away sales that should be yours.

You can stop this from happening by transforming. Combining style and quality with creativity, innovation, uniqueness and pizazz ... to end up with a business that flies.

Then, as an attractive, metamorphosized business, you'll attract more customers then you'll know what to do with!

The Good Guys Wear White Hats

How to engineer the PERCEPTION in the customer's mind, that YOUR business is the ONLY one to buy from!

Q: What is the most powerful marketing tool in business today?

A: The ability to create a crystal clear, succinct and favorable image of your business in the customer's mind.

And it's all about perception!

Developing a Unique Marketing Perception (UMP), then promoting that perception, will skyrocket your business growth. Here's how ...

Life was so much clearer way back then. The good guys in cowboy movies always dressed in white, and the bad guys in black. It made it easy to discern between good and evil, between right and wrong, between wholesome and crooked. Hollywood had it figured out. To make a hero on screen, just dress him in white. Give him a white horse ... and make that image 'sparkle'.

Our image can be discerned from afar, and it can literally make us, or 'break' us. We can sparkle, or look crooked.

And the amazing thing is we can <u>choose</u> EXACTLY what that image is that we desire to project!

Who Am I
and What Do I Do?

In business, you need to ask yourself the question: *"Who am I?"* You also need to find out *what* you do, and *why* do you do it. Without these simple questions answered you can never fully develop an image for your customers, to 'engram' into their minds. What YOU think you are in business is not necessarily what the customer thinks.

Let me explain more fully ...

- *You may think you provide a 'great' service, and the customer may think it is mediocre.*
- *You may think you provide a product that benefits customers, they may think otherwise.*

72

- *You may do things a certain way that in your mind, is the best way for the customer ... they may prefer you didn't.*

It's all in the *perception* ... their's and your's!

Today, businesses also wear white hats, or black hats, and in fact, many shades in between.

However, many times the people 'inside' the business (CEO's, Presidents, Managers,) are simply not aware - they just don't realize their business is displaying a hat for all to see.

However, the customers and clients do, and instantly discern if the business (including yours) is the good guy in a white hat ... or the bad guy in black or gray!

Shock, Horror! ... It's All in the Perception

It's lunch time. You're driving along the road thinking about various restaurants where you may like to eat. Your mind works at a rapid pace, mulling over different choices. You think of a number of places and immediately your mind gives you opinions about the choices, such as slow service, awful food, great food, friendly staff, surly staff, cheap, expensive ... or whatever descriptive picture your mind instantly displays.

What your mind is doing is 'perceiving.' And it's instantaneous. As soon as you think of a particular business to buy from, your mind will give you a green light to go, orange warning, or a red light to stop. As quick as that, and all based on the perceptive-mind-thought process you have about that business. Your mind is saying, *"Go there and buy, they're the good guys in white"*, or *"Careful, they wear gray hats and remember the service you received last time?"* ... or worse still; *"Stop, don't even think of going there, they wear black hats. They're the bad guys and you'll be sorry you ever went there!"*

Hollywood made it easy by the 'dress code' that made the good and bad stand apart. Today, although it is more subtle, we human beings are no different in our thought process. We still make 'snap decisions' on where to buy, or who to buy from. And every one of our buying decisions are based on the 'perception' we have of that business we are considering buying from - all in a nano-second.

YOU have 'perceptions' about businesses, products, and services, instantly and forcefully!
But what is really interesting is that everybody has a perception about every business they come in contact with ... including YOURS!

Shock, horror! Did you just realize? If we *all* have perceptions about every business we come in contact with, which influences our buying decisions, then it stands to reason that people must have perceptions about *your* business also, which in turn influences them to buy from you - or stay well away!

Every existing, or potentially new customer or client
has a perception about YOUR business.
That perception is either good, bad or indifferent
... ALWAYS remember that!

They may be perceiving your business as a black hat, or a white. Your *projected perception* may sparkle like the good guys dressed in white ... or it may be projected as the bad guy dressed in black.

We are no longer in the days of good old westerns, but nevertheless your perception is projected widely. Customers might perceive your business, from the perception you're sending them in a number of ways:

- *Your business' perception could be dressed in the clothing of poor service, or 'awesome' service.*
- *It could be dressed in quality, or dressed in shoddiness.*

- *It could be identified by powerful after sales service, or the lack of.*
- *Or it could be in how easy and fun it is to do business with you ... or not.*

Like it or not, your business projects a powerful 'perception' into customer's mind's. It is either good, indifferent or bad.

White, gray or black!

Lessons
From a Nudist

I learned a profound (if not hilarious) lesson on perception from a nudist! In fact, it's such a good lesson that I use it in all my seminars!

One brisk, cold weekend at a seaside resort in Tasmania, a colleague (no names mentioned here!) had joined me in a management retreat. We had chosen the location due to its quiet nature during the winter months. Both enjoying exercise, he suggested we brave the elements and go for an early morning run along the beach before the seminar, and so I agreed. That morning, it wasn't too long before I realized he was fitter than me, as he easily pulled ahead 100 yards or so. And that's when things entered the twilight zone!

As soon as he started to heat up he peeled off his shirt and dropped it to the sand ... then not much further along he stopped for a moment and peeled off his shorts. So now, about 150 yards in front, was this completely naked guy running along the beach! Unbelievable! Suddenly, this alarming thought went off in my head; *"What if someone is watching? If they are they'll see me chasing this naked man along the beach!"* Horror of horrors!

After what seemed like an eternity, (about 20 minutes) he finally stopped, turned around and motioned for me to run back the way, which I did. (Gladly!). But now, I was having this even more unsettling thought; *"Now what if someone is watching? If so, they'll see me being chased by a naked man along the beach!"*

When we finally reached the starting point, my wife was waiting ... and wondering! My colleague then told us he was a naturist, and enjoyed running naked. We all laughed ... and have laughed at the story ever since!

The Naked
Perception

But here's the lesson. From the point of view of onlookers (thank goodness there were none), I was the pursuer of a naked man. But then, one simple 180 degree turn changed all that. He was then the pursuer. The perception *immediately* changed. Simply by turning around, going the opposite direction, their perception of us would have changed.

Your business could be seen (perceived) by onlookers (customers) as going in a certain direction and doing certain things. Even unintentionally. I was not pursuing a naked man, but I would have been *perceived* to be. Your business could be wearing a black hat or gray. Being the villain. Then with an *immediate turnaround*, (change of hats, direction, service, quality etc.) a different viewpoint, (a totally opposite perception), is created. Therefore, a change of direction equals a change of perception.

A change of direction = A change of perception.

White Hats
Attract Rapid Growth

Imagine having every potential customer in your town or city perceiving YOUR business to be the white hat guy. The ideal, most perfect and attractive business to buy from. The business that is perceived to be *simply irresistible*. You would experience outrageous business growth and customers would drive clear across town to seek you out. And they certainly would *not* waste their time going to the black hat guy, or grey hat of mediocre performance when your business shines like gold ... their 'preferred choice' ... and as the leader in your field!

They simply would not!

Create Your U.M.P.
and Discover the Most
'Potent' Business Tool Available!

If you can gain an understanding of perception, and apply the principles, your business will rocket to the top. Understanding and developing your image will assist you to stand apart from the crowd as a Red Striped Zebra in no time flat.

But perceiving what your image is, through the 'eyes' of the customer, is so very different to the way *you* may perceive it. An image of the business could be presented as the decor, the signage, the displays, the products. These could all receive high marks by you and the customer. However, if poor service, sloppy attention to detail, poor or no after sales service ... or a host of other customer skills are left to slip, your customers will have a different perception of your business than you.

One thing is certain, the building block you have to work with is 'unique'. It's YOUR business image and it can be adjusted to the highest standards.

You can maximize your white hat image to attract customers like flies to honey, and it is not difficult to do.

U.M.P. - Your Unique Marketing Perception

Your *Unique Marketing Perception* is the white hat your business should wear, and once you become aware of it, how to develop it, and how to promote it, you will overtake your competition in a flash.

In fact, without a doubt, having a well defined and strong U.M.P. is the most powerful business tool available to you in today's market. A U.M.P. that positions you as the preferred choice in the mind of your customer is the essential undergirding and effectiveness of advertising, marketing, promotions and sales. These promotional tools are a necessary part of a Red Striped Zebra business, but it is the U.M.P. that magnifies their pulling power, or *Magnetic Value. (MV)©.*

Let's break the meaning of a Unique Marketing Perception down, word by word ...

Unique (rare, uncommon, unusual)

This means your business is 'different' from others. It may be like a host of similar businesses, but there is something 'very special' about it. It may be fast service, or the ability to work miracles for clients, or a caring attitude, a specialty product, or even a special Risk Transfer (see the chapter called; *Supercharging the Marketing Engine*). You *must* identify what is so unique about your business, for it is the very essence of success for you.

Marketing (promoting, projecting, broadcasting)

Your uniqueness must be 'promoted'. In your advertisements, yellow pages, corporate brochures ... even on your packaging, invoices, letterheads, business cards ... everything that leaves your business must broadcast the difference and uniqueness about your business

Perception (customer's instant understanding of your business)

Your customer, as explained, has a 'perception' of your business, either good, bad or indifferent. Realizing this, you can engineer a stronger, more effective perception (or instant understanding) and change their behavior towards your business.

Defining Your Unique Marketing Perception

Putting all this together, your Unique Marketing Perception is the business soul ... and a tool that can revolutionize your business. It is your white hat. It must be *clearly* and *precisely* elucidated in customers' minds. It must become part of the business culture, and it must be 'projected strongly'.

Federal Express identified their U.M.P. with their credo *"If it absolutely, positively has to be there"* which means, in the mind's of its customers, *urgent*

> *The UMP is the very* **essence** *of a business, the* **soul***, the* **spirit***, that invisible but very real substance that the customer has a perception about.*

overnight delivery, guaranteed!

Pepsi promotes their U.M.P. by telling you *"It's the right one, baby!"* which is perceived to mean a delicious cola drink.

The Peabody Hotel in Orlando and Memphis is world renowned with their U.M.P. of quality accommodation - somehow projected by the *Peabody Ducks* culture. Every day, a ceremony is performed that gives the red carpet treatment for the ducks to come from their home on the roof, down to the foyer by elevator and stay all day in the center fountain. Everything in the hotel has the ducks culture, from the name of the restaurants to the ornaments on sale.

And Northwest Airlines projects their U.M.P. by telling us they are the 'number 1' on-time airline.

Having a well thought out U.M.P. and promoting it, is the success secret to establishing yourself as the absolute leader in your field.

Following are a few U.M.P.'s that have been cleverly crafted into simple advertisements ...

The Vast Selection Business

Perhaps you have a wider selection than your competitor. State your UMP in the headline:

Drive to any one of our 14 convenient locations and choose from over 700 lounge suites and 1,200 separate pieces of beautiful (and always the lowest price), furniture.

Our bakery has 23 varieties of wonderful fresh, hot bread each morning, along with 18 types of delicious pastries, cakes and pies.

Or:

Perhaps you could feature your UMP in the body copy:

Many bakeries just make the same plain ol' white bread. Smith's Bakery specializes in eight best-selling brands - plus we are the authorized distributor for

Mrs. Munro's Pies and the Sweet Selection cake range. When next you yearn for some mouth watering cakes, pies and the finest, high quality bread you'll ever taste, come to Smith's and discover the widest choice in town. We have it all for you .... and we'll even bake special orders too!

Or:

Here's a Travel Store That Can Send You Anywhere

With a name like World's Fair Travel, we have something to live up to. Wherever in the world you would like to go, we can help you. We are agents for 21 cruise ship lines, 52 airlines, 7 major train lines ... and 1,000's of hotels. We are open 7 days a week, 12 hours a day ... and if you're in some foreign country and need assistance we have a toll-free, 24 hour number that keeps us in touch and working for you.

No longer will you have to be stressed with travel, because we do it all for you. From travel, accommodation, insurance and visas, our complete, personalized service is ready to work for you.

One visit will convince you that we are your total travel source.

Or:

When You Are Choosing Cameras, Don't You Want to Know ALL Your Choices?

Not only has the world changed, but the range of cameras has radically altered in just a few short years. From SLR's to advanced Digitals, there is now a sea of choices.

Do you know what is best for you? Perhaps it's time for you to have a look at the new Digital models and see how they can change forever the way you photograph. We can help you decide as we are here to demonstrate and show you all the features and benefits.

Our special XYZ imported model now has 15% more features than the normally accepted top-of-the-line model, and 20% less to purchase. It also has a built in GPS system that records exactly where the photograph was taken, the exact time of the day and the prevailing weather conditions too. Come on in and see this and the other 23 brands, along with 100's of accessories and 47 film types.

Price
Discount Business

If your business focusses on price-discounting, perhaps you could state your UMP by saying:

**We have Exactly The SAME Brand of Cameras Everyone Else Has...
But at 35% Less**

Or:

Five Relaxing Facials for $50
Most beauticians charge $20 per visit. We are offering you that same facial for only $10, if you buy the full five ... Just so you can feel the difference for yourself.

Or:

$760 Fifty-Two-Inch Televisions Only Cost $495 at CheaperTellies.

Or:

Brand new $21,500 Fords only $18,000 ... This weekend only.

Or:

How can those big department stores give you a discount, with the cost of their overheads, salaries, utilities and advertising? They can't, because they are forced to mark everything up about 98%

Our Price-Cutters Store Here Costs Almost Nothing!

We're a family run, family owned business ... and we've been doing it for over 20 years. Everything is paid for. We keep our advertising budget low and we all work six days a week to serve your needs.

If we make 20% markup we are happy. We also find our customers are happy too, because they get the same products at a very low price. Come check us out and discover what others already know.

Or:

When you buy your cleaning chemicals from those 'giants' in the hygiene industry, you're paying top price ... and sometimes it's just for water!

We manufacture ours with the highest concentrations in the industry, and at ISO9000 specifications. But, because we're small with low overheads, our costs are about 17% less than any others. We then mark them up only 29% above costs.
Where would you rather buy your cleaning chemicals? From the distributor who buys them in dozen lots, then doubles the price, so you pay the highest .... or direct from the manufacturer? Low priced - highest concentrations!

Or:

The Average Markup in the Suit Business is 43% ... ... Ours is only 15%!

The High Quality ... or Elite Appeal Business

If your business focusses on high quality, 'exclusiveness or 'elite-appeal' you could create your UMP similar to these:

Imagine! Living in a community where you share 1,000 acres of mountain views and pristine country with only 19 other aircraft owners.

This place has it all. A 5,000 foot paved and lighted runway. Your choice of 20 beautiful home sites, each with immediate access to the taxiway. A new clubhouse that has five pool tables, kitchen, entertainment area, conference room, swimming pool and sauna. Plus a beautiful clay tennis court and community barbeque.

Now, you will be able to have an exclusive retreat to live in full time, or simply as a weekend hideaway. Fly into the beautiful mountain valley and taxi right up to your home. Ride your horse, fish in the trout stream ... or just take it easy. Call for details: ...

Or:

Each Squire's suit has 1,500 miles of fine New Zealand wool ... and that's just the beginning

In fact, each suit has 1,500 miles, 379 yards to be exact, and only the finest New Zealand wool is selected by our fastidious buyers. There are over 432 separate procedures for crafting our suits, and each step is inspected thoroughly before proceeding to the next. All our seams have double stitching to ensure both strength and durability. The lining is the finest polished cotton on the planet, and even our buttons receive special selection. Those buttons are scrutinized for imperfections, and meticulously attached with special strength thread.

In fact, each suit comes with a lifetime guarantee. Just lose a button, or put on extra weight, and we replace it, or adjust the suit, even after ten years.

We have recently bought the entire shipment of New Zealand wool from the McGreggor Farm in Auckland. They have the finest wool production in the industry. From this shipment we will produce only 243 of the finest suits in the world. They will cost more than other brands, and you will have to wait two full months after your initial fitting and measurements, but the wait and price will be worth it.

Especially if you are a business executive with a discerning eye.

The 'Service' Business

If your business focusses on great service, you could develop your UMP using these ideas:

Many Lawn Care Businesses Charge $30 Per Visit, With Extra Charges For Edging and Raking

SunnyLawn Care will visit 26 times per year, care for your lawn, trim your edges, rake your leaves and leave a perfectly neat yard for only $21 per month, billed quarterly.

Or:

Not all restaurants charge extra for appetizers, dessert ... and even the coffee

Bruno's Restaurant gives you a 'Fixe Prix" price of only $23 per person and that includes a choice of three appetizers, four main courses, and five desserts.
Then, at the end, we also give you a wonderful free cappuccino!

Or:

Here's a guarantee that other painters don't give!

When you contract us to paint your home, you get a 5 year unlimited warranty. This means if there is any blistering, peeling or fading, we will re-do the home again for free. That's a guarantee!

Or:

Buy a hand-held GPS from Most Stores and it May Be Obsolete Before You Pay it off!

Not so at AirTech! We provide you with a guaranteed update service. This means that if your GPS does not meet your requirements within two years of purchase we will give you a guaranteed and agreed upon trade in price, before you buy.
We even offer you a 60 day trial period before you become committed to the purchase, just to help you into the world of GPS navigation.

We also provide a monthly newsletter featuring time-saving tips, and ideas to help you master your new GPS and keep you informed of the ever-changing world of navigation, moving map systems and accessories.

We are here to assist you!

Conference Planning Can Be a Daunting Task

No longer do you need to drop everything to organize sandwich platters, overhead projectors, space, whiteboards or flip charts. We take over the load for you and let you get on with what you do best ... running your business.
We do it right for YOU!

These examples shout loud and clear how a well defined U.M.P. can be broadcast (marketed) to people ... and how these U.M.P.'s could change perceptions.

You may have the worst business or service record in history, and yet your business could turn around overnight. Just clean up your service act, develop your U.M.P. and promote it to the customers, loud and clear, just like these examples.

The Power Duo - a Well Defined U.M.P. and Business Substance

Q: What steps are required to develop your UMP?

It would be ludicrous to promote your business as *unique* and *special* in a certain area if it does not stand up to the test. To say your restaurant has the best food, if indeed it was terrible, would be business suicide. To promote your service as the best when it may be the sloppiest would also be fighting a losing battle.

You have to boost your U.M.P. with substance.

Combining solid customer service with a U.M.P. statement, or great food with a UMP that states: *"We have the juiciest steaks in town"*, is a proven winner.

If Federal Express established their U.M.P. with the statement *"If it absolutely, positively has to be there"* and didn't deliver the packages on time, what a backfire this U.M.P. would produce! However, they state it, and it gets there.

That's a power duo!

Upgrading, Modifying, Improving, and Renovating

Would you advertize a home for sale if it required any of those abovementioned headings to be completed? Of course not, and in business the same applies. If you can upgrade, modify, improve, or renovate any part of your business performance, operations or service ... and then promote by incorporating your U.M.P. you will generate outstanding growth.

As a Red Striped Zebra, your business cannot afford to provide sloppy or unimproved anything. It must go *first class*. It must be the *best*. With this in mind it becomes easy to then proceed and identify your U.M.P. and promote that image.

Your Distinctive Business

Having a U.M.P. establishes you as 'distinctive' and 'distinguishable'. It creates a special appeal to your business and infers that your business is more 'worthy' to buy from than the competition. *U.P.S.* or *Airborne Express* may provide very similar services to Federal Express, and in some instances may be cheaper. However, it is Federal Express that has that catchy U.M.P. Even when people send a package by U.P.S. they say they are going to Fedex it!

There name has become a verb!

In a fiercely competitive world, with mounting competition from a myriad of businesses, and faced with customers who are armed with a mind-staggering array of choices, engineering your U.M.P. will be the most potent marketing strategy you can do.

A U.M.P. breaks you free from the crowd, and as a Red Striped Zebra business that is exactly what you are trying to do.

It is not only potent, but perhaps one of the most crucial strategies you need to 'get right' before you spend another cent on advertising.

Barry Bryant - Delivery Service Extraordinaire

Barry Bryant of Hamilton, New Zealand has perfected his parcel delivery service with the use of a very clever U.M.P. He doesn't use a motto or statement, he tells an 'enthralling' story. And he has it on his business card. That is a perfect place for a U.M.P., but this one is a little different (Red Striped Zebra different).

He 'identified' the main 'uniqueness' that set him apart from other local parcel delivery firms; his cheeriness and helpfulness.

To reinforce his happy attitude to life he had a business card designed that was amusing, cartoon like, and opened out like a birthday or Christmas card. The card features a cartoon drawing of him and his van, and brightly colored. And on the card is not just his name, business and phone number, (as most are) but a catchy story:

It reads:

Picture this. It's late at night. Your office is as empty as Rugby Park on a Sunday. Suddenly, you spy four parcels that were supposed to go that day. PANIC!
Then a happy face comes to mind, Barry Bryant! You call Barry on his 18 hour mobile phone. He arrives in his

sparkling new red Courier Post van. With a joke and a smile he helps you wrap your parcels and fill out the despatch forms. Before you can say "Thanks Barry" he is half way to the depot to get your parcels on the last transport out.

You shake your head and say to yourself, "Who was that masked man?" It was Barry Bryant, alright. Courier man extraordinaire.

Then printed on the reverse of the card is a bullet list of all his services.

WOW, and Wow again! That is a U.M.P.! It is long-winded, but it is humorous and his message cuts through like a hot knife in butter. Who would you use to deliver your local parcels if he lived in your town? With a card, U.M.P. and happy disposition like that, it would be Barry for me!

Selling
the Sizzle

In every newspaper of every city we see advertisements that focus on price. Car dealers are the main offenders. They are out their selling the price. No mention of their U.M.P. No mention of the attention to service, or after sales service, or quality of the vehicle, the pride of ownership you would experience buying one of their vehicles, or the feelings you would have just by driving their vehicles. It's always price! They are selling the steak instead of the sizzle, but they only refer to the price of the steak.

A U.M.P. tells a different story. It breaks you free of the price war and competition. It tells your potential customers that you are 'different', you have something special for them, and you are above the others.

Saturn cars identified this when they launched their new car and marketing program.

Their U.M.P. identifies them as a car firm which does not haggle, offers integrity, professionalism and an American made, fastidiously built, quality vehicle.

Your U.M.P. has NO bearing on price. It releases you from that. It is to do with perception. When we think about a Mercedes or Jaguar we immediately think quality. The price is higher, but the U.M.P. focusses on quality ... and people nowadays are prepared to pay more for quality!

Your U.M.P. may establish you as the provider of insurance with integrity and professionalism, or as a real estate person who cares. It may establish your restaurant as the finest food in town, or your dry-cleaning business as the quickest and best. It may establish your lawn service as reliable perfection, or your roofing business as efficient and high quality.

It is a powerful marketing tool that will carry your business to the top!

Identify
Your U.M.P.

It is now up to you to identify what makes your business unique, what sets it apart as special, or different from others. I suggest recruiting help from staff, colleagues, partners or friends to brainstorm with you.

And ask these questions;

- *"What makes our business different?"*
- *"What can I/we offer customers that will be unique?"*
- *"Is there a service, product, program or special offer I/we can install to differentiate the business from all others?"*

It doesn't have to be major. Even the 'smallest asset' in business can be enlarged to look BIG.

Bryant's 'happy disposition' was his asset. We all like dealing with smiling people, and just that smile alone was enough to develop his U.M.P.

Identify, modify or create your U.M.P. as quickly as possible, as this is an important step in establishing your business as a Red Striped Zebra.

Promoting
the Message

Customers and clients are important to business. So are staff and suppliers, vendors and distributors. When we engineer our U.M.P. we not only have to tell the customer, but also the staff members and all those outside the business, who are linked via trade. If we are establishing our business as the swiftest service, or friendliest, or the greatest food, or finest lawn care, we best make sure 'everybody' knows it. They need to be coached on what a U.M.P. is and how it works. This is very important.

Your suppliers also need to understand what you are doing, as they are out there talking to your competition and to potential new clients for you. Let them know what your new U.M.P. is and how you plan to back it up.

Boosting Your U.M.P.
by Empowering Your Words

Sticks and Stones
or Compelling Words

Sticks and stones may break my bones, but words? The old rhyme tells us how sticks and stones can hurt us. The stones thrown our way in business are many, from taxes to regulations, to competition and the economy. We have no control over them. However, in a U.M.P. we use words. And they should be very dynamic, clear, concise and forceful words that supercharges the U.M.P. But remember, words can either sound boring, uninspiring and ineffective, or crafted to engineer a U.M.P. that 'sparkles' ... like the good guy in the white hat.

You can state your U.M.P. by saying:
"We provide prompt lawn care"

Or you can say:
"We treat your lawn like our very own, with love, attention to detail and caring."

You can state your Travel Agency U.M.P. by saying:
"We supply worry free travel."

Or give it power by saying:
"At last, you can relax on your next vacation, knowing that we have taken care of everything for you. This means you can forget about insurance, ticket confirmations, hotel reservations or the myriad of things that could go wrong. We do it all for you so you can enjoy every moment."

You can promote your Realtor business with a U.M.P. that says:
"I will find your next house"

Or you can power it up by saying:
"I will closely work with you to find your new home, making sure it meets your exact needs and desires. This means the most major purchase in your life will become much easier to locate ... and will give you years of happiness because of the right choice."

You can take a word like efficient, as in 'efficient service' and change it to expert, skilled or professional service. The word service could be changed to assistance, or help. From *'efficient service'* we can search a thesaurus and create *'Professional, skilled assistance will be provided for you'*. It means the same, but is more <u>powerful</u>.

Federal Express could have just said *'Overnight service guaranteed.'* That sounds good! ... But; *'If it absolutely, positively has to be there'* were the powerful words that built the empire!

Many of our words have deep meaning. They can motivate a person to call you or enter your store ... or they can de-motivate and REPEL!

Slogans, Truisms and Descriptors

In essence, a U.M.P. can be a descriptive, wordy precis' of your unique business, or it could reduce down into a slogan, truism, or catchphrase to relay to customers. Or it could be a combination!

R.P. Adam Ltd., our chemical manufacturer client in Scotland, specializes in the health and hygiene industry. You would have read about them in the previous chapter; The Magic of Metamorphosis. With the help of management, we produced a wordy U.M.P. that is used in it's entirety in brochures, and exerts are used wherever needed, such as in letters, newsletters and advertisements. Here is the slogan, followed by their U.M.P.

Scotland's Other Cherished Liquid Asset

This slogan appears on all brochures, packaging, adverts. and literature. And now for their U.M.P., created over a day and a half retreat session.

It reads:
YOU no longer have to SUFFER paying TOO MUCH for a confusing number of 'run of the mill' standard chemicals and poor or mediocre service

Here's your opportunity:

Because other company's can't or won't, we can and will provide you with;
   1. *A reduced number of superbly effective products specifically crafted to your precise needs.*
   2. *Unique and easy to understand wall charts and training materials - to help you attain the ultimate goal of PRISTINE HYGIENE LEVELS.*

You'll have the advantage:
In partnership with you, we'll ensure your premises are maintained to the highest possible standards ... and your people trained to work in a RISK FREE environment.
In addition to this, you'll have the ADVANTAGE with our Technical Expertise. Our highly trained team are on line for YOU. You can pass your cleaning and hygiene problems on to us, allowing you to get on with what you do best .... running YOUR

business.

Your Risk Free Guarantee*:*

So confident are we that you will be delighted with your new products, new level of service and our refreshing new approach ..... and more importantly, your reduced costs ...... that we offer you a NO RISK TRIAL.

If you are not 100% happy within 14 days ...... We'll rip up your invoice

Yes, it's wordy, but that U.M.P. says it all for R.P. Adam. From this they have incorporated sections into brochures ... and even used the guarantee on their invoices for new customers. (See the chapter: Supercharging the Marketing Engine for more on Risk Transfers).

I repeat; it's wordy, but it tells the 'essence' of the business to new customers. It creates a perception in their minds. A perception that says;

"Why would I go anywhere else but to R..P. Adam Ltd.?
I simply cannot lose with them!"

And this U.M.P. creation has propelled them out of the stagnation that a firm over 100 years knows too well, to the ability to take on the big guys and win big!

Delighted
Distributors

I heard for myself the excited comments of some of their national and international distributors, at a conference in Scotland, after seeing first-hand the 'new' R.P. Adam Ltd. They were saying that from now on, they will only carry this firms products, rather than competitors', because of the whole Zebra process the firm had gone through had made their products much easier to sell. Everyone was happy with the result.

Helpful Tips

- Change your U.M.P. with different statements to test it out.
- Create multiple U.M.P.s for dissimilar business divisions.
- You may carry a number of unrelated products and each one could carry its own, unique U.M.P.
- For the fashion store with high quality garments, such as fur coats or stylish suits, or the luxury car dealer, it could have a built in 'class' appeal U.M.P.
- The electronic goods store could build a U.M.P. in slogan form that states how 'state-of-the-art' their products are.
- The travel agency that seeks the business travel market could build a U.M.P. slogan stating how they provide 'professional service to the discerning business traveler.'

Everywhere!

The place to promote your U.M.P. is <u>everywhere!</u>

- ▸ On your business cards.
- ▸ On your letterheads.
- ▸ On all your brochures and stationary, including envelopes.
- ▸ On your signs.
- ▸ On your advertisements.
- ▸ And spoken by voice on radio or television.

The message that you are sending is promoting your 'business', not so much your products. (That comes next.)

Your business is 'special', because your U.M.P. tells people it is. It is 'unique' because your U.M.P. tells them it is. And it provides superior, different, individualized, more efficient, or whatever ...

People will come to YOU because you are identifying your business as the ONE wearing the sparkling white hat ... and the one where they'll be 'better off' buying from!

... because your U.M.P. tells people so.

> *Your U.M.P. can be short, or in the case of Bryant's Package*
> *Delivery or R.P. Adam Ltd.; long. As long as it tells the story*
> *that you choose with FORCE and EFFECTIVENESS.*

Inexplicably Unexpected - a 25% Increase

At 7.42pm one Monday night in September 1984, Sir Tom Farmer and a group of *Kwik-Fit* executives stood glued to a bank of television monitors at their advertising agency in Edinburgh, to watch their new advertising campaign.

At that time, the firm was relatively small, not having yet reached the heady status of over 1,000 auto repair centers throughout the United Kingdom and Europe. This was a gamble for them, to launch such a huge campaign, for these advertisements were different from anything Britain had ever seen before. They had a mix of actors and real Kwik-Fit fitters dancing and singing their unique new U.M.P. message; *You can't get better than a Kwik-Fit fitter.* And that message was emblazoned in white writing on the back of their blue coveralls.

Overnight
Success

The results of this campaign, using this very catchy U.M.P., were astonishing. Paul Yole, who is now Marketing Director for Kwik-Fit, recalls that sales leaped an unexpected 25% that very next morning ... and kept rising. The U.M.P. instilled a new perception in customers.

From that time on, future advertisements featured actual fitters working on vehicle repairs, to further emphasize that Kwik-Fit fitters are highly skilled artisans. Price-cutting (endemic in the industry) was displaced by Kwik-Fit with this powerful U.M.P. that underscores high quality, expert repair work. *You can't get better than a Kwik-Fit fitter* is perhaps one of the most potent U.M.P.'s in use today and is a powerful lesson on changing people's perception overnight (the 180 degree turn) ... demonstrated by the astonishing overnight 25% sales jump. (Sir Tom tells it in more detail on our tape program; *PlanetZebra.*).

Chet's Way

Chet Whitsitt is in real estate. In fact, he's a life member of Crye-Leike's Multi-Million Dollar Club. That means he's good! He sold more than $10 million worth of homes in 1994 and more than that in 1995 ... and is increasing each year since. This 37-year-old dynamo is re-writing the real estate sales book with his monumental performance. His Unique Marketing Perception (U.M.P.) presents a 'mind-picture' of an extremely hard working agent, caring for his clients. That's not what sets him apart like a Red Striped Zebra business though. It's the 'way' he promotes his U.M.P.

Chet stepped out of the portrait gallery of grinning real estate agents featured in newspaper advertisements, to do something unique.

He decided the best way to promote his U.M.P.
and his name was to become his own media barrage.

He runs his own display and classified advertising, all with unique copy that sets him apart from the rest. He works his 1,000 plus list of former, current and potential clients every month. With the help of the Crye-Leike marketing department, his 'prospects' receive a bulk rate postcard with his photograph and slogan, Check With Chet!

His marketing blitz even goes further. Whitsitt asks his clients to fill out a form about family birthdays, and they all get cards. That's parents, children and even pets. Then there are his memo pads. Every person he comes in contact with gets them. Bank tellers to fast food staff. And every pad has his U.M.P. emblazoned for all to see.

Chet even developed a metal plaque, designed to hang from the bottom of a real estate 'For Sale' sign, bearing his name, number and his inescapable face. Chet says he was the first person in the United States to do this, and he even tried to patent the idea.

Chet even goes further down the experimental road in promoting his face, name and U.M.P. Working through a local company called Metro-Pop, Chet has bushel bags of popcorn, once again emblazoned with his face and the slogan, *'Chet's popping up everywhere'* delivered to prospects and media journalists or personalities. Through this 'over-the-top' promotion Chet has had three radio stations give him free 'exposure' by poking fun at him and having a great time in their morning drive-time shows. Although Chet's monthly advertising exceeds $1,000, he has no hesitation in spending, knowing it *"takes money to make money",* he says. And the results are certainly there.

Chet's U.M.P.

What sets Chet apart? Other people have mounted similar campaigns of self-promotion with limited success. So, what's his secret? First, his U.M.P. is down to earth. It tells people he is humorous, able to laugh at himself, a hard working agent who cares. You can see it in his promotional pieces. They are not flashy or sophisticated. In fact, many think they are downright 'hokey' and cornball. Here are a few examples:

> ▸ *There's the loud orange newspaper inserts with themes like Wanted, Chet Whitsitt. (front and side views of Chet's head).*
> ▸ *Another states:*
>   *It's 8:00pm. Do you know where your Realtor is? (If your Realtor is Chet Whitsitt, chances are he's still at work).*
> ▸ *The business card with a photograph of Chet posed near the goal line of an empty stadium under the slogan: Outstanding in his field. Get it?*
> ▸ *The direct-mail piece that shows Chet with his hands to his head, his eyes bugged out and his mouth distended in a wild hoot under the slogan: I'm crazy about real estate!*
> ▸ *And then there is his Halloween card. Another bright orange insert which features his face not once but fifteen times, his likeness transformed with marking pen into fifteen cartoon caricatures, from Chet Presley, Chetopatra, Dolly Whitsitt through to Gorbachet.*

Chet Whitsitt not only developed a strong U.M.P. that showed him as a funny, in-your-face type agent who loves life and people, but he also promotes that U.M.P. far and wide. Every creative method he can think of to get his U.M.P. message out there, he takes. You too can literally about-face your business by creating the U.M.P. then promoting it widely.

Your Business Will Shine like Gold

A clear U.M.P., well defined and constantly promoted, will establish your business as 'undisputed leader' in your field. It will give you an 'unfair' advantage over your competition, for to the customer, your business will be the one that shines like gold.

On the reverse of this, an unclear U.M.P. (black or grey hat variety) will give your competition the unfair advantage that will cause them to win by default. As mentioned, you *already* have an image, a U.M.P., a perception held by your customers or clients. It may be good, bad or indifferent, but nevertheless it is there.

Check-mate Your Competition

When you create and promote your U.M.P. you immediately re-position and place your business in *front* of your competition. You check-mate them. The owners or managers simply will not understand what is going on as many business people today simply do not understand what a U.M.P. is ... and what it can do.

Take a walk today and observe every business you pass. Chances are they do not promote their U.M.P. How many times have you gone into a business and thought to yourself that if you owned it you would change things? I have, on many occasions. And so do customers! If the owners of those businesses understood the concept they would experience a profound growth in their business.

> *It is the <u>clearly</u> defined, and <u>repeatedly announced</u> statement, called a U.M.P. that is important to the customer's buying decisions.*

U.M.P.'s, Red Striped Zebras and White Hats

Establishing a powerful U.M.P. means more than a good company logo or name. Our business name is important to us, but *not* to the customer. The logo is also important, but more to us than others.

Dr. Smith's Family Dentistry may be a good name for the dentist, but a statement that says: *Gentle care and beautiful results, at a moderate price, guaranteed!* ... means a great deal more to the potential clients.

Being Different

A Red Striped Zebra business, is one which explores 'every' avenue in order to be 'different' in a *world of choices*. The customer or client not only demands choice, but *retreats* from the business that is mediocre and average. In this world of fierce competition and customers armed with choice, a business must be very unique, very 'different' ... and it must provide over-the-top service to stand apart.

It is important to understand what hat YOUR business is wearing and how to project the perception YOU want. A perception that actually 'moves' customers to respond. That can only be achieved by developing your U.M.P. and promoting it far and wide.

YOU are the creator and author of your business's
*U.M.P. ... **it's very soul**. And 'what' you say as a descriptor,*
or 'how' you say it, is paramount to your success.

Choose your words carefully and promote
them to the world. Then watch your business grow!

Your Unique Marketing Perception is a manufactured statement,
designed to paint a 'word picture' or PERCEPTION in
customers' minds ... to COMPEL them to buy from YOU.

It must set you apart as the 'unique' and 'different'
Red Striped Zebra business
... the undisputed leader in your field!

And you do this for one major purpose ...
because the GOOD GUYS WEAR WHITE HATS!

Stripe 4

ZebraServe©

How to skyrocket your business by
supplying what others don't ...
Awesome Customer Service!

Q: How does a Red Striped Zebra business stand apart from the crowd and excel?

A: Simply by learning how to not just please, but to spoil and delight customers and clients.

They say if you build a better mouse trap, people will beat a path to your door. Presented here is a 'philosophy' to build a better customer service strategy, so customers beat a path to YOUR door.

It's been over two decades now! The fervor to embrace a passionate dedication to customer service has not abated. In fact, if anything, it's increasing. The utterance of corporate platitudes for 'quality' customer service are numbering in the trillions; telling people how to survive in the service economy has become an industry in its own right. Bookstore shelves groan under the weight of books with either 'service' or 'customer' in the titles, and each week yet another 'ultimate guide to winning' through customer service appears.

Also, a quick check through any number of training video catalogs will reveal 100's of entries under the 'customer service' title, plus the saturation levels from the seminar industry with these programs.

Placing a 'delighted' smile on the face of every customer or client has become an obsession. And who would argue with that? Certainly not the Chief Executive, President, or the Marketing director. Further down the line though, where front-line service staff work, there's a different story. That's the realm of the bank teller, waiter, flight attendant, sales person or hotel clerk who must try to meet the directives of the corporate decision makers, by 'pleasing' the customer. And many of these industries, such as the airlines, require, nay; demand, that their front-line people actually smile at customers. (Even when they simply don't 'feel' like doing so!)

This is where making customer service effective gets tough! Today's customers are demanding. They are sophisticated ... and are armed with a myriad of available choices for products, services or businesses.

A television that sells in one store is offered in a myriad of other stores, at a better price, sales price or matching price ... and usually with many other options. Same applies for lounge suites, cars, or clothing. Customers can buy anything they want and they hold the key to *your success* ... or your *failure*.

Because of the availability of products, prices, and choices, it is much harder to please customers than ever before. They will not accept, nor tolerate poor service, because all they need to do is choose your competitor in preference to you!

Red Striped Zebra Service

Trying to just 'improve' customer service is not sufficient enough for the Red Striped Zebra business.

It simply will not do.

What's needed is a 'brand new strategy' that surpasses all the performance standards of the past. A standard or service that is 'over and above' what customers are used to ... or what your competitors expect.

What Must I Do To Win YOUR Business?

Have you ever asked potential customers or clients that question? *"What must I do to win YOUR business?"* The answers might surprise. In business, we 'presume' to know what the customer wants or needs, and so we endeavor to provide for those wants or needs without asking.

Detroit thought this. The big car manufacturers 'thought' they knew what the public wanted to buy, or needed. They of course, were wrong. By presuming they wanted big, gas drinking sedans, with unimaginative styling, was a disaster. People wanted smaller compacts with style and high quality - hence the Japanese invasion that put Detroit on its knees. Detroit had to fight long and hard to come back and win the trust of the American people.

Just Black

Even way back in Henry Ford's day, the choice of color was limited. They would say; *"You can have any color you want, as long as it's black."* Why? Because black dried faster than other colors. The focus was on the needs of the business, NOT the buyer. They did not consult the customer, they were simply told what to buy. Presumption ruled! Not today though, it just does not work anymore. To thrive, we simply must ask the customer what 'we' must do to win 'their' business. That's correct, it's is not just the 'normal' service you supply. It has to be a very special and specific service. In fact, it has to be service that WOWS customers.

It's all about _special_ service that WOWS the customer. That's it! Do it right and you win, do it wrong and you lose!

Competition is fierce in today's marketplace, and those businesses which provide sloppy service will lose big time, as there are any number of others ready to replace the business that 'under-performs'. In fact, it's a dog eat dog world of business.

Better put, you're operating your business amongst a herd of black and white Zebras. If you're the Red Striped Zebra business, the one that stands apart from the crowd (represented by the *type* of service you provide) you win big time. If you fail to, you meld into the herd of indistinguishable black and whites - doing nothing out of the ordinary!

It's a world full of customers armed with choice, all desperately seeking out the Red Striped Zebra business, from the vast herd of indistinguishable black and whites!

The "Philosophy" of Awesomeness

Teenagers have some great words. Awesome being one of them, along with radical and cool, but why should awesome belong only in their world? A great word like that should be used to describe something of 'real value', such as the quality of customer service a business decides to provide.

Awesome means; *inspiring, amazing*, or *astonishing*.

It's a great word, and one which I 'reclaim' for the sole use of the Red Striped Zebra business, to describe the 'type' of customer service provided ... i.e. ***Awesome Customer Service.***
Now wouldn't that make a great *Unique Marketing Perception*? (Outlined in the chapter: *The Good Guys Wear White Hats!*). To state that you supply *Awesome Customer Service* would certainly establish your business with the perception in customer's minds that you're the leader in your field, and the only one to buy from, because you treat people in a way they've never been treated before.

Philosophy is another great word.
It means an *idealogy*, a *conviction*, or a *view*.

In the United States, customer service is generally taught and applied as 'systems', with specifics and clear job procedures that can be measured. (And recounted in a complaint before the Equal Employment Opportunity Commission). These 'systems' also include self-service displays, mail order catalogues, and serve yourself buffets.
Even in small retail specialty stores, these systems are demonstrated as 'selecting your own products' from the racks or shelves and finding someone to take your money. It is demonstrated every time you drive into a service station and pump your own gas. It is demonstrated by the drive-thru systems of the food chains. The 'systems' have replaced employee involvement, employee interest, product knowledge, personal pride, commitment and employee equity.
Amazingly, these systems do work. A bank drive-thru window can be efficient. Just don't go there on a busy Friday, or get behind certain folk with complicated transactions though ... It might make more than just your car fume!

What an opportunity for the Red Striped Zebra business to steam-roll straight past the competition.

Sadly though, the customer, non the wiser, misses out on 'experiencing' truly 'awesome' service. What they do not know, they will not miss. Or will they?

The Usher
on Y Block

Take the case of an Usher who works in London's Royal Albert Hall. A tall man in his fifties, who dresses in a distinguished red blazer, gray trousers, white shirt and black tie. He's in charge of Block Y in the third balcony. Endowed with personal pride, professionalism and a dedication to his career, he doesn't just collect tickets. He 'manages' that Y Block as 'though he owned' it. He takes patrons to their seats, helps them with their overcoats, helps people find better seats if they are available and does what he can to make them happy and comfortable. He smiles constantly, and gives the impression that it is his job to do 'whatever' he can to make certain the patrons have a 'thorough' enjoyment of the evening.

He's a Red Striped Zebra
(with a red blazer to match),
in the theater business.

Contrasting his professional performance and Awesome Customer Service, the United States Ushers have different guidelines. It falls under the systems approach. They would receive a job outline that would state;

> *Your job is to show patrons to their seats, give them a program and point out the exit doors in case of a fire.*

The theater management could not also say;

> *"....... and do whatever it takes to ensure the patrons are comfortable, happy and able to enjoy the performance."*

Systems ...
or Philosophy?

Most Western European countries still rely on professional and dedicated employees who 'take great pride' in their work, especially in retailing. When we take the systems and clear job procedures approach, we will get a 'measure' of performance, but how big is that measurement? Systems will guarantee performance levels to the 'set standard', but no more. They will also provide a cookie-cutter formula for service that works in the chain stores. But that is all!

These approaches that businesses have taken present an astonishing opportunity for the business that decides to put on the red stripes. They do not have to be locked in to 'normal' standards, systems or procedures. They can break free and excel.

- ▸ It's an opportunity to overtake competing business, or even businesses *many times larger*.
- ▸ An opportunity to capture clients by the bushel load.
- ▸ An opportunity to provide a service that 'spoils' customers, causes them to return at *every opportunity* for more.
- ▸ And an opportunity to provide a service so 'awesome' that your customers and clients become evangelists for your cause ... telling all their friends about YOUR business.

It's an opportunity, YOUR opportunity, awaiting to be embraced, and all you have to do is adopt a far superior standard of customer service than what the competition provides. This means rather than sticking with the systems approach, embrace an **idealogy** or **conviction**. It means making the rules as you and your team go along, changing, modifying and fine tuning to make sure the customer receives their *inspiring, amazing* and *astonishing* customer service.

Sounds good doesn't it? But can it be done? Absolutely! The usher in London does it. He doesn't need a set of 'specifics' written down, telling him what he must do to provide awesome service. It's already a *philosophy* in his mind. Whatever it takes to make the patrons happy, he does it, (with pleasure) and his only guide is the *conviction* or *idealogy* that tells him he provides inspiring, or astonishing service. He in fact, wants to *spoil* his patrons.

A customer service strategy NOT written as a set of systems, procedures or job descriptions ... but one that embraces a philosophy.
A 'philosophy' of Awesome Customer Service.

The Ideology
Permeates

When we introduce the philosophy of *Awesome Customer Service*, from the management down, we can throw away the rule book. People will not have to be told, threatened, cajoled, enticed or harassed into providing good customer service. The philosophy, or idealogy will *permeate* throughout the business and people will seek ways, on their own volition, to provide 'over-the-top' type service. If something has to be fixed for the customer, they will go out of their way to fix it. If something has to be found, ordered, or supplied by a certain time, they will go overboard to get the job done.

The philosophy of *Awesome Customer Service* takes on an identity of its own as people embrace its precepts. This conviction that we provide *'astonishing'* and *'inspiring'* service will be the fuel that skyrockets the Red Striped Zebra business to the top.

Extra-Mile Thinking

The Red Striped Zebra business which embraces the philosophy of *Awesome Customer Service*, always extends itself, going for the 'extra' mile approach.

The systems approach rule book doesn't allow for 'extra' service ... but the 'philosophy' style does. That little 'something extra' given by staff to delight customers, becomes a part of *Zebraising* (new word to learn) a business. It simply takes on a bold, new RED stripe, as in these following examples:

▸   *The Great Northern Hotel* in Launceston, Tasmania embraced the philosophy of Awesome Service. And it wasn't long before the 'extra mile' thinking came into effect. Management gave the housemaids permission to place gift chocolates on the turned down beds for guests, adding to the Great Northern experience. In the up-market *Tram Bar*, they gave Friday evenings a boost as they provided the after-business guests with free, hot finger food, brought around regularly by staff. Just small items really, but the Extra-Mile thinking generated more guests and patrons.

- *The Hacienda Hotel* in Los Angeles is a medium priced, mid-range hotel with a Mexican flavor. It also stands apart by providing awesome service, and the Extra-Mile concept, by serving guests champagne, along with Mexican food appetizers in their courtyard, in the late afternoon. Add a 'wandering minstrel' singer/musician, and you have a very pleasant hotel experience. An experience that causes you to bypass the systems type hotels and return to this Red Striped Zebra business.

- *The Holiday Inns Menzies Hotel* in Sydney, New South Wales adds the extra mile thinking. While in Sydney on business for a two-week period, I stayed at this fine old hotel. It is well known, but has to compete with many beautiful, new hotels in the city. As far as I was concerned, a stone jug of fine port wine showed their Extra-Mile thinking. It was placed in my room while I was away conducting business. That was a very pleasant surprise. I always remember that hotel with pleasure, and of coming back to the room in the evening to have a glass of port with my business colleagues.

- *Routley's* is another Launceston business that embraces awesome service, and Extra-Mile thinking. David Routley runs a tight customer service ship. He knows his clients and looks after them well. The last time I purchased a suit from David, I didn't even leave my office. I called him and described the type of look I was after. A charcoal grey, fine wool-flannel type, business suit. We discussed the type of image, cut and other details, and in a few days he called me to say he had ordered the suit in from the manufacturer. I went to the store, tried the suit on, and immediately purchased it. David, already knowing my size and required adjustments, sent the suit to his tailor for fine tuning, and once again called me when it was ready. Knowing I travel frequently, David always includes a plastic, zippered suit bag, which packs nicely into a suitcase. His business stands apart like a Red Striped Zebra, his service is definitely awesome ... and he goes the Extra Mile.

- *Axis Travel* of Adelaide, South Australia, is operated by Max Najar, a man who understands awesome service and going the Extra-Mile. This travel agency has won the Travel Agent of the Year title, and in the last eleven years has produced over 83% *repeat* business, plus a large following of overseas and interstate-based clients. How? By establishing the business as a high-quality provider of travel, undergirded by applied *Awesome Customer Service*. Upon entering the business, the client experiences designer decor, piped CD music, and on the tables are customized chocolates. His consultants are highly trained, and sent on regular educational trips to familiarize themselves with destinations. They operate the latest computer equipment, and they even have their own personalized, monogrammed towels and toiletries. The consultants are empowered to deliver awesome service to their clients. This, combined with the superb image of quality that Axis Travel projects, generate outstanding results. Discounting and competition has faded from view. The notion and belief that a travel agency has to discount to survive, simply are not true in Axis's business. The discerning business traveler who wants to be treated with class bypass the discounters and place all their travel business with Axis. They've set a new standard in quality that clients respond to. They do not have to seek the client who chases low prices, for their business attracts the discerning traveler. A business which has gone the extra-mile!

▸ *The Omni Hotel* in Hong Kong goes the Extra-Mile and provides its philosophy of *Awesome Customer Service* in an unusual manner. They supply one of the finest buffet breakfasts ever experienced, and served in their beautiful restaurant overlooking the harbor. Selected nights have differing Asian food tasting, further adding to their 'extra mile' thinking. To go for a swim in their pool is a great pleasure, an attentive attendant with a welcoming smile supplies you with fresh towels, locates a place for you and serves drinks as you require. On each hotel floor a security guard sits in a position that allows him to see along all corridors. Anytime of the day the guards are present, giving a feeling of security to overseas visitors. Tour groups are well cared for at this fine hotel. The individuals in any tour group have their baggage delivered from the airport, directly into their rooms. Upon checking out of the hotel, baggage is taken from outside the doors, to be collected at the airport check-in desks. No handling of heavy baggage and no security problems.

▸ *Bruce Hardwood Floors* went the extra-mile in service 30 years ago that won them real success. For years people had been writing to Bruce to ask how to take proper care of their new oak floors. This resulted in Bruce manufacturing their own brand of floor wax. The extra-mile was added by placing small stickers on every 20th or so piece of flooring. This sticker message instructed the floor layer to leave it on the floor ... and told the homeowner to pull off the sticker, stick it onto a postcard and mail it to Bruce for a *free sample* of wax and *instructions* on how to care for the new floor. This was extra-mile thinking ... but one that resulted over a period of years for a strong demand for Bruce Wax, which caused it to move onto the supermarket shelves rather than the lumberyard store. It literally created the Bruce Wax brand and a very profitable product family that is now owned by the Dial Corporation.

► *Linters Inc.*, is a Seattle-based manufacturing firm that has gone the extra-mile in producing a product that is totally different, yet competes neck to neck with it's competitors. The firm has developed a method of using 100% cotton for its tissue products ... instead of wood-based. (Even manufacturers, not just service industries, can go the extra-mile by developing *unique* products!). Trading under the name; *Purely Cotton*, and formed in 1994, they have taken on the giants such as Kimberly-Clark and Proctor & Gamble and are carving a niche market with all those folk who would prefer cotton for their toilet tissue, paper towels, feminine hygiene products and diapers. Linters was formed by two Scottish brothers from Hawick, a tiny borders town. Tim and Willy Paterson-Brown sensed that they had a winner with the cotton idea, and went through great hurdles to figure out how to create, develop and market such a product in an already saturated market. The extra-mile thinking was in giving people something *different* (there's that word again) than the other guys. Tests have demonstrated that cotton is the least disruptive product to the skin as a result of having a different chemical content than wood pulp products. These brothers felt this way well before tests were completed ... and today you'll find their extra-mile product on your supermarket shelves. A testament to breaking the rules or the accepted ways of manufacturing ... and going the extra-mile to produce something more highly desirable than other goods. Their goal for 1999 is $50 million in sales ... and climbing as they go nationwide ... and then Europe!

► *Zoo Doo Inc.* was founded by Pierce Ledbetter as an extra-mile firm after he read an article in an Asian newspaper during his travels, about the wonders of elephant manure for gardens. This got him thinking. He talked to zoos in the United States and found that many neither had the time nor the resources to collect and transform animal manure into compost for gardens. Most of it was sent to landfills which cost the zoos money and time. After caring for animals all day it was simply a time-consuming and thankless task for zoo workers to rid their zoos of all the animal waste. He found that there was even less resources for zoos to undertake nationwide, let alone regional, marketing campaigns to make compost selling a success. That's when he formed the *Zoo Doo Compost Company Inc.* As he puts it; *"Wherever zoos had the poop, I had the time!"* His extra-mile thinking for customers was quite simple; turn the manure into sweet smelling compost for plants, then package and merchandise it in the most clever and advantaged based way possible that would help the gardener customers. From large plastic buckets with attractive labeling to visual tools, instructions ... and even novelty items in zoo gift stores as well as garden and nursery shops, Zoo Doo offers a twofold benefit; zoos prosper by supplying the firm the 'raw' product, cutting down costs and time ... and customers are advantaged with perhaps one of the best organic fertilizers available. And with his highly humorous brochures which read; *Ever wonder why jungles are so lush?* gives him a great extra-mile thinking business venture that benefits everybody. (I wonder if there is any zebra doo in the buckets?)

➤ *Disney* is an extra-mile business. Everybody knows that and the stories are many, however, I prefer the ones that change the *names*. All customers to Disney World are called *guests* ... and employees are known as *cast members*. That makes for an instant *re-focus* on how to go the extra-mile. If a guest asks a staff member; *"What time is the three o'clock parade?"* the cast member doesn't roll their eyes and give the person a bad time ... but presumes they mean 'where' is the parade held ... and goes out of their way to help them. The also have names for any problems a guest may have. They call these *tragic moments* ... and try to replace those tragic moments with a number of *magic moments* to make a guest happy. Mickey's magic moments are really extra-mile thinking strategies to delight customers and bring them back to the theme parks time and time again.

These are all examples of *Awesome Customer Service* and going the Extra-Mile!

The 5 Advantages of Awesome Service

Replace the systems approach with the **philosophy** of *Awesome Customer Service*, and your business will benefit in these five ways.

1. *You will eradicate competition.*

2. *You will eradicate price-cutting.*

3. *You will increase customers.*

4. *You will make more money.*

5. *You will stimulate employee satisfaction.*

Mediocre performance is the general rule today. Your competition's customer service, in general, is weak and your opportunities are *great*. When you understand the pulling power of *Awesome Customer Service,* and understand how all your people can embrace it as a *philosophy*, or *ideology*, rather than just a 'rule book' or system, the gains for your business will be substantial.

1. Eradicating Competition

> **Don't compete, change the game!**
> Dr. Robert J. Kriegel Ph.D.
> *"If It Ain't Broke, Break It!"*

Embracing the Philosophy of *Awesome Customer Service* will change your service game, making competition, for all intensive purposes, obsolete. You eradicate competition because your business no longer competes. (The Red Striped Zebra *never* competes - he changes the rules).

As with Axis Travel, by presenting an image of well-trained professionals supplying over-the-top service, they attract the business traveler, along with discerning travelers who want to be assured of a problem free journey or holiday. Axis does not need to compete against the local market, nor the Australian market. The business has consultants who are educated professionals, qualified and oriented toward the world market. If an enquiry comes in for discount travel, they refer them elsewhere. They don't compete, because they have 'invented' a *new* game.

For the hotel guest, a home away from home is always preferable than a sterile hotel situation. Chocolates on pillows, hot food in the bar, champagne and musicians, it all adds to the perception of inspiring service.

The customer or client is a human being. They have needs, wants and desires. They want to be satisfied. They want to be made to feel *important.* They want to be educated about their potential purchase, and they want to be treated as though you were serving your own mother.

Customers WANT satisfaction. They desire and secretly crave being spoiled.

If your business can do all that, competition fades into insignificance, as the satisfied and happy clients return many times over. (Refer to the *Customer's Long-Term Value - CLTV.*)

2. Eradicating
Price-cutting

Competing on price also becomes secondary, as you provide awesome service. If you provide over-the-top service, AND inform your potential customers and clients that you do, the 'perception' of a quality business, supplying quality products and service, will take pre-eminence over price. This further undergirds the business U.M.P. that's covered in the chapter: *The Good Guys Wear White Hats.*

It has much to do with perception
... not just price!

We expect a Ferrari should cost far more than a Mazda because we *perceive* the value to be more. If you produce and sell the 'Rolls-Royce' of hamburgers, the customers will *expect* it to cost more than a simple burger. The perception of value is higher.

So too is the supplying of *Awesome Customer Service*, which further fortifies a quality product or service. The customer, client, guest or patient will *expect* it to cost more. Again, the perception of value is higher. (see; *Perception of Value Education - POVE*, in the chapter: *Supercharging the Marketing Engine That Drives the Machine*).

3. Increasing Customers
and Return 'Buying' Visits

What is your reaction when you visit a restaurant that supplies *inferior* service? Have you ever sat in disgust, waiting for your order to be taken, and then waited for ages for the meal? Have you ever had to wait for an eternity for the check? Rather than cause a scene, have you quickly paid the bill and left, vowing *never* to return? I have! So have many others.

On the reverse, have you ever visited a restaurant that has provided over-the-top service, a friendly caring server, superb food, and prompt attention to the bill? Of course you have, and chances are you *still* frequent that establishment.

An inbuilt guarantee
of repeat sales

The philosophy of *Awesome Customer Service*, along with going the Extra-Mile, comes with an *inbuilt* guarantee. Poor service, or systems approach service, does not. That guarantee is that the customer, client, or guest 'will' return, ... *time and time again*. In Axis's case, the guarantee stands at 83%!

The normal black and white business which has provided job descriptions and systems to its people will of course have return customers, but simply not at the same rate. They have educated the customer to *expect* that type of *mediocre* service, so they take it for granted. However, the Red Striped Zebra business which embraces a philosophy of *Awesome Customer Service* has a 'secret weapon' guarantee.

The spoiled, pampered customer 'always' returns!

Once you expose a customer or client to inspiring service, they will always return. They cannot help themselves, for you will have 'spoiled' them. Once they experience quality service, they will not want poor service anymore. They will perceive the business offering the systems approach as *substandard* in comparison.

Once you have made customers feel good, made them feel respected, made them feel happy and excited about your business and their purchases, there will be no stopping them. They will hone in on your business as their *preferred choice*.

4. More Money
with the CLTV

Awesome Customer Service guarantees customer returns. Coupling these returns with an understanding of the *Customer's Long-Term Value (CLTV)*, outlined in detail in the chapter titled: *'Supercharging the Marketing Engine That Drives the Machine'* will provide you with the second most powerful marketing tool on the planet. (The first being the development of your U.M.P.).

Most businesses do not understand this amazing phenomenon, and consequentially lose out. They see customers, clients or guests as a *one-sale* transaction. They of course would like the customer to come back. Yet if you were to ask most business owners or managers what is the long-term value of a customer, in dollar terms, they could not tell you. They do not know if the customer who just bought an item for $300 is worth more in the long-term. If they knew that the opportunity existed to sell that same customer $3,000 or $10,000 worth over the next two, five or ten years, would the service be different? Sure it would! The problem is, most do not know, nor have ever taken the time to find out the *potential true value* of a long-term customer.

- Do you know what that dollar value of your customer is in your business?

- Do you know how many times your average customer buys from you in one year, three, or five?

You should! If you do, you'll be staggered at the amount a customer can be worth to your business - and you will understand clearly why Awesome Service is necessary, to keep them returning and buying repetitively!

Imagine the possibilities for you!

A business embracing the philosophy of *Awesome Customer Service*, and Extra-Mile thinking, has a distinct advantage over the competing systems approach business. The customer will keep coming back, and consequentially the CLTV will increase. That is obvious.

What would be an added bonus though, would be if the Red Striped Zebra business embracing this philosophy were to 'actively concentrate' on building the CLTV. Imagine the possibilities.

5. Inspiring Staff to
Perform Awesome Acts

Equity partnering is a phenomenon that develops when the business embraces awesome service. The staff act and perform as though they had an equity, or investment in the business. The truth is, they do. Their investment is their job. If the business performs well, their job, future and family are secure.

If you empower the employee to act, (not to just please, but to WOW the customer), they receive satisfaction from those happy customers, and from seeing the business grow. They can *see* and *feel* the difference their performance makes. They see it in the smiles and comments of the customer. They see it in the degrees of growth the business makes, as they perform cach *awesome* act. And in the long-term they experience it in their salary increases and promotions.

Equity partnering comes about in those businesses which fully liberate staff to 'perform' at awesome levels.

When you expose them to a philosophy of *Awesome Customer Service*, they discard the rule book and limits disappear. They will continually find ways to outdo each awesome service performance.

The usher at the Albert Hall does not own the block of 200 seats on the third balcony, yet he certainly acts like an equity partner. He acts and performs as though he does, as he skillfully moves throughout the area caring for his patrons. Because he provides awesome service, he acts as though he has a strong financial interest in that block of seats, but the truth is he is experiencing the *phenomenon of equity partnering*, caused by embracing this inspiring service.

The people in your Red Striped Zebra business will function at higher levels of performance, and act as equity partners, when you allow the business to adopt the philosophy of Awesome Customer Service.

How to Install Awesome Service as a Philosophy

Hire Attitudes ...
Teach Skills.

Howard Putnam, the former CEO of *Southwest Airlines*, was responsible for taking the airline from $80 million to $240 million in revenue, and tripling profits to $24 million in just three years.

Howard and I recorded an audio-tape program, titled; *The Magic of Metamorphosis*, in our studio in Memphis. This four-tape program proved to be a potent mix of success-secrets and formulas for growing any business. (Contact our office to secure your copy). Howard mentioned that Southwest became the most copied and envied airline in the United States, and in fact representatives of airlines worldwide, such as Ansett in Australia, traveled to Texas to see what gave them the runaway success.

Was it great marketing, promotions, cut-price sales? No, none of those. We tend to think that good marketing is all that is needed to build a business, but Howard emphatically attributes the airline's success to one major principle ... *We hired attitudes and taught skills!*

Wow! That goes against all business thought doesn't it? To make a major airline overwhelmingly successful one would think of catchy advertisements, good ticket prices, on-time flights ... anything but hiring attitudes. But, that's exactly what happened! The right attitudes made everything else work well!

The Personality Profile

The airline had a personality profile in place. They figured that if they wanted to build an airline with a 'fun' customer service philosophy, they would have to hire 'fun' people. They looked for cheerleaders, baton twirlers and women who had high energy, gregarious, fun attitudes. The hot pants and boots added to the pizazz, but it was in the *hiring of attitudes* first, then teaching the necessary skills to these people.

I doubt if you could build a business on hot pants and boots today, but most certainly the right attitudes will. In recent times, I have spoken to people who have traveled on Southwest and on some of the 'majors'. They tell me they notice a big difference in the friendliness between Southwest and others - a legacy of awesome service that still exists today. In fact, as of this writing, *J.D. Power and Associates* reports that on the Power/*Frequent Flyer* survey of 6,250 frequent business travelers, Southwest ranked *first* with the most helpful flight attendants among the top nine airlines!

Attitudes = Awesome Service

Hiring of staff in most firms always takes a totally opposite approach. It's hire *skills*. They make sure applicants for a position have the right degree, the right experience. In many cases they overlook personalities and end-up paying for it in the long run.

A grumpy person, an uncaring person, one that ignores or overlooks customers will drive them away, even though that person may have academic degrees, knowledge and experience. Worse than that, in an effort to pay the lowest wage, many firms will employ people with neither skills nor appropriate attitudes.

More than ever, in this fiercely competitive world, if you are out to out-do competitors, you better make sure you use Howard's 'proven' success-formula; *hire attitudes - teach skills later!*

> ➤ *Do your existing employees have fun attitudes?*
> ➤ *Are they gregarious and do they enjoy making a 'difference' in customer's lives?*
> ➤ *From the customer's point of view, do you think your business is a fun place to do business with?*

Bob's Approach

Bob Ansett is a leading personality in Australia. He was the man who established the *Budget Rental Car* franchise in the country, and developed it to great heights. Starting with six vehicles in Melbourne, he built the business nationwide on the 'awesome service' philosophy. Although he was the Chairman of the corporation, Bob worked shoulder to shoulder with counter staff if demand was great, and was not averse to joining the cleaning crew and washing cars. Today, Bob is a sought after consultant and speaker teaching businesses about awesome service.

Prior to Bob starting the business though, he lived for some years in the United States. He tells how he learned his over-the-top service strategies and philosophy from his working in a service station, of all places.

Groceries ... or Gas?

Today, to drive into a service station for fuel, we witness how systems play havoc with business. Gone is the need for awesome service. It is replaced with an insulated clerk behind a glass screen, who collects your money. If you want to buy groceries your in luck, but don't try to get your oil checked and topped off. You will have to go to a grocery store to buy oil. Service stations do not see the need for providing such a service. They have reduced it down to the bare minimum.

In fact, I object to the word *service*, in service station. Now that they've reduced the service, surely they should reduce the name too, like everything else, to just station ... or; *No-service* Station!

Uniforms
Inspire Service

Back in the early sixties, when Bob Ansett learned service, he tells how a car would drive in, and the staff would go into action. Dressed in white coveralls with a red hat, their uniform reflected quality in service. They would clean the glass, check the oil, check the tires and pump the gas. Then they would collect the money, make change and wish the customer a great day. That was awesome service!

Nowadays we have to get our hands dirty and pump our own gas, check our own tires, oil and glass. We have to make the journey into the station and pay the cashier through a glass petition. So, we must ask the question;

> ▶ *"If we have to provide our own service, or accept less-than-before service, is a systems type service better than the 'philosophy' of Awesome Customer Service?*

Pyramex, a supplier of products in the health and safety industry, and one of our clients, have incorporated the 'uniform' approach to building their service industry. They purchased made-to-order shirts, blouses and even baseball hats, with their corporate name, and a Red Striped Zebra on the pocket or hat, to remind themselves and their customers, the level of service they supply - being awesome service - Red Striped Zebra variety!

Waist-Coats Too

Arpal, another client in the United Kingdom, have chosen waist-coats with red stripes, to be worn by staff members and management, whenever they man their booth at large trade shows held throughout the country.

Perhaps it's just a small thing, but as Bob Ansett states, the wearing of those uniforms did much to lift the service philosophy, in everyone's minds. (Including customers). It's not a matter of wearing uniforms with stripes or Zebras as some of our clients have chosen to do. It can be anything, from matching ties, shirts, blouses or scarves. What matters is the solidifying of the team ... and the inference of service that excels!

Leading
by Example

Bob Ansett took his training in awesomeness and built a national car rental giant with it. He set the example to his people by *physically showing them* that it is a ***philosophy*** ... NOT a rule book, simply by rolling up his sleeves and washing cars. An *inspiring* leader who inspired his people to *inspire* customers!

> *Systems tend to diminish productivity and performance.*
> *The philosophy of awesome service builds national giants!*

Rose by Any
Other Name

They say a rose by any other name is still a rose. Maybe so, but name changing can cause *mind-sets* to be broken. Having people embrace a new way of presenting customer service, is done by actually *revising* the names. The wording 'customer service' has become quite boring. Like a word that we repeat many times over, the actual meaning becomes meaningless.

Q: So, how do you introduce a 'philosophy' of awesome service?

A: *Just change the names!*

The wording we have been using throughout has done just that for you. *Awesome, inspiring, amazing, astonishing* are all words which immediately cause 'excitement' in people. Telling your staff, or yourself, that you want to give *astonishing* service to your clients will 'rewrite' your mind-set rule book.

You create a new ideology

... or *belief system.*

If you and your people know they provide service to *inspire* and *amaze*, immediately their minds will go into action to generate innovative strategies to do just that.

Customer Became *Member*
... and the Business Flourished

In the chapter titled: *The Magic of Metamorphosis,* you would read of the men's clothing store which changed the name customer, to *member*. Because of that simple name change, an immediate new mind-set sprang into place. A member is more than a customer. It means belonging and being someone *special*. In this case, changing the name actually changes the whole flower, and in these times of tremendous change, we need a few name changes also.

A Red Striped Zebra business can re-invent the customer service issue by changing names and creating a new, fresh approach. The word rose does not do justice to the actual flower, a flower of exquisite beauty and fragrance. Maybe they named it wrong in the first place, and maybe they also named *customer service* wrongly.

In summary, your Red Striped Zebra business can achieve outstanding growth by:

- ► *Embracing the philosophy of Awesome Customer Service.*

- ► *Going the 'extra mile' to WOW and SPOIL the customer with extra service, thereby guaranteeing many happy returns. (And many happy new sales!)*

- ► *Calculating the CLTV and being aware of the extra opportunities this gives you to sell more product or service to an already convinced customer.*

- ► *Building of a 'totally satisfied' and 'delighted' customer's data base to give you control of your future ... and place you way ahead of old 'systems' type black and white competitors.*

And in addition, try making these changes:

- *Do a check-up from the neck-up on your people (yourself included) to gauge and install fun, friendly and personable attitudes. (Hire attitudes - teach skills).*

- *Use stylish uniforms as an image and service builder.*

- *Change tired, old and meaningless names ... to ones that excite, inspire and motivate.*

- *Then lead your business by example - from the front! (The sleeves rolled up, Bob Ansett model.).*

> *In a rapidly changing world, with infinite choices available to a better educated and fastidious customer, your goal of achieving success is easier than you may have thought.*
>
> *Simply cut a path through your competition by embracing the philosophy of 'awesome' customer service. Service that is over and above customer's expectations ... and competitor's standards.*
>
> *Your business will stand apart in a sea of mediocrity and be unique, as a Red Striped Zebra!*

Supercharging the Marketing Engine That Drives Your Business

*How to make your business BOOM
... with creative Red Striped Zebra
marketing strategies*

Throw away your marketing books.

As a Red Striped Zebra business, your marketing strategies follow a different path. A path that opens the door to new, exciting opportunities for business growth.

And it's all about understanding what motivates the customer to buy from YOU!

Is there anything new under the marketing sun? With all the advertising firms, PR firms, marketing consultants, books and information available to us, it would appear that everything to be known about marketing has been covered. Or has it?

Standing your business apart like a Red Striped Zebra requires a NEW set of strategies. A Zebra with red stripes must run a different race, travel in a different direction and travel at a faster speed. That Zebra stands out from the crowd. It moves at a *different* pace, with a different set of rules!

A Tale of Two Emus

To introduce a fresh marketing approach into your business, one that will help you supercharge your marketing engine, the following story will reveal a mystery. The mystery of understanding what motivates the customer, or client, to buy ... and to buy from you.

This story is about Emus, those large flightless Australian birds which until recently, had been the subject of intense interest and large profits.

An enterprising American couple had read about the huge profits that Emu farming could generate, from the bird's oil, hide, feathers, meat and offspring. They owned fifty acres of good land and were looking for a hobby that they could perhaps grow into a new, lucrative business for themselves. One weekend they consulted the 'Livestock for Sale' advertisements in their newspaper and noticed two separate advertisements for Emus. *"Let's go see!"* they said, and immediately called both Emu farmers for directions.

Arriving at the first farm they were greeted by a somber man who pointed out his breeding pair of Emus he had for sale.

"The birds are over there. I'm selling them for $9,500 for the pair. You can go and have a look if you want. If you take them the delivery fee is $100. I sell my birds with a money back guarantee if anything goes wrong in the first month. If you want to know about Emus there are some books available that I will sell you."

As he turned to walk away, he stopped and then said:

"Oh, I must tell you, you better make your mind up now if you want them, because I have some other people on the way out and they are really anxious to buy the birds!"

Sound familiar? Similar to what takes place in many businesses once the original advertising entices a potential customer? Sure does! A 'not to interested in you' type person, who says; *"You better hurry 'cause we only have this one left, or; I have others interested, or; it's only on sale for today, won't be here tomorrow"* ... etc.

Service is certainly there, albeit very basic service. There's also some imparting of rudimentary information. Just to clench the deal for the farmer there's some added pressure in the form of a 'hurry up' and buy, or else the other customers (or fictitious customer) will get the sale.

Let's now look at what the prospective customers decide to do as a result of the failing of the farmer to market his birds well.

We'll Think
About It!

Before spending such a large investment, they decide to go to farmer number two. They tell the first farmer they will just have to *"Think about it."* Sound familiar? Customers all use that one to get off the hook. They are reluctant to give their money away too soon. In reality, they were NOT convinced that these were the right birds.

Do customers tell you they have to think about it for a while? That's because they are not convinced yet that what you are offering is exactly the right product or service. Or is it the 'lack' of a powerful, convincing sales proposition that makes them reluctant to buy?

An Offer to
Good to Refuse

Finally arriving at the next farm, a jovial, friendly man immediately approached. He has a spring in his step and a smile to greet them. After the initial greeting he takes the couple over to the breeding birds in his holding pen and then states:

> *"Let me tell you about our Emus. I've been in this business for twelve years now. I was one of the original breeders. I've been over to Australia often and studied everything there is to know about Emus. I've selected the finest bloodlines, the biggest birds, the ones that have given the best meat, hides and feathers. Over the years I've religiously kept records and only bred those birds that I consider the very best. These two birds in front of you are, in my opinion, the finest examples I have ever bred, with excellent parentage. I guarantee you'll be totally happy with the results!"*

He then went on to say:

> *"Now, these birds are a little more expensive than what other breeders charge. They're $10,750 for the pair, but the price is justified in the high quality of the birds.*
> *If you decide to take them today I'll deliver them to your place for no charge. I will also let you have them for thirty days before I even deposit your check. If at the end of the thirty days you find that you both are totally thrilled with them, then of course I'll deposit the check. But, if you're not totally thrilled with the birds at that time, just tell me. I'll come and pick them up, no questions asked, and you will not owe me a cent."*

The farmer then added:
> *"During the thirty days I'll periodically come out to your place to check on the birds, show you how to care for them, feed them, keep their pens clean, check for parasites, and administer vitamins. That way I will know that my birds, which represent the*

126

name of this ranch, will be well cared for. You'll also receive a good education on the breeding process with this arrangement."

Walking over to a large wooden cupboard inside his barn the farmer gathered a few small objects and handed them to the couple. He then said:

"I'm giving you two months supply of vitamins and medicines that you may need, and here's a free book on breeding that will become your bible on the art. Take them with my compliments."

The farmer was nearing the end of his story and in his reassuring, friendly voice he then said:

"I must tell you something important. I reserve the right to make two inspections of the birds. The first in six months and the second in twelve. This gives me an opportunity to make sure you're on track and to check if the birds are breeding O.K. I can then correct any errors you may be making and see how the egg incubation is going.

At the twelve-month inspection time I'll also bring my Veterinarian. He will give the birds a thorough examination. That visit will cost you about $200 but it's money well spent, especially if you want to have a very profitable future in Emu breeding."

Finishing his story, the farmer finally said:

"One last thing you need to know. During the next twelve months you're going to need accessories, such as incubators, vitamins, medicines, and other items. You can buy these elsewhere for sure, but if you buy them from me I will sell them to you for twenty percent cheaper. Just give me a call and I'll get them to you.

These birds also thrive well on our own brand food pellet formula. We mix it ourselves and it gives startling results in growth. I will also provide the pellets at 20% cheaper rates than any other food pellet available."

So, which farmer do you think the couple bought from? The first,
(cheaper product) one, or the second? This is a fictitious story, but if
this was real the answer would be indisputable, farmer number two of
course. But why? What was it that would cause the couple to buy
from him and not the first farmer? The first one had a cheaper breeding
pair at only $9,500. The other pair were $1,250 more at $10,750, so
why buy the more expensive pair?

Doesn't this go against all we know about marketing, such as
cutting price to make the sale? If we look at any newspaper of any day
of the week, we see pages of car dealers, clothing stores, and many
more offering their products on price only. Emu farmer number one,
(or should I say car dealer/retailer/small business person) would have
missed out on this sale!

What did the second farmer know, or do, that the first didn't? In brief, he understood the psychology of *buying*, not selling. In other words, he understood what *motivates* a customer, what makes them buy, and what makes them *not* buy.

> *Obviously, there is a better way. The farmer understood the psychology of buying!*

The Psychology of Buying

To understand why his offer was *irresistible*, we need to dissect
the story into separate sections. If we do, we will find six significant
strategies that act on the buying psychology of the client. A Red
Striped Zebra business is one which fully understands what motivates
the customer. It understands what words can be said, what offers can
be made and what is that motivating force inside a customer's mind
that causes them to come and buy. Conversely, a black and white zebra
business only sees the business through their own eyes, NOT the
customer! And because of that, every promotion, every sale, every
advertisement and brochure is produced with words that infer they
only care about the business, not the customer.

The six strategies appearing in the second Emu farmer's story that give it such potency are:

1. *Perception of Value Education (POVE)*
2. *Added Bonuses*
3. *Risk Transfer*
4. *Customer's Long-Term Value (CLTV)*
5. *The Back-End*
6. *Customer's Perpetual Buying Habits (CPBH)*

These strategies, placed end to end, join to create an *Irresistible Sales Offer (ISO)* for the couple.

Breaking your business free, like a Red Striped Zebra, means understanding those strategies, and incorporating them into *all* your marketing efforts.

1. Perception of Value Education (POVE)

The first strategy the farmer undertook was to *immediately educate* the couple on the history, make up and current information about the birds. He went into detail of how he was an *expert* on the subject, how he made trips to Australia, and how he kept detailed records of the birds breeding history. Farmer number one probably had 'exactly the same' expertise and history, but herein lies the secret; he *never told* the couple. B-I-G mistake!

A shirt is a shirt?

Lands' End, a Dodgeville, WI. catalog company has a superb advertisement that promotes its shirts.

It has a headline that reads:
It takes 12 miles of cotton to make a Lands' End Pinpoint Oxford. And that's 'just' the beginning.

> *It takes 12 miles of cotton to make a Lands' End Pinpoint Oxford. And that's 'just' the beginning.*

Wow, this must be a great shirt! This is a profound, attention grabbing

129

headline, but the real story starts in the three-column body copy. It reads:

"When you put on a Lands' End Pinpoint, you notice right away how silky smooth it feels. That comes from the extremely tight weave of our Oxford fabric - a weave that wouldn't be possible without a very fine cotton yarn ... it's what shirt makers call an 80's 2-ply yarn. And actually, it takes more than 12 miles ... 12 miles, 946 feet to be exact."

The copy then goes on to read:

"Each one takes 69 different sewing steps, for example; the shoulders have an authentic English-style split back yoke, which simply means the yoke - the part that goes over the shoulders - is cut in four, then sewn back together. This allows it to g-i-v-e a little when you move."

The copy goes on to say:

"We're even fussy about our buttons. They're classified as 'super durable' in the trade. (Only 62 buttons in the world are.) And our buttonholes are just as durable; each one is edged with 120 lock stitches, so it won't fray."

Now, this *seems* to be a fabulous, top-of-the line shirt. Or is it? How do we know if the shirts sold by the stores in your own town have 12 miles of fine cotton, or not? Or if their shirts also has 120 lock stitches on the buttonholes, or 'super durable' buttons, or not? You don't! They could be *exactly the same*, or *even better*, for all you know.

The difference is that your local stores which sells shirts, if they resemble most other retail stores, *do NOT tell the customer how good they are*. They do not express the 'specialness' in a concise, compelling way. They do not supply the customer with a 'Perception of Value' *Education* about their shirts. *Neither did the first Emu farmer!*

Winning by a nose

Dr. John Hodges, a facial plastic surgeon, has a powerful advertisement undergirded with the *POVE* approach. In his 8 inches by 5 inch advertisement that runs in the major newspaper, he gives the reading public an education about nasal surgery, under the heading;

Nasal Surgery, The Most Requested Facial Procedure.

Dr. Hodges revolutionary approach *transports* the reader *into his practice* as he describes in detail what Rhinoplasty is, who needs it and why. He then goes on to mention how his initial consultation takes place, what they can expect in the way of results from the operation, and what his qualifications and experience are.

It reads more like a story than an advertisement as he states:

> *"The initial consultation is important. I carefully explain how the surgery will be performed and what you can realistically expect afterwards. The rhinoplasty provides physical advantages such as unimpaired breathing which improves general health. As a facial plastic surgeon, one of the most rewarding aspects of my practice is seeing the psychological benefits that my patients receive as a result of an improved appearance - the size and shape of the nose becomes more harmonious with the rest of the face."*

The advertisement goes on to say:

> *Dr. Hodges goal is to produce a result that goes unnoticed by those who meet his patients.*
> *"My patients report that their friends ask them if they have had something done to their hair, or if they have lost weight ... not if they've had a nose job."*

Not only is Dr. Hodges providing a *Perception of Value Education* on Rhinoplasty, but on his service as a plastic surgeon. Prior to this advertisement, a potential patient/client could ask who is Dr. Hodges. After they read the advertisement they not only know *who* he is, but *how* he cares, *what* his methods are, how the *results* should be, and more importantly; *who* to go to for their nose work.

It matters not what business we are in. It could be small business from retail to wholesale, or a service industry from insurance to real estate, or even a medical practice, such as a surgeon, dentist or chiropractor. What matters is that to be unique like a Red Striped Zebra we need to provide an 'education' to our potential customers, clients and patients. An education in the form of a *Perception of Value Education* ... Educating, informing, instructing and transferring pertinent knowledge about the business, product or service to the potential buyer.

The Perception of Value Education of your potential customers will boost your sales more than any other single strategy, and as a Red Striped Zebra business it is imperative to develop and use its power.

It is amazing how even the smallest detail can make a huge difference in sales. You'll remember reading in *The Good Guys Wear White Hats*, how Barry Bryant had even mentioned on his business card the 'color' of his courier van. It works! I have witnessed this many times, but none so dramatic as in Scotland, at the oldest whiskey distillery in the land; Glen Turret.

Glen Turret; Scotland's Oldest Whiskey Distillery

I've visited this distillery three times, with three separate people, to demonstrate the power of the POVE. It is nestled in the hills of Crief, in Perthshire, and for a small fee you are taken on a guided tour of the whiskey process. (Whiskey is called *Eskavar* in Gaelic.).

The guides explains in detail how the barley is smoked over peat fires to produce the golden color and flavor. They explain how this barley is ground and then mixed with 1,200 gallons of water at a temperature of 120 degrees, and this is then called the Wert.

Then this Wert is pumped into huge casks where fermentation takes place, then it is pumped to the huge copper kiln for distilling. From there they show you how it is pumped through a system that divides the 'head' the 'middle' and the 'tail' of the brew.

A second distilling takes place in a smaller kettle, then the mixture is sealed into oak casks for 12, 19 or 25 years.

The tour group is then taken into the foyer of a theater, where they are served 'drams' of Glenturret whiskey. A movie is then shown, called; *The Water of Life*, (the Scots have it all figured out with that phrase) or *eskavar* in Gaelic, which once again shows the age old process, while the group sips on the samples.

From
Now On?

I've always delighted in turning to my friends after this movie finishes, to ask them what whiskey they will buy from now on. Glenturret of course! Why? Because they have just received a *Perception of Value Education* about the product, in sight, sound, smell and taste.

What is so amazing though, about this wonderful and potent strategy, is that in Scotland there are over 300 *other* whiskey distilleries. They ALL use the same highland water, same barley, same Peat smoke process, same copper kettle distilling and the same Oak casks. The 'difference' is in the *telling* of the story in detail. That's what makes one business break free from all others!

An Art Lesson
in Edinburgh

You can learn a great deal about business from art galleries. Especially about the perception of value. I did in Edinburgh, Scotland. (And I thought I knew it all!).

My son and I had finished viewing all the masterpieces on both floors of this great gallery. I particularly liked the work of the nineteenth century artists; John Glover and John Constable etc., but the very old renaissance work is upstairs. And to my mind, not so attractive.

Just as we were about to leave, a security guard asked us if we had viewed the Raphael's (Raffaello Sanzio) upstairs. I said; *"Raphael who?"* He then went on to tell us in great detail all about this famous Italian renaissance artist and about the three works the gallery had secured; the Madonna and Child. I then quizzed him on the cost to the gallery, and finally he told me. It was *twenty million* pounds! After I got up off the floor I asked him was that for the three paintings. He said; *"Oh no, that's each!"* Sixty million pounds for three Raphael's.

Well, my son and I went (nay; bounded, leaped, ran) back up the stairs to find these paintings, and we stood in awe at something so small and not so spectacular that cost so much.

We had received from that guard a *Perception of Value Education*. Before, they were merely three not-so-spectacular paintings. In fact, we could hardly recall seeing them. But, after the education of value we received, they were seen in a very different light indeed. We viewed them differently. We could understand the value, the age, the craftsmanship ... and the power of the art. And to this very day I still can vividly see them in my mind. Sixty million pound Raphael's ... indelibly engrammed in my mind by a Perception of Value Education from that guard! It worked for me ... and it will work for your customers too!

Sixty million pound Raphael's ...
... indelibly engrammed into my mind
*by a **Perception of Value Education***

- ► *Do you have many competitors?*
- ► *Do you have 300, or only 30?*

It doesn't matter how many you have (or how many black and white zebra are in the herd). Just start using the Red Striped Zebra strategy; POVE ... and take the lead position.

Much of this information given in these examples could be rather small and relatively unimportant to the actual product on sale, but is important for the application of four vital processes.

134

I.   *Perception*
II. *Compulsion*
III. *Price*
IV. *Memory*

Perception of Value Education establishes your business, product, or service as the *absolute leader* and *preferred* choice in your field. The only product or service to buy, and the only business to buy from.

- It presents a ***perception*** that your product, service or business is of supreme quality, very 'special' or 'distinct' from all others.

- It ***compels*** the customer to come to YOU for the product or service, and *bypass* your competitors, even if it means going out of their way to get to you.

- It eradicates ***discounting of prices*** by presenting your product, business or service as higher in quality, therefore 'justifiably' higher priced.

- And it etches into your customer's ***memory*** for 'long-term' buying performance.

It can also take a product or service that at first glance may appear ordinary, and 'empower' it with its own magic. An insurance agent may promote his *"13 step plan for reviewing the needs of his client"* with a POVE style. He may tell how he provides an ongoing service to keep the client abreast of the latest changes, tax laws, financial savings, best coverage and best returns on any retirement investments.

The house painter may explain in a *POVE* type advertisement his 17 years of experience and expertise. He may explain how he finely sands and prepares a room ready for painting. How he first applies a sealing coat, then an undercoat with the finest latex paint. How he provides three more covering coats of the primary coat, lightly sanding the entire walls between each one. He could explain how he does all the finishing touches, how he fastidiously cleans up, and even how he arrives at the estimate of the job so people feel secure in the quotation.

Readers of an advertisement know how a painter works - but a vivid, in-depth, *Perception of Value Education* undergirds his offer with its own *importance* and *specialness*. It sure beats the: *House painting - free quotes* operator - every time!

The secret of a great POVE is in giving people lots of details and information. You can never give them too much to read, as long as it is pertinent to *their* decision and targets THEIR needs, wants, desires and feelings. NOT yours!
You will read more about the power of a POVE and why it works, in the zebra copywriting chapter; *ZebraWrite.*

Perception of Value Education treats people like the educated and sophisticated customers they really are.

It demonstrates to them that you respect their intelligence and their ability to choose.

It alleviates their fears and gives them the knowledge to make an informed buying decision.

---

2. Added Bonuses

Our farmer added real, touchable value to the offer by giving something for nothing. Giving the couple complimentary vitamins, medicines and a reference book on Emus. Total cost? Who knows and who cares! If it secured him a sale of $10,750 does it really matter if it cost him $20, $50 or even $100? Losing a little money is preferential to losing a sale, and yet most businesses refrain from giving the customer anything free.

Many years ago, in the late 60's, I bought three new cars, at different times and from different dealers. The competition now faced with foreign and Japanese cars was not present, and yet the dealers were always interested in adding a few 'free bonuses' to *secure,* or sweeten the sale. A radio, or whitewall tires, mud flaps or wheel spats, (remember the 60's styles?) one could always ask for, and usually get these items if it meant making the sale.

We wouldn't expect to receive spats or whitewalls now, times have changed, but neither would many dealers consider giving us accessories for free. A clothing store seldom 'throws in' a tie and shirt to go with the new $400 suit, nor does the furniture store enthusiastically offers to supply free some new cushions to go with the newly purchased lounge suite. Why?

Simply because they do not understand the power of:

Low-Acquisition Cost (LAC) - High Perceived Value (HPV)

When we take on the role of a business owner or manager, we sometimes distance ourselves from the customer. We forget that they are human beings and see them as a *sale* only. People like to get something for nothing, especially if it is something of *High 'Perceived' Value*. (Remember; *perception* is a powerful ingredient of zebra strategies).

By including a complimentary gift, accessory or extra product we touch a deep psychological nerve that creates a *warm response* in customers. A sale can be won simply by adding something extra for free, or irrevocably 'lost' by stinginess.

The farmer knew these people were new to the business of Emu farming, so by helping to further educate them with a free book, plus saving them some money with the vitamins and medicine would add weight to their decision to buy.

The choice a customer makes is somewhat like a pendulum. It can be weighted in your direction with a few added bonuses that add high perceived value to the customer, and adds power to the sale.

The added bonus is a *Low Acquisition Cost*, costing you a small fraction of the sale, yet is seen by the customer as *High Perceived Value*. It makes their decision to buy 'easier' and automatic!

Q: What can you add to your product or service, to entice customers and secure sales?

It could be a complimentary product or service, or like some magazine subscription firms, it could be a supportive product to get the potential customer to buy. It could be a fabric protector for the furniture store, plus free home delivery. The accounting firm could offer free newsletters and advisories, the dentist could offer free first check up or cleaning. The idea is to give that 'extra' something that really does not cost much, but in the mind of the customer, it means a great deal.

A small offering in return for a big sale!

3. Risk Transfer

Invisible though it may be, nevertheless there exists a *wall of resistance* between a customer and the seller. This wall is built from the bricks of mistrust, indecision, and a lack of commitment the customer experiences. Some bad buying experiences in the past also help to cement it in place.

This wall can become an *impenetrable* barrier to making a sale for the business. It can confuse sales people who are trying to understand how to get through this buyer's *wall of resistance*, causing them to take on pressure tactics as did our farmer number one. He used the old standby, telling the couple that other people were interested ... so they better make up their mind's now.

That's a Guarantee!

Farmer number two made a brave and profound offer. He told the couple to take the birds home and keep them for 30 days. If at that time they were totally thrilled, he would cash their check then, and only then. *That's a guarantee!*

Most businesses offer some type of money back guarantee. In fact, that type of guarantee has been around so long that it has become a 'Dinosaur' and lacks power. No person really likes to come back to

138

a business and ask for their money back.

It doesn't make buying FUN!

Transferring
the Risk

The farmer *transferred* the *'risk of buying'* the couple may have been feeling. He didn't tell them to bring the birds back if they were not happy, as did the first farmer. He almost inferred the birds were free for thirty days. They could 'put off' the buying decision until then. He knew there was virtually no way they would return those birds, because they would have fallen in love with them by that time. He believed in his 'product' ... and he knew that he would have his money. He had their check for thirty days, it only had to be deposited. He removed, or transferred the risk, from 'their' shoulders, to his!

Many clients have initially told us that this would not work for them, people would take advantage of the offer or not want to pay when the time is due. This argument may sound fair, but the truth is it is their 'mistrust' of the customer that causes this remark. I always tell them that there are only six dishonest people in the world ... and they move around a lot! The real fact is, *risk transfer is simply not done.*

The percentages of business people who make such an offer are very low indeed. Those who discover this most potent and profound marketing tool will put their businesses light-years ahead!

When used, it is *instantaneous* in gaining results. The Red Striped Zebra business can use the Risk Transfer strategy to set itself apart from the money-back guarantee crowd, and dramatically enhance the business of making sales.

The 'real'
guarantee

When we offer a money-back guarantee, what are we really

saying? Are we simply guaranteeing to return the customers money if they complain, or are we somehow inferring that our product or service is superior, and therefore the customer should buy it? The argument for a risk transfer type offer becomes more feasible when we decide to go back to basics, (or forward to basics?) with our guarantees.

What ARE you in business for? To 'rip' people off, or to supply them with the very best product or service available? If the Emu farmer knew his product and service was superior, then why wouldn't he offer such an exciting concept to his potential buyers? He just couldn't lose!

If your product or service is as exceptional as his birds, then wouldn't you also be in a position to offer a powerful, rock-solid guarantee that transfers the risk from the customer and back onto you - where it rightfully belongs in the first place? If so, what are you waiting for?

If you truly believe in the quality of your product or service, you are in a powerful position - one on which to transfer the perceived risk of buying from customers and directly onto you - where it belongs.

Start offering powerful risk removal and transfer offers now on everything you sell. Once you do, and promote that guarantee both verbally and in print, you will experience overwhelming responses from NEW customers.

Of course, there are problems, especially in large cost items that may require insurance coverage, or in the gaining of possession of goods if the occasional 'bad egg' customer is involved. However, these are problems that can be overcome though, in the way you offer your risk transfer, but remember, there is a majority of honest, responsible people who greatly outweigh the dishonest and who will respond to your guarantee.

Modify
the Risk

A Red Striped Zebra business will always operate differently from all others, and so the Risk Transfer is one strategy you should include. Perhaps it could be used to persuade a vacillating customer, or as a reward to a loyal customer, or even in the launching of a particular product. It can be *modified* and adjusted to fit the circumstances of the business on any given day, or simply to increase sales during a slow month.

Not Only
Money

Rather than offering a return of monies, the risk transfer could be the guaranteeing of intensive after-sales service, or 3,6, or 9 monthly visits by your technicians. It could be in the form of "keep the bonus as our thank-you gift for trying" if they return the product for any reason. One client which installs equipment to dispense their chemical products in factories actually states that they will: *"Tear up the invoice" and uplift the stock and equipment for free - if the client is not thrilled after 30 days.*

---

*Do whatever it takes to **remove** the risk of buying from the customer's shoulders ... and **transfer** that risk back onto you.*

What is the risk to you if you transfer the risk from the customer? That question arises time and time again in my seminars. When we coach participants in this strategy there is usually a silence when they consider it for their own businesses. They comment that it *could backfire, it could cost them plenty, it could cause people to take advantage, it could cause a large return of products, it could ....*

But the gains always outweigh the could's. I have never had a client who hasn't tried the *Risk Transfer*, because eventually they see how it makes a difference, and once it is 'trial run' the actual results have been overwhelming. In fact, people prove to be less likely to return products, less likely to take advantage, less likely to cause a problem ... because they are much happier buyers, with an assurance that they have made the 'right' buying choice from a firm which 'backs' the purchase with a solid guarantee.

I have a client firm which sells safety eye glasses to distributors. They are in competition to many other, much larger firms. And most of these firms have the 'normal' guarantee on their products. So, we developed a unique guarantee that solidly transfers the risk of buying from the potential new distributor and back onto my client. The result has been exceptional, for they have captured many new distributors to sell their products.

It reads:

We guarantee you'll MAKE
sales with our products!

"Here's a guarantee that means you're TOTALLY protected! Not ONLY do we give you a 'lifetime' guarantee on our frames AND on the lenses of all our safety glasses from breakage .... but we ALSO guarantee the SALEABILITY of our products for 90 days! This means if they don't sell within 90 days, ship them back.

Try them out, show your customers, and if they don't sell, we take them back. You simply cannot lose with that solid guarantee. How can we do this? Because our distributors have runaway success with our products ... and so will YOU!"

That's a guarantee - and a transfer of the risk!

Whatever your business is, the very essence of risk transfer can be incorporated and modified to best suit your product and service. One thing is certain though, whilst your competitors *sweep their guarantees under the carpet*, you will place yours right 'under the nose' of your prospect customer .... and experience runaway success!

---

*TRANSFER the risk of buying from your customer .... and back onto YOU, with a **solid** Risk Transfer guarantee!*

---

4. Customer's Long-Term Value (CLTV)

The farmer was astute! He knew that Emus eat, lay eggs, require vitamins and medicines. He knew the customer would need to buy Emu feed, incubators, vitamins and medicines in the future. He was a futurist! He was a rare breed of business person. One who knew that having a customer buy something, then buy again, and again, and even again, was the true secret of ongoing business success. He knew that 5, 10, 20 or 40 sales from one customer is better than 1. And he also knew that the 'back-end' of the customer can be worth MORE than the front end. In time, if he worked at it, the couple could actually spend more buying products from the farmer than their original $10,750 sale! He was a 5 year man with a 40 sale plan! His goal was to 'convert' his customer into a 'long-term client'. From the initial sale, he expected them to stay with him for up to 5 years and buy feed, vitamins, medicines and accessories for up to 40 more times. He had calculated, from past experience and sales, the *Customer's Long-Term Value*. He knew these people were worth many thousands to him over time.

Lunch is Served - Long Term

I frequent a gourmet sandwich restaurant for my lunch. I once calculated how much I spent in this place over one year. It worked out to $1,150. I told the owner about this calculation and asked him what his thoughts were, knowing now that I (and most of his other customers) actually spent more than just a $6 lunch, but over time (one year) we averaged over $1,000 each. He was astonished, saying he had never realized it. I then asked him if his service (and that of his staff) should 'go up' knowing that every customer (and every 'new' customer) is worth $1,000 to the business. Obviously, he said yes, and in fact I noticed a big improvement, with staff going out of their way to *delight* customers.

I then asked that as he now knew the *Customer's Long-Term Value,* if he also realized the necessity to try to 'never lose' a customer, as every customer 'lost' is $1,000 lost from the business. His mind reeling from that question, he started working overtime on all this new 'revelation' to make sure that his business 'keeps' customers ... and 'extends' the life of a customer's sales.

Knowing your customer is not only worth $6, (or $10,750 for the farmer) but will in time be worth $1,000 (or possibly $20,000 for the farmer) changes the game plan. For these reasons:

- *You will guarantee your firm's future with long-term sales and profit*
- *You will work harder at 'delighting' your customers with great service to extend their lifetime value and perpetual sales*
- *You will make certain not to 'lose' customers by pro-actively working at keeping them buying from you.*
- *You will start building a data-base of their names to make sure you have a 'contact' if they stop coming to buy.*

Keep
Them Buying

The *CLTV* can be increased. A sale to a new customer should NEVER be the last sale, just the beginning, and throughout each year your mind should be working overtime on ways to INCREASE the *CLTV* of EVERY new and existing customer. How? By writing to them occasionally with offers of:

- *Exclusive bargains and unique offerings, only available to them, as long-term 'special' clients.*
- *Invitations to join exclusive 'insider's clubs', with advantages and benefits not available to the general public.*
- *Special buying arrangements with businesses you are in synergy with.*
- *At times, when you may be experiencing a cash flow problem, or when buying has slowed, you could write them with offers they simply cannot refuse.*
- *At other times you could give them the opportunity to add accessories to, or upgrade their original purchase.*

The list is endless!

144

What is essential though, is the need to discover 'your' *Customer's Long-Term Value*, rather than seeing customers as one-hit sales.

Ascertain your Customer's Long-Term Value

1. What is the average sale in your business?

2. How often does your customer or client buy over one year?

3. Over two years?

4. Over five years?

    Multiply No.1 by 2,3 or 4. Result: $ .... (the CLTV)

Without this information, a true understanding cannot be arrived at about your business, about your customer and about the potential for growth in your business. If your average sale was $70 what would your attitude to the customer be if you ascertained they buy from you six more times over a year, and spend $420, or over five years and spend $2,100?

The *CLTV* of a customer must be known. Ascertaining this is imperative for it establishes the foundation for future growth. When the sums are tallied, the averages are known and the true value of the customer is understood a new realization takes place.

Increasing the CLTV
With a Data Base

Simply *keeping records* can ascertain and increase the CLTV. When a customer or client leaves your business, how can you get them back for further sales? The *Awesome Service* you learned about in the chapter; *ZebraServe*, will bring them back of course, but wouldn't it be more advantageous to have rock-solid control? To be able to know *exactly* what the average customer is worth and to also know *who* they are would certainly put you in control. How do you do this? By building a *data base*.

Have you ever been to a hairdresser, shoe store, dress store, restaurant, food store (and plethora of other businesses), and been asked for your name and address, for their data base? They just don't seem to bother ... and what a tremendous waste. What lack of foresight, lack of an understanding of the *CLTV*, lack on knowing the importance of bringing customers back, time and time again. They all would gain tremendous advantages by building their data bases.

The restauranteur who understands the worth of a data base, coupled to the CLTV, would seek names and addresses from patrons, simply by asking for a business card to go into a prize drawing for a free dinner. With this information a client's data base could be developed from which letters and cards could be sent, offering special invitations, locked-in prices for a number of meals, free wine evenings ... and any number of options to *habitually* re-sell his customers.

Your Red Striped Zebra business is different, isn't it? You do keep your customer's names and addresses right? If so, then you could also add to the base the value of customer's purchases, and tracked.

Dividing the total sales for the year by the number of customers will give you an initial 'average' *CLTV*, and as time goes on your understanding of the *CLTV* will increase.

Even certain individuals could be tracked, noting those who tend to spend far more than others, keeping them in mind for 'special offerings' or the 'exclusive insider's clubs' I mentioned. The control you then possess will place your business ahead of competitors.

Every person who does business with you should be on your data base. It should be the lifeblood of your business, and should be constantly built up, fine-tuned and added to.

Once you know the CLTV, you and your staff will have the extra motivation to provide over-the-top service to keep customers buying from you, again and again.

And you'll constantly find ways to work your data base for profit, so that you guide your customers into 'five-year' clients who buy forty times more - or three-year clients who buy twenty times more - whatever you decide - as long as its 'long-term' and 'many' sales!

Your creative genius within will have a field day with your new data base. Creating powerful promotions, writing creative letters to motivate your customers toward a new offering, and selling more products or services. It will be like a breath of fresh air that sweeps your business, as you take control armed with your *CLTV, data base* and the philosophy of *Awesome Customer Service.*

5: The Big Back-End

Yes, our farmer was a forward thinking man. He knew the true worth of a customer. That worth is NOT the sole domain of a single sale, rather it is in the cumulative effect of selling not only the initial first item, but the selling of additional items over a period of time.

He knew the couple would need to buy incubators, vitamins, food pellets, medicines and other accessories. The amount of money a customer was worth to him was far greater than that original $10,750 and so he offered items that they would not only need, but were imperative to the breeding process, and items that had an irresistible discount of 20%. The sum total would be substantial for the farmer, and so he was very prudent in *loading his back-end.*

Knowing your customer, or potential new customer or client, will provide your business with not just a *once only* sale. If treated properly, you can commence selling the 'back-end' on every sale.

One would think that purchasing a new car should be a classic scenario for selling the back-end! Apparently, this is not so in many car dealerships. I experienced this lack of attention to the back-end on my last two purchases of corporate cars, one an American, one a Japanese. Not a word was mentioned about purchasing a few 'accessories'. Not the ones that come as almost standard these days, such as air conditioning, CD players, electric windows etc. but the 'other' accessories we go *elsewhere* to purchase. If the sales people had asked they would have found that we do not garage our cars. Therefore this could have been a signal to offer and sell us dust covers, burglar alarms, steering wheel club locks, polish, chamois, car detergent, lamb's wool seat covers and upholstery cleaners.

These were all items I purchased, but NOT from
the 'dealer' ... they missed out on selling the back-end!

Too simplistic to fool with? These items added $185 to the 'back-end'. One of the dealers, (the Japanese version), mentioned that they sell 300 used cars per month. Add to that the new car totals for the month, multiply the figure by the accessory dollar total, then again multiply it by twelve for the full year and the 'back-end' starts to look very healthy indeed! They could package their back-end into a nicely presented 'basket of accessories' and do very well!

The Care Factor

Disregarding the back-end' sale also shows a disregard for the customer. It tells them that the sales person or firm is not really *interested* enough to add further value to their purchase with some well chosen accessory or service. Even to call or write a letter a month or two later offering a unique, 'special' product or service to enhance their original purchase never seems to figure into the back-end equation.

Failing to sell the 'back-end' results in missed opportunities for MORE profit.

My car dealers have never called, never written a letter to offer products, or even to thank us for buying the original cars. They have beautiful show rooms that they could stock with car-care accessories, but they have overlooked the back-end and the true worth of the customer.

In our case, we will not return to buy future cars, nor advise our clients to buy from those dealers. How many thousands of dollars were we worth to them over a few years because they didn't understand the *CLTV* or selling the back-end? They will *never* know!

Painters,
Luggage and Socks

Real estate is an 'open house' for enhancing the 'back-end'. Most home buyers are never quite satisfied with their purchase. They like to add a coat of paint, wallpaper, modify and landscape to personalize their purchase. The agent has an open opportunity to enhance that sale by having 'connections' and an 'arrangement' with the local painters, gardeners and carpenters.

The goal is to *enhance the value* to the customer, not 'rip' them off, so by introducing them to the very best, most reliable and favorably priced tradesman the clients are thrilled and the sale is enhanced by a commission back from those tradesmen. If there was $5,000 of painting, modifications or landscaping done, and the agent received 10% commission from his recommended trades people, that would be $500 extra for every home sold ... not a bad back-end sale.

Not to mention that the future then would look brighter for further home sales. Many people buy homes more than once in their lifetime, and some almost make a hobby out of it .... and they have friends whom they refer. By providing these 'extra' services and assistance, especially to new-comers to a town who need the help, the agent builds trust. And establish their Real Estate business as the Red Striped leader.

A Sydney-based travel agent has learned the value of building the 'back-end' by giving them a letter of introduction to a luggage store. They can purchase their complete travel luggage at a specially crafted price, simply because the agent and the luggage store put their heads together on a mutually beneficial arrangement. The agent reports their repeat business from happy clients has increased 43% since they embarked on a 'long-term' attitude to their travel clients.

They keep data bases and enrol their clients into their special 'club' ... offering them unique travel adventures via personally written

149

letters at great prices.

Have you ever bought shoes and had the store offer you quality socks? The shoe store that sells socks would be a rare animal indeed! In fact it would be a Red Striped Zebra business! Simplistic though it may be, no person wears shoes without socks. If this is so, why doesn't the shoe sales person offer us a choice of their fine range of socks, or hose to compliment our new purchase? Why not?

A:

Because they do not understand the wealth and power of selling the back-end!

Every business could, and would benefit from selling the 'back-end'.

- ➤ *The dentist could supply oral hygiene care kits*
- ➤ *The car mechanic could offer a long-term service agreement for a set price as an add-on to the original work.*
- ➤ *The appliance mechanic could do likewise*
- ➤ *The florist could sell an up-market greeting card to add further impact to a bouquet, rather than the basic free store card.*

Q:

- ➤ *What can you add to the back-end of every sale to increase revenue?*
- ➤ *Could it be a special service, an accessory, an extra product?*
- ➤ *Could you synergize with another business and offer their product or service?*

The possibilities to sell the back-end are endless and well within the creative ability of you and your Red Striped Zebra business.

6: Customer's Perpetual Buying Habits (CPBH)

Our farmer knew another secret that most business people do not. He knew about habitual buying. People buy from 'habit' and will frequent a business many times, simply out of the habit they have developed for that business.

It's been said that it takes 21 days to either make, or break, a habit. Totally abstaining from something that is a habit in your life, or totally immersing yourself in something, for 21 days, is usually enough time to either break, or make, that habit.

Are Your Customers Addicted Yet?

Wouldn't it be great to have customers in the 'habit' of doing business with you. Every time they were to buy, they came to you, simply out of habit. What would that do for your sales and profit? Every time they came back to buy, out of habit, it would be like having a new customer come in the door. Better still, you would not have to spend money to 'buy' that customer, with advertising or promotion. They just kept coming back and back, two, ten or twenty times a year, year in, year out, simply through habit ... or better still, addicted to YOU!

But what is a habit, and how do we get them hooked? My dictionary states a habit to be an *addiction*, or even a *"pattern of behavior"*. Addiction seems harsh, a habit that cannot be broken. But, are habits all meant to be negative and destructive? What about a habit of discipline, tenacity, neatness, cleanliness, moderation, positive speaking and honesty? All good habits. So, if we focus on making our customers *positively addicted* with the habit of regular visits, this too is a good thing, for the business and for the customer.

Creatures of Habit

It's interesting to note that humans are creatures of habit. We run our lives on habit, in the time we get out of bed, the way we shower, dress, have breakfast. We follow the same pattern daily. Why?

Because it builds a *comfort zone* of security into our daily lives.

It adds substance to the way we live. It creates peace and lessens stress when we follow a 'pattern' of behavior.

And herein lies a key.
If you can help customers build a 'comfort zone' when they
visit your business, then their visits will build into a
'pattern of behavior' or habit ... A buying habit.

And as the 21 day formula suggests, if we can do it for a *consistent* and certain *length* of time, we then end up with an *happily addicted* customer.

A Habitual Buyer

Tapping the *Customer's Perpetual Buying Habits (CPBH)* is the ultimate goal for any business. We skirt around the issue of continued business by calling it *repeat* business. But repeat is not the aim. It's the *result* of converting a customer into a long-term client. (A habitual buyer). If your business is to really take off it must be one that knows how to tap those perpetual buying habits.

People frequent the same restaurant, lunch store, service station, coffee shop, dentist, doctor and hairdresser, sometimes for years. Why? Because of the *CPBH*. They *know* these services, quality, prices, people and they are addicted. Even when the service slips, or the quality deteriorates, still, they keep returning, because a habit has been formed.

> ► *But what makes a habit?*
> ► *What makes a customer into a habitual buyer?*
> ► *How do we tap the CPBH?*

Here's some Zebra strategies that will do it for you:

152

The 5 Elements to Create a Habitual Buyer

1: Familiarity
With People

Ever gone into a business to buy a product and felt intimidated? New customers coming to your business may feel the same, unless you have 'familiarized' it.

Customers (people) prefer to do business with those whom they know, rather than strangers. There is less fear of being 'ripped off', being treated discourteously, being ignored. And in today's overcrowded world, people *gravitate* to the *known*, rather than the unknown. They prefer 'friendly' reassuring faces that they've done business with before. People who know them, who understand their needs, who will give them the warm treatment they crave.

You can easily make your zebra people (staff and management) familiar to customers, just by personalizing . Using photographs with bios and stories about your staff in newsletters or brochures, and photographs on business cards, letterheads and thank you notes. We always encourage our clients to personalize their businesses in this way, so they can break down the unfamiliar walls and re-build them with personalized, familiar walls of friendship and relationship. It's a vital step in converting customers into long-term clients.

If you operate a factory or 'behind-the scenes' operation where customers do not come in to buy, you can take your people AND the inside, to the outside, to further familiarize or personalize the business. Photographs of 'Jim' operating a particular piece of machinery, with a story about him and his experience, along with 'Patty', 'Bruce' or Steve' doing what they are good at, also builds immense relationship value for the customer. When they receive your product, they know exactly who has built it.

Personalize your business to make it familiar to potential customers, thereby reassuring them ... and encouraging their buying decisions.

Dentists or Doctors, Accountants, Lawyers and most professionals miss out on this great opportunity, because many times these people are backed up and served by very skilled individuals, who form part of the practice, or business. The dental assistant, the receptionist or researcher behind the scenes, the nurse or hygienist, they should all be featured to personalize the business. It's a reassuring strategy that they could be using, and one that you could well use to transform the perception of what potential customers may think about your business.

Your Red Striped Zebra business could be seen as the firm with the friendly, *familiar* faces - and the *only* business to buy from.

2: Customer Advantaging (CA)

This is a *major* key to success in tapping the *CPBH*. Giving an advantage.

The restaurant that I frequent for lunch, (and have calculated that I spend $1,000 plus per year) is my 'preferred choice' because of the *advantages* I get. Ample food, quick service, great taste, quality and a superb atmosphere that offers a place to escape for an hour or so.

I know of another restaurant that offers even better food, but the atmosphere stops people returning. The music is too loud and inappropriate. The seats are arranged so you are staring at the next person on the nearby table. The place seems dirty and floors grubby. The first store has tapped my *CPBH*, the second hasn't. Why?

Because the first has given much thought to giving me MORE advantages, and they now have become a *valuable* part of my life.

The second store seems only interested in 'their' interests, 'their' music preferences, 'their' lack of inactivity in keeping a fresh and clean premises. No *advantages* for the customer, only *disadvantages* (disadvantages that *break*, not *make*, a habit)

The more ADVANTAGES (CA's) you give customers,
the more VALUABLE you become to them.
(And the quicker the formation of a buying habit - or CPBH)

Here's another Zebra Strategy to use:

3: Locking In

I know of a hairdresser who sells a 'block' of haircuts to new customers. Twelve cuts for $85, a saving of $59 over the regular rate. He has found that these twelve cuts 'lock' the customer in to keep returning for up to a year. After this time, they automatically return as habitual buyers, and many have brought in friends as new customers.

Locking in customers for long-terms is a key to tapping the *CPBH*. It may be three months, six or twelve. It could be a number of visits, or a fixed amount of products, to be paid for in advance for a much lower price, and collected over time.

Twelve lawn-care services for a set price will lock that client in. Three restaurant visits for a *Prix Fixe* will also do the job of building the confidence with a guest. A local gym offers 20 visits for $70, knowing full well that after this time people buy yearly memberships because they have become *familiar* with the gym, the service, the equipment, as well as making new friends with other patrons.

What about oil changes? Aren't they similar to the ongoing food pellets habitually and continuously required by the Emus? Every 3,000 miles a car needs a change. What a pleasant change it would be to be offered a coupon book containing 10 oil changes at a once only special price! The hairdresser could lock-in a year of haircuts at a set price, or a family membership at a set fee for a year to seek the habitual sale.

4: Time

The key here is time. To become addicted to your business and to build a habitual buyer from a first-time customer, that customer has to experience your business, product or service *a number of times*, over a period of time. Your job is to entice them, give them a 'reason' to return, delight them, do what you must to keep them returning, until the *CPBH* kicks in.

> *To become addicted to your business, customers have to 'experience' the business, product or service a number of times over a period of time.*

You would have read about the farmer thinking about making 40 sales over 5 years. This of course is a fictional story, but the concept that has proven to work outrageously well in client's businesses is to remove forever the focus on the first sale, and see the repetitious buying as the formula for success. Hence the number 40. And to buy 40 times, or even 10 times, there has to be an element of time. The customer must come back 10, 20 or in this case, 40 times. This is the 'key' to building a habitual buyer; the CPBH.

To buy the customer in the first place is a costly exercise. Why then, would any business person in their right mind only focus on the first, initial sale? This should 'only' be the *first step* to a long and rewarding relationship for 'both' the seller and the buyer - you and your customer. Think L-O-N-G!

5: Pleasure

Why do we prefer certain foods, drink, friends, places? Because of pleasure. We want to *feel good*. That's a basic human need and a very powerful one. The need to feel pleasure, to be rewarded with good things that delight and satisfy. If you can do that for a person, you have a friend for life. Give them pleasure.

Is buying from your business a pleasure?
Or a punishment?

I know of an outdoor camping equipment store that dishes out punishment like no other. People constantly complain about the very unfriendly service from staff. Why do they do that? I do not know, but they do. I ask the offended people if they go there regularly and most simply say that they *stay away*. That store has no chance of creating a *CPBH*, let alone tapping the *Customer's Long Term Value (CLTV)*.

Another store has opened up (and since become our clients) becoming the first store's direct competitor. Guess what undergirds the marketing strategy for this new store? The providing of *outrageously* friendly service! They are there to make it pleasurable for people to buy. To provide fun, and delight the customers.

> *Habits of buying are formed by p r o v i d i n g pleasure and fun to customers.*

When a customer is delighted and their pleasure has been fulfilled, they return, because they know what buying experience they are in for. With that second and third return, a further reinforcement of pleasurable buying is experienced. You can see that with perhaps five or six visits like this it's enough to convert those customers into *habitual* buyers!

156

In Summary

It is *Personalizing, Customer Advantaging (CA), Locking-in, Time,* and *Pleasurable Experiences* that will help you tap the *Customer's Perpetual Buying Habits. (CPBH).* Once this is achieved, your future is guaranteed, as you have a steady stream of continued business.

In YOUR Business

- ➤ *What can you do to personalize your business and make it familiar to customers?*
- ➤ *What can you do to give the advantage and make your firm a customer's valuable asset?*
- ➤ *What can you do for customers that others are NOT doing?*
- ➤ *What can you do to add pleasure and make every visit a habit forming opportunity?*
- ➤ *What locking-in strategy can you develop that causes the customer to return, until their habit is formed?*

Make a list - and then do it!

Synergy Selling

Our farmer had one more 'strategy' up his sleeve. He understood synergy - the working together of two entities for combined strength. In this case he pre-sold the visit of his veterinarian for two visits @ $200 each. As a wise businessman, this farmer had arranged with his vet a commission on the fee - *of course!*

He was also aware that more than one visit would be required over a lengthy period and would have arranged for an ongoing commission for this referral business.

Customers are *assets* ... that has been established. (Although you will not find them listed on corporate balance sheets - I wonder why?). And these assets can be ethically capitalized on by referring businesses to them with whom you have a synergy arrangement.

You could also allow access by these synergy businesses to the new data base that you have built - *for a fee of course!* Learn much more on *Synergy Selling* in the chapter: *Clydesdales and Geese!*

Become a Red Striped Zebra marketer, using the Emu farmer as an example ...

... to supercharge the marketing engine that drives YOUR business machine!

This is not just the 'end' of the chapter on supercharging your marketing, but the beginning. For already, as a Red Striped Zebra business, you should now be working on ways to put these strategies in place, and to start growing your business for RESULTS.

So, put in place these Zebra strategies ... and grow:

1. *Perception of Value Education (POVE)*
2. *Added Bonuses*
3. *Risk Transfer*
4. *The Customer's Long-Term Value (CLTV)*
5. *Selling the Back-End*
6. *The Customer's Perpetual Buying Habits (CPBH)*
7. *Synergy Selling*

Samson's Pillar's of Destruction

How to strengthen and expand your marketing to make more sales ... and profit!

For decades, businesses have relied on one, or two pillars of income. But, in these tumultuous times, having only one or two pillars courts disaster

Red Striping your business with give you multiple marketing pillars to add stability, strength and outrageous new growth.

Two key pillars supported the entire Philistine temple! Fascinating! What architectural madness would allow a building to be designed and built incorporating such a design fault?

The story we read in the Bible, about Samson bringing down the entire building on his enemies, contains a lesson for modern businesses to learn. As the story unfolds, we learn how Samson was God's strong-arm man. A man who had God-given strength, which enabled him to overcome his enemies by sheer force. In one incident, the Bible reports that he fought and overcame 1,000 enemy soldiers, using nothing but an animal's jawbone as a weapon. However, being human, they soon captured him as he buckled under a temptress's spell. The symbol of his strength; his long hair, was cut and his eyes were put out.

Samson was a sad and sorry man. Over time, his wounds healed, his hair grew back and as his recommitment to God ensued; his strength returned. As the story tells us, a young boy brought Samson into the presence of his partying enemies, so they could use him as the object of their fun. Some three thousand and more, laughing, drunken enemies.

But Samson had other plans. This man knew something about architecture and physics. He knew the inherent weakness in the building was embodied in those two middle pillars. Two columns of solid stone that *appeared* (the key word to this Zebra strategy) very strong and supportive, yet their strength contained weakness of design.

To everyone concerned, the building was solid. People would not party inside a structure that appeared weak and ready to collapse. This building looked good. A great place to party. A great place to feel *secure.* A building that will last for years, despite what goes on outside ... Or so they thought!

Samson, in chains, asked the young boy leading him around the room, to take him over to the two main supporting pillars, so he could lean against them and rest. The obliging boy did so, and positioned Samson between those pillars. Samson started pushing with his outstretched arms. When the surge of mighty God-given strength coursed through his body, he pushed those columns out of plumb, causing a chain-reaction collapse that brought the entire building down on his enemies.

Two Solid Pillars

Two single pillars! Very solid, stone-hewed columns that looked as though they would last a lifetime. Two pillars that supported the roof, bearers and other supporting material. Two columns positioned parallel, perhaps no more than five feet apart, and so when pushed out of plumb, caused the entire structure to collapse, crushing all those inside.

> *Everything depended on those two supports; the integral strength of the building.*

That recorded collapse was not just partial, but the collapse of the *entire* temple. For all those present, those mighty stone pillars were symbols of strength, resource and power. But NOT to their enemy. To Samson, they were simply; *Pillars of Destruction.*

Samson's business pillars

Business is *supported* solely by *marketing*. The promotion and selling of products and services. Without that marketing support, there is no business ... or no structure. Simple as that!

And it's usually only *two* marketing pillars that support most businesses today, sometimes more, sometimes less, but usually two. They are *Samson's Business Pillars of 'Destruction'* in this world of competitive enemies.

Changing Times
Erode the Pillars

In the decades since the Second World War, most businesses have functioned comfortably with two marketing pillars. Times were easier, products almost sold themselves, competition was mild, and the world had not become a 'global' village. The customer complied with the wishes and directions of business. Customers then were not as sophisticated and demanding as today. Foreign products were considered inferior and they were no threat to our own homemade varieties. Advertising had not reached the gigantic proportions of today. Creative television advertising, home shopping channels, Internet marketing or direct-mail were all still futuristic. In short, business could run on *simplistic* marketing endeavors.

The *business* temple was supported by solid stone and had many years of strength remaining. The Bible does not mention how long the temple had stood before Samson destroyed it. It obviously was considered the place to hold the big celebrations. It was the main gathering place and focus of the town. It obviously had stood and functioned for many decades ... as have businesses throughout our decades.

A Competitor
Called Samson

The Samson of competition is ready and poised to push down *your* marketing pillars, like it or not! Competition is fierce and increasing. Every competitor out there is trying to steal away customers and sales that should be yours. As the world grows in population, the global warriors of competition are also growing rapidly. Countries involved in international trading are not just flooding our land with quality goods so we may have a better standard of life. No, they are doing so to *compete* with *your* business, to sell *your* customers *their* products ... and to take the profits home. Many of these foreign companies establish plants, employ local workers, manufacture their products on our soil ... and still take the profits home.

To remain in business today, the dual

Then Samson came! And in business today, the Samson of competition has arrived on YOUR doorstep!

pillars of marketing are no longer sufficient to protect you from the assault of competing forces. You *must* undergird your business with new marketing pillars, new supports, new columns of marketing strength.

The Dominating Temple
of a Red Striped Zebra Business

On being unique, as a Red Striped Zebra, your business will stand apart and dominate by *installing* new marketing pillars. Not just propping up the old. The fact that most businesses stick with the old supports and never consider adding new pillars, gives *you* the edge.

By adding extra pillars, you will become the stronger business, because:

- *Each marketing pillar will <u>attract</u> a fresh source of customers*

- *Each pillar you add will further <u>strengthen</u> your business with new sales and profit.*

- *Your business will become <u>invincible</u> as the competition beats against your door.*

- *Your business temple will not fall if one pillar fails, because you will have many others to help you stand <u>firm</u> and <u>strong</u>.*

- *Your business will be seen as being <u>unique</u> in a time of chaos.*

- *Your business temple will <u>dominate</u> the field, unshakable, unmovable and commanding attention.*

Two Standard
Issue Pillars

Focus on the marketing of any category of business today and what do we find? Two pillars! The real estate business has two. They are *standard issue* pillars. One is the newspaper spread with a sea of houses (or agent's faces) for sale, and the other is the open house pillar, where an agent sits all day to show prospects through a home.

- *The car dealer has two. Once again, a newspaper spread, and the other is the television advertisement.*

- *The lawyer sometimes runs television advertisements and a yellow page advertisement.*
- *The dentist usually goes for a newspaper advertisement, along with a yellow page space, as does the plastic surgeon.*
- *The mechanic, service station or lube business relies on newspaper or coupons.*
- *The builder takes the display home and newspaper approach.*
- *The carpenter usually takes the small newspaper advertisement, and word of mouth pillars.*
- *The retail store goes with the display newspaper and brochure insert method.*
- *The magazine publisher relies on direct mail, along with news stands*
- *And many service businesses use both newspaper and direct mail.*

All tested marketing methods that produce some results. But in most cases, just *two* marketing approaches.

Seldom do we find a business that consistently uses 'many' marketing efforts, or pillars, to undergird their business temple.

Pillars of Profit for the
Red Striped Zebra business

What are the profit pillars that will undergird your business, and bring in fresh streams of customers, sales and profit? They are the *borrowed* pillars from other industries.

It's *customers* that are the *life-force* of a business. NOT management, staff, products or service. Without the customers and clients there is 'no' business.

Adapting and adopting the *borrowed* marketing pillars from various businesses will not only strengthen your business, but will enable you to penetrate new customer markets previously *unknown* and *untapped* by you. The bonus that comes with new marketing pillars is the recognition your business gains by being unique. This means your business will shine like gold as you undertake marketing in areas previously untouched by your competition.

Using marketing strategies from other types of businesses (albeit shaped into Red Zebra format), will dramatically boost your business.

Different Tools
For the Job

A carpenter uses different tools than an electrician. The plumber uses something different again. The dentist has a completely unique set of operating tools ... while the accountant, lawyer, and investment advisor use equipment esoteric to their needs.

None of these trades or professions would consider adapting and using tools from outside their realm. That's a pity. The very essence of *creativity* in business (or becoming a Red Striped Zebra business) is in the ability to *open* one's mind to *new concepts* and ideas from others. What's needed is a perceptive-mind-shift, the very essence of business success.

If the carpenter were to examine the dentist's tools, or the plumber looked at the accountant's procedures, from this, new ideas could flow to enhance each other's professions. In the same thinking mode, when it comes to marketing many people run businesses following very *myopic* and *limited* thinking patterns. What has been done for decades is adhered to, without any thought of trying other 'tools' from different sources. What has worked for the accountant, retailer or restaurant in the past, must be the way to do it now and in the future ... Or is it?

Problem is, these chaotic times we find ourselves in simply will not allow 'business as usual' anymore! It's undergird the building, adapt new pillars, or have the business temple fall.

Undergird the building, adapt new pillars,
... or have the business temple fall.

Here's 13 Pillars of Profit to Renovate Your Business and Create an Unfair Marketing Advantage

Advertising in magazines and newspapers is one main pillar most businesses build their temples on. Yellow pages advertising is another. It is surprising that most businesses exist on these two alone. In undertaking our 'business renovation' we can add many marketing pillars, borrowing from other industries. Some of our clients have developed 10, 12 and as much as 14 separate pillars, with each one producing its own revenue. One firm in particular had a goal to achieve $20 million in sales per year, thinking that it would take at least five years to reach that target. After the 'revelation' of the pillars, they could easily see how they could bring that goal forward to only two years ... and started doing business quite differently.

Here's some examples of pillars you can put into your business:

1. *Results-driven advertising*
2. *Yellow Pages*
3. *Telemarketing*
4. *Direct-mail*
5. *Synergy*
6. *Back-end*
7. *Publicity selling*
8. *Referred leads*
9. *Endorsements or testimonials*
10. *Creative selling*
11. *Internet*
12. *Television and radio*
13. *Direct selling.*

Separate marketing pillars, and each by itself is a strong selling tool, a strong pillar of support used by some form of enterprise or industry. But, each will only hold true until eroded or attacked by competing enemies. In combination though, they will strengthen and establish your business, giving you outstanding new growth. Pillars in *combination* to create an *unfair marketing advantage* in your Red Striped Zebra business. Unfair for the competition that is, and an advantage for YOUR business.

Let's look at how they can work for you.

Borrowing, Modifying and Installing Marketing Pillars

1: Results-driven
Advertising

Newspaper and magazine advertising, as mentioned, are the realms of the real estate, car dealer, retail stores, professionals and a few others. It is an excellent pillar if used correctly, or a sheer waste of time, space and money if used wrongly.

In the chapter; *ZebraWrite*, results-driven advertising is shown to be the most *potent* form of any advertisement. The wasteful style of 'corporate' advertising that 95% of businesses use simply does not work efficiently enough to warrant its' consideration. Yet, every day we see in every paper or magazine in the country the same old format.

Red Striped Zebra businesses incorporate *results-driven* newspaper or magazine advertising, thereby creating a strong marketing pillar that actually generates sales. Installing this *results-driven style advertisement marketing pillar* with will not only strengthen your business, but attract a constant stream of customers or clients, wanting to buy what you are selling, every time. No ifs, no buts, no maybes.

For the business which *never* uses newspaper advertising, borrowing this pillar and adapting it into a results-driven style will establish that business as unique and worthy of attention.

For instance, a house painter, who in the past may have never used a newspaper advertisement, could borrow this pillar and develop a results-driven advertisement to attract a new source of clients.

The same applies to the mechanic, accountant or appliance technician. If you are not currently using the advertising marketing pillar, borrow it, (modify it with results-driven advertising), and add it to your marketing temple.

(You'll learn how to create these type of adverts in ZebraWrite, or by contacting our office and ordering our powerful audio-tape programs.).

2. Uncovering Gold in the Yellow Pages

Many businesses see yellow page advertising as a 'necessary' waste of money. When the sales representative calls, business managers try to avoid taking out anything but the bare minimum. Mainly because it is costly. Still, others have experienced its profound value. They consider it a benefit and not an expense. The outcome all depends on *how* the advertisement is constructed.

The yellow page is the realm of many professions, but those who see the potential will add it to their marketing pillars, and enhance their business temple. Again, the need for a *results-driven* advertisement is paramount. One that will actually get people to respond! (Once again, *ZebraWrite* will show you how).

People do read the yellow pages. Newcomers to town immediately go through the book when looking for products or services. People who are looking for a new service or product usually consult those yellow pages. All these people can become a fresh, new supply of customers and clients, simply by having an advertisement that establishes your business as the leader; one that stands apart from the crowd.

And if you have established your *Customer's Long Term Value (CLTV)* you will know how much over one year a customer may be worth to you - and from that you can ascertain how much to spend on *buying* that customer. Perhaps the cost of the yellow page might diminish in size when you compare it with the amount you are willing to spend to buy the customer, and how much that customer will be worth to you over time.

- *Your yellow page advertisement should be the one with the powerful headline, to flag the reader.*

- *It must 'stop their fingers in their tracks' by grabbing their attention, instantly, with a big, bold promise.*

- *It must tell a story about your product or service, in vivid detail, explaining how your product is manufactured, developed, endeared with quality or pizazz. (i.e. a POVE)*

- *It must explain how your service is one of caring, quality, speed, attention to detail ... or whatever 'sets you apart'.*

- *It must be content-rich in benefits and advantages that the reader obtains by using your service or product.*

- *It must be designed with your business name last, and their interests, desires, and needs FIRST.*

- *And it must explain why they'll be 'better off' buying from you.*

In short, it must be a results-driven yellow page advertisement that COMPELS them to reach for the phone and call YOU.
This then, becomes an 'ideal' marketing pillar. One that generates its own separate sales calls and income.

---

3. Telemarketing Pillar

Telemarketing has a strong role in your business temple. It is the realm of the insurance agent, investment advisor, the wholesaler and a host of other businesses.

However, telemarketing now has a soiled reputation because of the unscrupulous 'boiler-room' sales people who prey on the elderly with various schemes to channel their money from them. But, used in its correct place, it can become an extremely strong tool for gaining new business. And coupled with direct mail, the telemarketer has a strong advantage that produces strong results.

Calling a potential customer cold usually attracts a cold response. Calling the same person to follow up a letter, especially a letter that mentions a call will be coming, is far more expedient. If the letter that preceded your call made an *irresistible* offer of your product or service, or contained the opportunity for the receiver to gain a substantial gain when purchasing your product, they would readily receive your call.

Dentists, Accountants and Plumbers Calling

The despised sales call has earned its reputation because the sales representatives do not belong to Red Striped Zebra businesses. There are no *Irresistible Sales Offers (ISO's),* no special bonuses, no special treatment, no risk-transfer strategies. Just a cold, hard sell. By paving the way with a profound substantial letter, then followed up with a call, the telemarketing pillar becomes a vital, effective pillar of business.

- The car dealer who adheres to the newspaper/television pillars could extend into the telemarketing realm. Wouldn't it by pleasing to receive a letter and call from a dealer, offering a test drive in their latest luxury car? The sales person would bring the car to your home and allow you to drive the car in your own suburb, on your own turf. It's simply not done.

- The accountant looking for new clients could send a letter and arrange for an experienced telemarketer to call the prospective client, with an offer to review their accounting needs for free.

- The dentist in search of patients could easily gain a 10% to 20% increase by sending out letters then following up with telemarketing, offering a free initial consultation or teeth cleaning.

- The plumber could write to homeowners to introduce a new device for saving water, or offering a new service, then follow with the telemarketing calls.

- The lawyer could secure new clients by offering *two hours free service* through his letter and telemarketing call.

170

Who receives calls like this from plumbers, lawyers, accountants or car dealers? Not me ... and probably not you. Here's your chance to add this pillar to your Red Striped Zebra business and excel. And here's another clue for you, set yourself a fixed number of calls to make per day. That's what the real pro's do, they make 20, 30 and 40 set calls every day, in a *content-rich* hour or two ... to increase their contacts and sales. One client calls it their *Quality-Time,* or *QT.*

Telemarketing is a much overlooked pillar, because it's usually left to those who constantly use it. People never think or realize that it could be used with even greater results in their own businesses.

---

4. The Direct-Mail Pillar

Sadly, the direct mail letter has been designated 'junk mail' ... and rightfully so. Yet, it is one of the most vital pillars in marketing today.

There is so much *deceitfulness* attached to direct mailing. Take the letter that screams out in large type that we have just won a million dollars, then to read in fine print that we will have won the money *only* if we have the winning number. *Downright deceitful and absurd!*

The problem is, there is *so much* direct mail. To compete, advertisers think their letters need to be crass to get noticed. The more bizarre the envelopes, the more glitzy and slick the contents, the more special prizes ... that's their thinking. They believe their methods of over-the-top promotion is supposed to attract our attention and gain the desired results.

The customer is educated. They know a con, or a deceitful attempt to gain their attention. That is why the mail has become JUNK mail.

Not so! It doesn't!
(Except for the attention of the trash can!)

We can make the offers and benefits attractive so that the receiver would be *pleased* to get their mail, but the *offenders* have made it difficult for the 'good guys' to get noticed. Or have they?

Your Red Striped Zebra business letter is unique. It arrives in an envelope that is business like, but it has your *Unique Marketing Perception, (UMP)* as outlined in: *The Good Guys Wear White Hats,* as a statement or logo on the front.

The receiver reads immediately 'why' you are different.

Upon opening the letter they could read a headline with a big, bold promise to make them curious. Then you begin your letter not by the done-to-death Dear Sir/Madam, but by the date, precise time you wrote the letter, and a *Good Morning* (Name), or *Good Afternoon.* (It's more 'refreshing' this way.)

The letter then takes on a personal, intimate feeling as you relate your special offer, your added bonus, the advantage and content-rich benefits they gain by buying *your* service or product. You then relate the risk transfer statement and the special gift for a quick response, then you'll have a letter that gets read and responded too. It becomes another marketing pillar to generate sales and income.

People want and 'expect' proper treatment. If you construct a *Perception of Value Education (POVE)* for them about your product or service, in the fullest detail ... coupled with the most compelling word pictures possible, they 'will' read your letter.

Adding the
Personal Touch

Our clients have found the letters that attract the largest responses, are those written as though they were to a *friend*, (the personal touch) explaining as clearly as possible the offer, and providing a reward for a quick reply.

The *direct mail marketing pillar* is an effective support in any business. Again, it is the realm of specific businesses, but for you, the prudent Red Striped Zebra business person it can rewrite the rules for you.

As indicated in the telemarketing pillar, all those businesses that never take this road are missing a huge opportunity. A letter bearing an accounting firm, legal firm, medical practitioner or dentist's name on the envelope *will* get read. This then is NOT junk mail. It is mail that invites a prospective client to come and try, plus receive something of real value free.

The landscape gardener, tree trimmer, house painter, car detailer or mechanic. All businesses which *never* use direct mail ... are all missing out on great opportunities. Their letters would not be considered junk mail. Prospects would read them. If the offer was genuine, and a gift or service was available, their responses would be overwhelming.

Your business may never have used a direct mail letter ... if not, then *now* is the time to break it free, like a Red Stripe Zebra, and do it!

If you find it difficult to produce such a letter, contact our office for help ... but whatever you do, decide to add this valuable pillar to YOUR marketing temple today.

5. The Synergy
Pillar

Combining forces with other businesses provides for a marketing pillar of immense proportions.

The combined efforts, data bases, promotional offers and results can be profound. Outlined in *Clydesdale and Geese*, working in synergy with compatible businesses, (or even with your competitors), provides exponential boost in growth. The competition you experience can almost disappear when you *combine forces* with others.

You can offer a better *package* of goods and services ... to a much *wider* range of potential clients, than by working singularly. The synergy pillar stands supreme.

Your other available pillars, such as direct mail, telemarketing, advertising and testimonials are enhanced many fold in synergy. Your synergy partner endorses your business, products or service, while you in turn endorse theirs. You have more people to write to, more to call, and your advertising dollar is combined to give greater spending power.

The synergy pillar is one of the most powerful yet overlooked pillars available in business today. But it is available to your Red Striped Zebra business.

6. The Back-end Pillar

In business today, one of the most overlooked marketing pillars is the pre-existing customer or client. The person who has already bought from the business.

Many business people who attend our seminars have admitted not having a full understanding or knowledge about the *Customer's Long-Term Value (CLTV)* and they *neglect* to follow customers up at *regular* intervals to offer new products or services to entice them to buy repeatedly. But, seeing a customer as a 'one-shot' sale is myopic. Seeing the customer as a *long-term potential buyer* is the thinking of a Red Striped Zebra.

Because of this lack of understanding of the long-term value, many businesses do NOT gather names to build a comprehensive data base. If they did, they would have the *tools* available to entice customers back to buy more. They could first be selling the *back-end* of the original sale ... then following on ad-infinitum with further offers over the ensuing months and then years. It is with this in mind that back-end selling becomes a marketing pillar.

The cost of *buying* a customer can be very expensive. Once you have sold them, it is so much easier and *cheaper* to sell that *same* customer other products or services. To call them in three months, six months or a year ... or to write to them with new offers, new products, add-ons, trade-ups or new contracts ... that all makes sense. Why?

➤ *Selling the back-end increases your sales and profit.*

➤ *The customer already knows your business.*

➤ *They have already experienced your service.*

174

▸ They know your quality.

▸ They have tested and had usage of your products.

▸ They are natural, pre-sold clients.

All it takes is some thought of what to offer them and how to go about it. An example could be a 'special offer' to new and existing clients that is NOT available to the public. An exclusiveness, or club membership, will give them the *prestige* of belonging.

The strategies are endless, but what is paramount is that your customers, even 'cold' ones, are the *least expensive* and the *hottest* prospects in your entire marketing endeavor.

Don't neglect the back-end of every sale, because it starts a cycle of endless reselling to existing customers and is far more profitable than seeking costly, new replacements! Install the back-end marketing pillar into your business!

---

7. Publicity Pillar

What is better than free publicity? Eric Brown is a young man in Georgia who runs a watch supply business. Send him your corporate logo and he will have it made into a watch face. Taking advantage of a controversy that was embroiling at the local high school regarding the confederate flag, he had watches made up incorporating the flag and the school motto.

Eric sold a few watches to various students and even teachers, until news of his product was picked up by the media and *featured* as a story. Eric then experienced an *immediate* and *dramatic* upswing in sales as people called from all over the state asking to buy a watch. This young entrepreneur discovered the value of *media promotion* in a dramatic way.

Press releases, stories about your new product or service,

television, radio or newspaper coverage you do not pay for. These are magic for the Red Striped Zebra business.

Publicity selling can become a vital marketing pillar in gaining attention. All it takes is a willingness to prepare press releases and submit them, or to call business journalists whenever you have an interesting service or new product to launch.

Virgin's
Success

Richard Branson's (founder of *Virgin Airlines*) financial services company in Britain; *Virgin Direct*, uses this pillar constantly. Branson suggests that money spent on publicity in the form of public relations is 30 times 'more' effective than that spent on advertising! When the company launched a new PEP (financial package) they spent £18,000 on a six-week public relations campaign in the run-up to the launch, and actually generated funds of £22 million, while an advertising campaign run at the same time generated less at £20 million. Their research also showed them that those who first learned about the PEPs via press stories were 40% more likely to invest than those who had heard about it only from an advertisement.

Further research of the *Virgin Direct* product launch found that the combination of editorial AND advertising in a June issue of the *Mail on Sunday* newspaper generated sales of £722,000 ... while two weeks later an advertisement run on its own in the same paper generated sales of just £182,000. Editorial stories speak volumes and gain huge responses!

Public relations and media coverage, either paid for by engaging a PR company, or by doing it yourself on a small scale, obviously is a strong and effective marketing pillar for you!

In fact ...

- *You can gain this exposure by presenting a 'vibrant' story (rather than a dull one) in your local paper about a new service, product ... or for the professional; a new procedure.*

This is exposure that most likely will bring in scores of new customers, clients, guests, patrons or patients ... and it could be done without costing you a cent.

- *Gaining attention by establishing your business as a sponsor of local community events, is another proven method.*
- *Staging free educational seminars and inviting guest speakers also opens the exposure door to your business.*

Even Eye
Doctors Do It!

Doctor Gentlefinger, (yes, that's his real name) a Memphis based professional, specializes in Radial Keratotomy, the operation on eyes to correct vision problems.

His practice gains enormous interest, and secures clients, because of the *free information seminars* they regularly offer to prospective patients. This is a vital marketing pillar that he uses to gain wide exposure for his business.

If you have a product or service that can be adapted to an educational or information seminar, it could be advantageous to offer these to the public for free ... to attract interested potential customers and eventually make sales. And the best thing about this, if you are creative at writing a press release, with a *scintillating* headline, you may capture the attention of a journalist who will cover your seminar offer for free.

What You *Must* Know About Press Releases

A press release is 'not' meant to just get a little piece of editorial in the 'news briefs' section of a paper or magazine. As a Red Striped Zebra business thinker you should write the release to 'capture' the attention of a journalist so they decide to do a *full story* about you and your product or service. That's it!

This means; an exciting headline that 'tempts' them to read more ... and riveting copy.

(If you have trouble writing press releases, contact our office.)

As a Red Striped Zebra business you can gain expansive exposure to the buying public by installing the Publicity Pillar ... and maximizing its usage with press releases, free media exposure, sponsorships, and information or educational seminars.

8. The Referral
Pillar of Gold

Referred leads and names are the primary marketing tool of the insurance agent, investment agent and other service businesses. Until now! Because now you can borrow and use this unique strategy for tremendous gains in your business.

Here's the reasoning for 'asking' for referrals from your customers:

- *Your existing clients and customers respect you. (Do they?)*
- *They know your business, products and service - and see it as outstanding. (We hope they do!)*
- *And they know many other people who do not buy from you now, such as relatives, friends and colleagues. (They do!)*

So, if you had 100 clients, and each was to give you two referred leads, what would you do with 200 more prospects? You would try to sell them of course.

The insurance representative tries to obtain more than two names. They seek six and more from every client. They ask permission to use the client's name, *purely as an introduction*, and 'not' to say that the client sent them. It's as simple as that.

However, you, as the Red Stripe Zebra business person can install this marketing pillar and do it differently, more effectively. How? By not just asking for names. No, you use the opportunity to 're-sell' the original purchase, pointing out that by buying from you the customer is now *better off.* You can explain how you have saved them money, or added extra value to the purchase. How you have saved them time, or given them a better product or service for the same price of the competitor.

By pointing this all out to the customer (in letter form or verbally) you gradually build a 'high perceived value' into the product or service, along with the 'real value' of the product or service you've sold them. Thereby, you are building rapport, trust ... and establishing yourself as their preferred choice to do business with.

This 'layer' effect of *high perceived value* and *real value*, along with *trust* and *rapport,* gives you greater leverage that opens the door for referred leads. By explaining to the customer that you wish to offer the same value, bargain, deal, offer etc. to their friends, colleagues, and family members, it makes them enthusiastic to offer you names and hot leads.

If you were also to offer a reward to your customers for referring names of potential new prospects to you, this can make it easier to gain leads. A reward would be a *High-Perceived Value (HPV) ... Low Acquisition Cost (LAC)* product or service that you can give the customer as a gift. In other words, something that costs you *little*, yet is perceived by the customer of being of good value.

The referral pillar is vital for your business. It cuts down the cost of advertising, and is a powerful key to unlock the doors of buying resistance. It shouldn't be left in the realm of the insurance and real estate agents ... but should be incorporated into YOUR business. It's a brilliant method for undergirding your business temple. The referral pillar!

Draft a script for a referral letter, one that points out the high perceived value and the real value, and ask for one or two names of people your customer or client could refer you to as an introduction ... then send it out to your entire customer data base.

You will gain a solid response if you've crafted your letter correctly.

(But once again, if you have difficulty, contact our office for assistance.)

9. The Magic of the Testimonial and Endorsement Pillar

An endorsement can work like magic. Especially an endorsement from a prominent community figure, celebrity, business leader, author etc. If you were to arrange for your product or service to be endorsed by a sports figure, arts figure, high profile business person, or a person of prominence in your industry, the weight of that endorsement can be *gold* for your marketing results.

Endorsements and testimonials are marketing pillars. They can be singular, or a compilation of satisfied clients. You can work them into the body of your advertising, brochures, and special promotions.

When a potential customer reads your literature and sees the endorsement from some person whom they respect, your product is assured a good hearing. Why? Because people like to associate with successful, high profile people, and if your business carries an endorsement from such an individual the customers will respond. It's also to do with believability.

What someone else says about us is ten times more readily accepted and believed than what we say about ourselves!

What someone else (a believable person) says about us is ten times more readily accepted than what we say about ourselves!

Endorsements From Celebrities

For many years in Australia, John Laws has been the leading radio announcer in the land. He has been known as a widely listened to man with a wealth of knowledge and insight into people. A true celebrity.

During all those years, to have John Laws announce and endorse your business or product assured success, listeners believed this man's word as the final authority, and his endorsement as sacrosanct. It cost plenty though, but produced results!

If you are selling golf equipment or services to golf courses, having a celebrity golfer, or a business 'legend' associated with the industry to endorse your product is tantamount to success. A celebrity who has his own 'home improvement' show on television could endorse a building firm, or a host of a cooking show could endorse a restaurant, a hotel supply house or cooking utensils firm. There is a celebrity for every trade ... and for a price (in trade or money) would endorse your product, business or service ... providing of course what you do is ethical and of good quality. And there is an agency somewhere that manages these people ... the Internet will help you track them down.

Testimonials
in the Copy

In my experience, if you have performed a service or sold a product to a customer or client who is *truly satisfied*, especially a 'high-profile' business client, they will be more than willing to supply you with a testimonial. (It's also good exposure for their business).

However, the secret in using the testimonial is NOT to just add the comments in an ill conceived fashion at the base of your brochure or advertisement. You weave it into the very fabric of the story. Remember, the Red Stripe Zebra business does it differently!

In other words, rather than place in your advertisement or brochure a testimonial like this:

"We believe this service is excellent value ......" Joe Smith Inc.

It is much better to write:

Joe Smith Inc. were seeking answers to some production problems in their factory. In desperation, after some shoddy treatment elsewhere, they contacted us after being recommended by a mutual client.

We were able to work with them quickly to solve their problems, then we installed a new servicing contract to reduce their ongoing costs. A delighted Joe Smith states:

"We believe this service is excellent value and right on the money for us."

By telling the story around the testimonial you build the perception that your business, product or service is superior to others, simply because someone else just said it was!

This 'building into the body copy' of your brochure, letter or advertisement adds

181

power and more believability. It also cause the reader to be well into the reading of the testimonial before they even realize it.

Do not be fooled into believing that brochures and advertisements must be graphic in nature. It is the power of words that motivate ... and especially the power of a well written testimonial or endorsement that motivates people to buy.

Install the *Testimonial/Endorsement Pillar* into your business and make more sales, because it will increase the *believability* of what you are saying about your product or service.

10. The Creative Marketing Pillar

Ray Evans sold Toyotas in Murwillumbah, New South Wales, Australia. For a few years, prior to branching out into his own retail business, he worked as a sales representative for *Hayes Toyota*. However, when Ray joined the firm he did not come from a car selling background. In fact, he did not know the first thing about selling new cars. (Probably a good thing!)

It wasn't too long though, before Ray was selling consistently, and in time he became the leading Toyota representative in Northern New South Wales and Southern Queensland. And as a result of his success he was invited to visit the Toyota factories in Japan as a recognition of his high selling rates.

What caused this man to outsell all others?

He sold creatively!

His marketing pillar was unique in the industry. Rather than wait around the showroom for potential customers (as most do), Ray would drive around suburbs and streets looking for cars in driveways that looked like good trade-ins. He would then knock on doors, introduce himself and ask if he could bring a new car to the people for a test drive in a day or two. He covered many miles visiting surrounding towns, always on the lookout for potential customers. And he was only in the office to do paperwork, the remainder of the time he was *on the road*.

Ray had the ability of *taking the showroom to the people*. A simplistic strategy, but one that worked. And besides, he didn't know anything about selling cars, so he simply *invented* a way. He did know about people though! He knew they liked his preferential treatment, his friendly, courteous manner, his obliging way of doing business. He impressed people with this reverse selling approach, and as a result he sold cars. Lots and lots of cars!

In marketing, it is easy to get 'bogged down' in *old* methodology and miss many opportunities for sales. The creative marketing pillar is one that requires you to find *new methods* of selling your products or service. It means taking your product or service *to* the customer. It means finding *creative* ways to expose your business, add to the offering, or doing things differently to all others.

Creative marketing *attracts* attention, and that then becomes a marketing pillar. An example of this is Federal Express. Creatively, they color their world orange and purple. That strengthens their creative marketing pillar, because those colors emblazon into our minds and motivates us to choose their service, over all others.

The Creative
Bagel Bar

The *Bronx Bagel Bar* (a new franchise) outperforms its competition because this Deli does not just sell bagels. It has created a New York theme, from the uniform the staff wears, to the New York street scenes on the wall, and even the name of the bagel sandwiches, such as the Yo'.

That's creativity.

It is a creative marketing pillar that breaks their Red Striped Zebra business free from all the other 'sandwich' stores. It attracts attention, and attention means *more* customers, clients or guests.

The creative marketing pillar is one that *must* be incorporated. It will help you develop new concepts and ideas to win customers and gain much exposure.

Creatively Promoting Where
You're Least Expected

Which business advertises in a car magazine? What about an aviation, shooting, fishing, or home furnishing magazine? One glance through each magazine shows us that the businesses which sell products in those industries, are the ones which are endemic. Those which 'function' in those respective industries, naturally advertise in those associated publications.

The people who sell the GPS tracking system advertise in aviation magazines, or the wallpaper supply firm advertises in home furnishing magazines.

But, one could think that the people who read such magazines do not buy any other product. Doesn't the man who reads fishing magazines have teeth that require dental treatment? Or a car that needs a service? Does the pilot ever come to earth and cut his grass?

We become very myopic in promotions and marketing ... thereby missing great opportunities!

Your business, product or service would certainly stand out if you were to advertise in a magazine that had *nothing whatever* to do with your offering. People would read your advertisement, simply because it stands apart. And the people who read those magazines most probably could use your product or service.

In a recent *computer* magazine from Scotland I noticed a Glasgow Lingerie firm had placed a display advertisement with the heading *"Software"*

... That advertisement stood apart!

- *The dentist who advertises and states that he takes care of the teeth of the fishing community will attract clients.*
- *The investment adviser can do likewise in an aircraft magazine to the many well-healed aircraft owners.*
- *The car dealer could feature his car in the driveway of a beautiful home, in the furnishing magazine.*

184

- *And you can feature your business using this creative marketing pillar, reaching an abundance of people who may never see your offering in your usual trade magazine.*

Some people only read certain magazines. They may never read a paper, yet would never miss their subscription to their favorite magazine. You can reach them at their source with your creative Red Striped Zebra advertisement.

Be creative in your advertising. Look for ways of doing it differently. The black and white Zebra businesses are still doing it the old ways ... but your bold red stripes will stand apart with a creative marketing pillar.

11. The Internet
Pillar

They are now telling us that if we do not have a home page on the Internet we will lose out.

Mind-blowing numbers are connected via computers to the electronic information world. However, as well as huge benefits there certainly are drawbacks. It depends on what you sell.

The average Internet, Prodigy, CompuServe, America On-Line, and other services user is a 31-year-old male with a $45,000 income. If you sold recipe books or dolls, you may waste your time and money in this medium. One thing is true though. The system is one of *information.* Receiving unsolicited E-mail sales pitches is annoying, and expecting users to spend all their time browsing *advertising* is to say the least, naive.

However, if you were to build into your advertising a *Perception of Value Education (POVE)* style, simply to inform and educate the reader, your chances of success will dramatically rise. Treat the Internet like an information medium and *inform* the users. Give them 'inside' information about the manufacturing, quality and use of your product. Explain how your service can be advantageous to them, in precise detail. Inform, and your electronic marketing pillar will stand true and effective.

Having a Web page allows for a great amount of trial and testing.

You can change and modify a Web page until you obtain maximum results, much easier than changing a new printed brochure, yellow page advertisement or direct mail piece.

In essence, you could save a great deal in advertising through this medium, and attract a whole new range of customers or clients from afar.

Word Direct Travel, a travel agency client in Glasgow, is owned and operated by George Glen. They had been receiving a large number of enquiries on their Web page, from people asking about discount airfares. George and his team were spending four hours every day sending quotations back to the inquirers, but *not* making any sales. Their problem was not in getting people to their page, but in making a sale from those potential customers.

We experimented with a specially crafted letter, written in a *POVE* style and telling the potential customer *why they would be better off* buying from Word Direct.

We mentioned all the unique and good things that WDT offered and exactly what these things meant to the customer ... then, at the very end, the quotation was mentioned, along with a final post script, just to mention one last advantage.

This letter was used for every enquiry, with just a cut and paste for the quotation. It resulted in an immediate increase in sales, because there is more to buying than just the price ... or a fancy Web page. More importantly; the people using the Internet are real 'people' - real flesh and blood human beings with *needs, wants, desires, feelings* and family members to consider.

The people (potential customers) using the Internet are real 'people' - flesh and blood human beings with needs, wants, desires, feelings.

They can be reached by treating them as such ... and by offering your product or services in such a way it touches them where they sit ... at their computer!

Just because the Internet has the potential to tap untold millions does not mean peanuts if we forget who is connected to every terminal.

This letter that WDT used touched needs, answered questions, fueled desires, created opportunities to act and gain real advantages ... and it was read by people who needed all those things in their lives. When they enquired about airfares or holiday prices, they were really saying; *"Can you help me have a great holiday or trip?"*

WDT became, through this e-mail response letter, a valuable asset to the people, not just a commodity, because they answered that question, instead of just dishing out quotes. And the wastage of time in answering enquires turned to valuable sales and long-term clients.

From Glasgow, George services the travel needs of clients as far away as New Orleans and Chicago ... simply because he has incorporated Red Striped Zebra strategies into his Web page design, e-mail responses and his business. You can too! Don't just blindly go to any ol' Web page designer, but find one who *knows* how to write copy that motivates and answers needs. Send e-mail letters or create Web pages written in a style that *makes people buy* ... and then you will have an Internet Marketing Pillar working for you!

12. The Direct
Selling Pillar

The strength of most businesses is in the sales people. The ones out there doing battle each day to secure sales.

This marketing pillar is vital for the business temple to survive, for it is the 'feet in the street' for your business. The sales person behind a sales counter, or out on the road, or behind the telephone, is the real force behind any business. They are the ones in constant contact with the customer, and they can *make* or *break* a business.

Sales people have a unique advantage over other forms of marketing pillars. They can have immediate and first-hand knowledge of the effectiveness of a particular sales presentation. They can test various presentations on their potential customers and report their findings to their managers. And they can ask the customer to buy more products, accessories, complimentary products or services.

When you buy a burger at a fast food store, do you think the sales staff is just being pleasant when they ask you if you would like *fries* with your order? No, they have been directed to make that request, and rightfully so. The asking for fries adds literally millions to the bottom line on the national chains. A simple question asking you to buy fries, is called *up-selling*, and it is an easy task to do for the direct sales force ... but more difficult for other forms of marketing. It has been found that people buy more when asked, simply to please the 'asker', in many cases.

Two out of every three buy more when asked!

Ken Bone owns *Bone Petroleum Services* in Australia. Jay Abraham, a Californian based consultant, who has Ken as a client, reported that the petroleum business was having some acute marketing problems.

Ken markets petroleum products through a service station network of about 20 stations, along with food products through the convenience stores. As a trial, they agreed to direct their sales people to ask each customer when they came in to pay for their gasoline, if they would like to *buy something else* from the store. At first they found it a little awkward, but soon learned an easy way of asking.

They also found that by *reducing* their fuel price, *more* customers started driving in to refuel, and upon entering the convenience store, were buying more products. And in fact, they reported that *two out of every three* people bought something else when asked to do so!

The direct selling endeavors can be further enhanced by directing sales people to ask the customers to buy something else.

Now, the business is booming because this simple strategy was added to strengthen this direct-selling marketing pillar.

- *The car dealer could direct sales people to ask the customer to buy accessories, such as car cleaning products, chamois, tarpaulins, or prepaid maintenance services.*

188

- *The furniture store could ask the customer to buy cushions, fabric protectors and wood preservatives to compliment new furniture.*
- *And the shoe store could offer shoe care cleaners and polishes.*

Using the direct selling efforts of the sales people in this way adds many dollars over a year of trading.

The testing and modifying of every presentation can also maximize results. There is no rigid way in which a sales person can talk to a potential customer. The *normal* method is to make the same presentation to many people each week ... and from that number they will sell a small percentage. The Red Striped Zebra business will have the presentations *tested*, trying different methods of presenting the benefits and advantages, and testing different closing techniques. By doing so this marketing pillar is strengthened and adds to the growth of your business.

But, no matter how prepared and tested the presentation is, what really is the undergirding strength of your sales force is simply this; sales people must present the sales message to as many potential customers as possible. It's a numbers game. Throw enough spaghetti against the wall and some of it will stick. The stickier the spaghetti the more of it that will stick. (The better the presentation, the more sales made).

Content-Rich
Hour or Two

Some of our clients have had sales teams who work exclusively on the telephone. And some of these teams have been operating at low call rates, simply because they had numerous other tasks to perform, papers to shuffle, disturbances from sources outside their control and a host of other problems. To be Red Striped Zebra businesses, they had to become *unique* in *everything* they do ... and that included telephone work. We instructed the sales teams to set apart *content-rich time periods*. One or two hours at a time when they could not stop, could not be disturbed, could not do anything else but make the *set number* of calls ... to be *unstoppable* during those content-rich times ... until *every* call was made.

And the results? From running at around 70% of goal, they are achieving 100% and more. In other words; a 30% increase in outgoing calls. Sales have increased and new customers are continuously being found. It works! And it's amazing how a new name, i.e. *Content-Rich*, or *Quality Time (QT)* spurs people with a new vision to win.

The *Direct Selling Pillar* should be a vital tool in your business temple, but like all others, it needs to be a true Red Stripe style. Sales people can be molded to become as innovative and creative as you desire ... for they too want the tools and support which will cause them to win big in business.

13. The Radio and Television Pillar

As a Red Striped Zebra business, the normal television and radio advertisement should be *forbidden* territory.

Effective marketing means embracing uniqueness and creativity. Getting <u>*noticed*</u> and *breaking free* from the crowd. In television and radio advertising, you must ask yourself if your message can be given, the public educated and motivated, and all within the normal thirty-second time-spot. Large amounts of money can be spent on this medium, but before rushing in you should study the advertisements, and note which ones motivate you, and why?

This marketing pillar can be used to benefit if you have the opportunity to *Perception of Value Educate* your viewer or listener. Trying to do that in thirty seconds may be difficult.

Better yet are the larger space advertisements. Not so much the long-winded infomercials, but those that take a few short minutes to tell the story. Better still, if you can have access to your local radio stations and obtain a community help segment where you talk about your industry and products. This gets you exposed and your business becomes recognizable.

Many radio stations and some cable television stations provide very cheap air time. For instance, the Christian, public access, library channels and other such broadcasting stations provide much lower rates than the big name stations, and yet their listening audience is strong.

190

Radio and television is a marketing pillar that you should not overlook, but for the Red Striped Zebra the rules still apply ...

Perception of Value Education (POVE)

Irresistible Sales Offers (ISO's)

Added Bonuses

Risk Transfers

And your Unique Marketing Perception (UMP)

... to name just a few.

If you can build all these into your advertisements or selling stories, you will have a winner ... and another strong pillar that can produce more sales and income for you.

And There's More ...

Now that you've read and thought about installing these 13 Pillars, here's a few more that you can dwell on ... and ascertain if they could be installed into your business to add further strength and money-making sales opportunites.

- Trade Shows
- On-site Demonstrations
- Distributors
- Manufacturer's Representatives
- Private Labeling
- Newsletters (results-expected style)
- Scheduled Promotions
- New Product Launches

(Want to know more about adding pillars, or about how to install and undergird them to gain maximum results? To find out more, contact our office.)

In summary, your business temple will thrive in these highly competitive times simply by adding marketing pillars.

Borrowing marketing pillars from other industries and incorporating them into your business will add strength. You will attract more customers, clients and consequentially make more sales. Not to do so is folly. And to continue with only one or two pillars is courting disaster.

Incorporate these thirteen into your strategy and you will establish your business far ahead of the rest. This will give you an 'unfair marketing advantage'. Unfair for the competition that is, and the lead advantage for your business!

Clydesdale
and
Geese

How to dramatically multiply customers,
sales and profit with synergy!

Nature can teach us powerful lessons. Working together (synergy) is one. And working in synergy with other businesses results in outstanding opportunities for the Red Striped Zebra business.

Mark Steinman has discovered a marketing secret. He is the owner of *The Reader's Nook* book store. Mark does things much differently than his competitors. He has to, because his surrounding competition is the *big-box* super book stores. Mark has discovered a *synergistic* approach to selling books. His store serves the browsing customer coffee and cappuccino. It's just a small secret really, but a synergistic strategy that *actually draws customers* to the store.

What is better than to browse throughout a bookstore with a cappuccino in hand? The customer has a relaxing time, drinks the coffee, buys the book, and returns *often* to repeat the experience. A superb synergistic approach!

Clothes, Shoes, Jewelry and Coffee

Launceston, Tasmania is a city that embraces synergy. Some years ago the city closed off one full block of Brisbane Street, converting into a beautiful pedestrian mall. Then the retailer's stores opening onto this new exciting mall pushed the trading envelope to the fullest, by working in synergy with other businesses.

Neil Pitt's Menswear, is an up-market quality fashion store that has introduced a small cafe in the rear. To reach the cafe the customer walks *through* the length of the store and up a small flight of steps, to this unique balcony eatery.

A few retail doors along, the mall's jewelry store also introduced the same concept. Directly across the mall the high fashion shoe store has combined with the cafe that backs onto their building. They simply cut a wall out and incorporated an archway, thereby combining the two businesses. Many similar ventures in the same city have followed, giving the retail atmosphere a boost that provides a unique shopping experience. In fact, it's become *customer friendly!*

In all these cases store traffic has increased. Customers who enter the cafes for lunch, or cappuccino, usually take time to browse and look at the clothing, shoes, jewelry and giftware, thereby increasing sales.

Other customers who enter the stores to buy clothing or shoes also take the time to have a coffee or a snack, thereby increasing the cafe's business.

When the mall first opened, there were the usual cries from merchants who were saying their businesses would suffer by cutting off vehicle access. But they soon found that it actually attracted more customers ... and with the synergy approach that later followed, this mall has become the hub of the city, a place to meet and greet, to shop and spend time. A place to spend dollars too!

In fact, since that mall proved so successful, the city has turned two more streets into pedestrian walkways. But it is the synergy that has given the businesses the added clout!

Synergy in action!

In Mountain View, Arkansas there's a *Hardee's* restaurant with *gasoline pumps* in the drive. This combining of businesses, or synergy, has been a very successful partnership for the owner of the franchise. His restaurant business in this quaint Ozarks town, has had a major boost with this marriage of gas and fast food, with his performance being 50% *above* Hardee's national average. That's synergy!

Anthony Conza is the founder, President and Chief Executive of *Blimpie International* in New York. Through Conza's efforts we are now seeing Blimpie teemed up with Shell stations. Conza believes that this combining of businesses reduces costs. The building and facilities, such as rest rooms and refrigeration, are in place with a service station, thereby making the cost of establishing a Blimpies far cheaper.

We are now seeing this synergy taking place with TCYB Yogurt and Subway sandwich stores, with Exxon service stations. And as I am writing this, Exxon are transforming fifty service stations in Memphis (we're we are headquartered) into synergistic *super* stations. They look more like grocery stores that just happen to sell gas.

One-Stop
Shop

The thinking that goes into this synergistic approach concludes that a customer would prefer to make *one stop than two*. To be able to buy gas, then go inside to purchase a sandwich, makes for better service, and stronger business.

A client firm of ours which sells safety equipment, is now taking on more product lines to broaden their horizons. They are now announcing to clients that they are a one-stop-shop. They realized that synergy in product offerings will give them increased sales. The customer is saved the effort of purchasing from a number of various suppliers, by buying from the one-stop shop.

Sales performances of businesses which become involved in synergy arrangements are increased. Results show <u>exponential</u> growth that far outweighs expectations.

Not Just
About Coffee

These stories are *not* about coffee, cappuccino, sandwiches or gas. They are *not* about every business incorporating a restaurant. Due to various cities having differing regulations, what is mentioned here may not even be allowable in other places.

It is about *synergy* ... and how to increase 'your' business growth by *joining forces* with complimentary, or even competing businesses.

Clydesdales, Geese and Red Striped Zebras

Clydesdale horses are remarkable. They are big, strong and powerful. Very big! In fact, many farmers in certain situations still use them in preference to tractors,.

In clearing bushland and scrub country, some farmers believe it is much faster to attach a chain to small tree and tell the Clydesdale horse to pull it out. Driving the tractor, they need to bring it into position, get off, fasten the chain, then board the tractor again to start the pulling process. In these and some other situations, a farmer and his Clydesdale can work far more efficiently than a tractor,

The Synergy
Miracle

Interestingly enough, the Clydesdale horse can out pull all other horse breeds, and can pull up to *two tons* of weight. However, far more remarkable than that, *two* Clydesdales harnessed together and *pulling in synergy* can pull up to 23 tons. We would presume that two harnessed together would pull four tons, (double the two) but twenty three?

What makes the difference, what secret power can cause this six-fold increase in performance? In a nutshell, it is *synergy!*

In researching these facts, I made a special trip to the *Heavy Horse Center* in Perth, Scotland. I drove the two hours after a seminar, just to see these magnificent animals at work ... and to understand fully how the synergistic concept can be applied to increasing the 'pulling power' in any business.

The Performance V

The V formation's we see in the sky during the cooling season, signals us that winter is on the way. The Geese are on the move, heading for warmer places across many air miles.

Scientists who work with these migrating birds have tried to unravel the mystery of the V formation, and arrived at interesting conclusions. The Geese know something we don't. Why don't they fly in straight lines, or in random groups? Why don't they just fly *every*

Goose for itself?

We do it that way, we run our businesses in *competition* to others. We do our own 'thing' and fly blindly on, in straight lines, in random ... and *every business for itself.* Why do the Geese do it differently?

The 71% Effect

Research shows a solitary Goose flies 71% *less* distance than if he flew in a V formation. In other words, the V formation group can fly 71% *further* than flying singularly.

Isn't that remarkable? Geese have known that secret all along, and have been flying that way since creation.

Apparently, because each Goose is positioned behind, and slightly to the side of the preceding Goose, they experience less frontal and skin-friction drag to hold them back and tire them out. Engineers design aircraft this way, to lessen the various drag elements. Skin friction drag, frontal drag, profile drag etc. Those Geese simply tuck in behind each other to gain a free ride and reserve their strength. It is noted that they also use the updraft caused by the preceding Goose to aid with their lift.

Leadership
Roles

Scientists have also noted the Geese take turns at the leadership role. That Goose out in front simply drops back and tucks behind, while another, fresher Goose takes over the lead role. (While all the others honk encouragement!). This *synergistic* approach increases their migration performance many times over, allowing them to travel *further* and retain body condition. They get *more* results!

Coffee, Birds,
Horses and Zebra

Cappuccino, Geese, Clydesdales and Red Striped Zebras. What's the connection? The connection is in *joining forces* and *combining efforts* with other entities, (businesses) to *increase the performance* of your Red Striped Zebra business. That's the connection and lesson to learn about synergy.

If I could put it into a scientific formula, it would be this:

The sum performance, (sales results), of two or three entities (businesses) in synergy is far <u>greater</u> than the individual performance of the various entities.
(Horses, Geese ... or Businesses)

By learning these lessons from nature, you can develop a perceptive new mind-set that seeks out synergistic opportunities, incorporating them into your business, and gaining staggering new growth.

- *Synergy has its own performance magic.*
- *It produces 'unexpected' results.*
- *It produces results that do not require any extra effort.*
- *And it produces results that far outweigh the 'individual' efforts of each synergy partner.*

What's Really Expected?

When the Geese fly in V formation shouldn't they expect just a small increase in performance, such as 10%, 20% or maybe 30% maximum? Yet, they end up with a whopping 71% increase? That is *unexpected* and *remarkable*.

The two Clydesdales should by rights only pull 4 tons together. Yet their astonishing effort produces 23 tons! That too is both unexpected and remarkable.

Success Formula

This is a little understood success formula in both nature and also in business that can cause equally profound results for the Red Striped

199

Zebra firm, willing to explore the parameters.

We do not fully understand why this phenomenon works, or why synergy increases the performance level *exponentially* when two forces join in harmony. However, it really does not matter how it works, why it works, or if anyone fully understands it. What you only need to know is that it *does* work well and in knowing how to introduce it into your own business.

Discovering Synergy's full potential

You may not have a retail store that would lend itself to incorporating a coffee bar or cafe. However, synergistic thinking can take on even *grander* forms than these simple examples.

I do *not* believe for one moment that any business has *fully explored*, or developed their maximum potential for synergy. The surface is not even scraped yet and is a gold mine for the Red Striped Zebra business willing to investigate synergy's potential.

You may be in a service business, a medical practice, or conduct a real estate, insurance or investment agency. Whatever your calling, there is room for synergy. There is room for joining forces with other businesses and reaping the harvest.

Birds of a Feather

A medical practice, such as a dentist, plastic surgeon or family doctor cannot introduce a cafe or sandwich store into the practice. How absurd! But, the secret in synergy is to find a *compatible* offering that will fit hand-in-hand with the business.

The natural synergistic business for a medical practitioner is one that would *benefit* the patients. *JuicePlus* is a multi-level marketing business that has a superb product. It sells fruit and vegetables in a capsule. This firm process freshly picked fruits and vegetables into a highly

Geese do not fly with Crows, and Clydesdales do not work well with Quarter horses.

You must first find a compatible bird to fly with, or horse to pull with.

200

concentrated supplement, in capsule form. This product is very high in antioxidants, enzymes, fibre, vitamins and nutrients, and many people are claiming outstanding health and energy improvements after a few months of daily usage.

Many doctors and chiropractors who have become distributors for JuicePlus are dispensing and advising their patients to take the product. What a natural *synergistic* approach. They combine their medical practices with a business that supplies health products. Birds of a feather!

Synergistic Success
in Real Estate

I bought a home in Tasmania in 1984. I had recently arrived from another state and was a 'newcomer' to the area. Not knowing any person, or any real estate agent, I was fortunate to locate a very friendly and efficient Realtor who catered exactly to my needs.

I had him drive me all over the city searching for the 'perfect' home, and when I found it, I had him negotiate back and forth with the owner until we reached an agreement.

From that point over the next few months I bought two more homes, both smaller and for investment purposes. I eventually sold these and moved on to other things. However, during this buying and selling experience, I uncovered powerful opportunities for synergy in real estate.

Selling
Services

Being new to the state and city, I had *needs*. In fact, every person who moves into a new town, city, or state has needs.

They usually approach an agent and go through the process of buying a home. After the deal is completed, they *may* receive a card, or home warming gift from the agent, and perhaps *never* see them again.

That is the typical scenario of most newcomers. The agent *presumes* they will own that home for many years, therefore the possibility of another sale may be remote.

In a synergistic approach though, the agent should *become aware* of the client's needs. To transform the house into their personal 'vision' of a home, they may 'need' (besides other trades) a:

- *Painter*
- *Carpenter*
- *Landscape Gardener*
- *Pool Cleaning Service*
- *Heating Specialist*
- *Maid Service*
- *General Gardener*

Keep in mind the client is new, and does not know *who* to contact, who is reliable, who does a quality service or who is prompt. They are at the mercy of the trades people whom they may call.

The prudent, synergistic thinking agent can boost their business by arranging contacts with all of these trades. For referrals and recommendations to each of these businesses the agent could earn a percentage, perhaps 10% or more, on the value of each of the jobs that the homeowner and trades people undertake.

A $3,000 paint job could net the agent $300, paid by the painter to the agent. A pool service, maid service or gardening service could also net the agent an attractive fee.

This is synergy. It combines the service of the real estate agent with the service provided by the trades people, resulting in an *increase* in the performance level and results for *all* parties. Everyone wins.

- *The homeowner is introduced to the finest and best in each trade group, saving them many hours of searching, or worse; being ripped off or receiving shoddy work.*
- *The trades person gains a new client and makes a sale that they never had before.*
- *The agent makes a commission on the work, over and above the original house selling commission.*

In the long-term some of the trades people, such as the pool service business, gardening or maid service, could earn many times the initial amount with the Customer's Long Term Value (CLTV). All because one prudent agent understood synergy.

- *Are you starting to see how synergy could increase your business?*
- *Are you starting to 'identify' which businesses could be an ideal 'birds of a feather' synergistic partnership for yours?*

Opportunities Abound

Taking this homeowner/agent scenario even further, those newcomers to town would also require recommendation or referrals to a lawyer, family doctor, dentist, hairdresser and even the best restaurants to try. If the agent had developed a synergistic business with each of these, he could present a special book of *introductory coupons* to the client as a complimentary gesture. When they redeemed them at each business, the agent would receive a percentage of the money spent by the client at that particular business ... simply for the referral.

The agent profits, the host businesses all gain a new client, and the client wins by receiving introductions to reputable and quality businesses or practices.

That is synergy in action!

Insurance Synergy

Insurance agents know everybody! So it seems. They gather a range of clients that is staggering. Painters, lawyers, mechanics, truck drivers and chefs. Unless they work specifically within certain industries, most of their clients have wide and varied occupations, and many of those are self-employed.

Unlike retailers, restaurants or service stations, the insurance agent knows his client better than all. They have inside information, so to speak. They also have a unique opportunity to synergize their insurance agency with all their clients and earn extra *commissions*.

Their builder client may be looking for a painter, drywall tradesman or bricklayer. The agent could recommend one of his clients, and receive a commission from that client for securing him a contract. The retail client may require a sign writer or cleaning service. The same 'bringing them together' applies.

Working in synergy means 'looking' for opportunities and making financial arrangements with synergy partners.

Missed Synergistic Opportunities

Synergy can work wonders when two businesses get together to promote a package.

- *The hairdresser joins with a dress store to offer a make-over seasonal package.*

- *The men's suit store combines with a shoe store to offer a complete 'executive' package.*

- *Or the wallpaper store joins with a carpet retailer to offer a 'complete room decorating' package.*

One major problem exists though in developing synergy. It is the *negligence* of *not* keeping records.

Have you ever been to a hairdresser who *asked you for your name* and address, so the salon could keep a file on your requirements? Not likely! How often have you been *asked* for your name and address from a clothing store, apart from your credit card requirements, so they could serve you better? Probably not often, if at all!

When you bought your last piece of furniture, did the sales person enter your name and address and other details into their data base? Have the trades people you contracted to do work on your home, or car, ever asked you for personal details for their records?

The answer to these questions will usually be no. It simply is not done as a normal part of business. Unless we run an account at a store, or a business, seldom are we ever asked to supply our name, address, age, phone number and our likes or dislikes. Bad mistake! And what a missed opportunity in laying the foundations for a synergistic approach in business.

> *The Red Striped Zebra business 'always' gets the name, address ... and as much information as possible!*

Synergistic
Data Bases

If that same hairdresser had asked his clients for names, and built a client data base of 500, they could approach the dress store manager and immediately construe a synergistic arrangement. If the dress store had also asked for names of their customers, and developed their own client list, (say 500 also) they too would have the foundation for a synergistic offering.

If you were given 500 *new* names, what would that be worth to you? What would that new list of names be worth if it came with a *recommendation* of your business to each and every client? *It would be worth many new sales, to say the least!*

Promotional
Strategies

The two businesses, working in synergy with 1,000 combined names could work out many promotional strategies. First, they could create an invitation letter, written on the dress store's letterhead, stating that the two stores have developed a new *joint alliance*. If the client would take the *letter of invitation* to the hairdresser, they could have a special style-cut or perm at an introductory price. The client acts on the *recommendation* of their dress store manager, and gains a special price hair service.

The hairdresser gains with the *influx of new clients*, and in turn pays a commission to the dress store for every new client.

Likewise, the reverse could be achieved, by sending letters to the hairdresser's clients, *inviting them to attend* a fashion showing and special sale on a certain evening at the dress store. *Synergy in action!*

Expanding the synergy envelope

The results of synergy when joining data bases is far more effective than just the referral example, simply because of the new numbers involved. Not just 500 customers to approach from each, but 1,000. And sending a letter is just the start of many offerings throughout the year, to an ever expanding base of names.

> *The 'combined' forces of two businesses takes on the 23-ton pulling power, rather than the two tons each approach.*

What makes it so potent is that these are actual trusting customers and clients of the hairdresser/clothing store ... and many will *act on the recommendation* and invitation.

Once established, working in synergy can in effect, create a third business. In this hairdresser and dress store example, a fashion show incorporating clothing and hairstyles could become an event, run three times per year. The promotion could not only focus on the combined data base, but be opened to the public through newspaper, radio or television advertising.

Special Clubs
for Special Boys

Executives do not by suits. They buy an *executive image*. With this in mind, the men's wear store could easily join in synergy with a shoe store ... and they in turn could join with a leather store that sells briefcases, belts and compendiums. Then, a triune synergy evolves!

Combining all three data bases would produce a burgeoning list of customers to promote to.

Now, if they were to establish a unique *'Executive Club'* that was *not* open to the public, but *only available to the invited clients* of the three synergized businesses, the businesses would have a tremendous marketing advantage. This club could supply a unique offer to its members. An 'executive image' package comprising two new suits every year, combined with four shirts, two pairs of socks, three leather belts, two pairs of shoes and a 'free' leather briefcase. All for one *'special member's'* price.

The suits could be the finest wool blends, double breasted and hand stitched. The shirts would be French-cuffed works of art. The matching leather belts and shoes would be the finest leather, and the complimentary briefcase would come with the client's gold initials. And this special offer for the *'Executive Image Club'* would only be to discerning clients who seek an image commensurate with their position.

Because it combines three data bases they can make the offer to a far wider audience than if the suit store acted alone.

The triune synergy has produced a fourth 'ghost' business ... one selling packages for executives. And this 'offer to good to refuse' would be promoted 'within the ranks' to the *already existing clients* of all three businesses.

Synergy works for these 'birds of a feather' businesses because:

- *The promotions come with 'combined recommendations' and invitations of those businesses that customers are 'already' buying from and have relationships with.*

- *A synergistic promotion like this example paints the picture of 'exclusiveness', 'image' and executive 'excellence' ... and provides customers with an Irresistible Sales Offer (ISO).*

Do you see the possibilities of synergistic thinking for *your* business?

As the manager of a Red Striped Zebra business, collecting names is crucial and vital for you. Every person you do business with *must* end up in your data base. If you do not have a computer, write them in a book and have a commercial computer firm develop a data file for you.

The names can be collected via a direct request, or even through offering prizes in a competition. Whatever it takes ... get those names!

If you are currently thinking of synergistic opportunities and you have a business in mind to approach, *they too must be encouraged to develop a data base ... if* they have not already done so. In a nutshell, this synergistic concept is an easy four-step process.

> *Maximizing the synergy strategy by data base building is paramount to real success.*

You must:

1. *Collect names/addresses of customers in your business.*
2. *Encourage your synergistic partner to gather names.*
3. *Share all those names.*
4. *Develop a joint promotional campaign ... and fire away!*

Restaurant Synergy

In the United States, serving staff deem it necessary to introduce themselves. It's customary.

Over the years I have been told the name of my servers hundreds of times. Not once though have they ever asked for mine, or my guests. What a missed golden opportunity!

What could a restaurant do with this gold mine? Plenty! They could check to see if certain customers have stopped coming, or have not been to the restaurant in some time, and write them a *'We miss you, please come back soon'* customer service letter.

More importantly though, in a synergy situation, the restaurant could join with a theater, movie theater or nightclub, and offer their restaurant customers a *'night on the town'* package: A three-course meal, plus tickets to the movies, theater or a nightclub for a special price. Once again, they attract customers and the restaurant makes *more* money.

Plus ... they receive a small commission from the synergy business. Multiplied over many customers this commission can grow into an impressive sum, and the businesses both grow synergistically.

What if the nightclub or theater develops a data base? (Ever had a theater of nightclub ask for your name for their data base? Missed opportunity!). They could then join forces with the restaurant. What a powerful list that would be. The theater would not have to pay a commission to the restaurant in this case, due to the new combined mailing list, but they would both benefit with their ability to do cross promotions to each other's data base or in a joint promotion.

Please ... give me your name

How would the restaurant gain those names though? Would it not be *distasteful* to do so, in a restaurant setting?

I've noticed many restaurants, either privately owned or chains throughout the United States, the U.K. and Europe, have barrels or bowls for people to drop their business cards into. Each week some lucky person wins a dinner. What an easy way to collect names. But unfortunately it is an inferior method for the Red Striped Zebra business. Why? Because many people do *not* have business cards ... and many others do not even bother with the barrel.

However, bringing attention to a 'competition' by mentioning it to customers would be easy for a food server, then leaving a pen and coupon on the table will gain the desired results. If the prize is substantial, such as a dinner for four or a bottle of champagne, the customer will definitely begin writing.

The hairdresser already has the trust of the client, so asking for a name and address to maintain accurate records should be a cinch and no problem.

It seems such a pity and *shortsighted* that many businesses do not see the benefits of gathering clients names and looking for further opportunities to expand the performance of the business. It would be easy to say that a hairdresser, dentist, optometrist or similar service industry would not need to write to their clients or patients. Would they? They *already* come to get their hair done anyway, don't they?

That's not the point though ... the primary purpose of a synergy application data base is to have a *tool* to use in *joining forces* with other businesses. It gives you the 'leverage' to make deals and synergistic opportunities.

> *That list of shared new names is a valuable tool in which each business can use to make more profit!*

If you went to a business owner and told them you have 200, 500 or 1,000 customers on your data base and would like to share both their's and your base in a joint promotional activity, then that person would jump at the opportunity.

The owner of a dress store, shoe store, beautician or any compatible business to yours would *love* to get their hands on 500 or 1,000 new names, especially when they come with an endorsement.

Health Clubs
in Synergy

Most body building gymnasiums and health clubs constantly advertise for new clients. Your business could take advantage of that, and join in synergy by securing a number of free, one-month memberships to one of these gyms.

Perhaps you work out an arrangement where they supply you with 100 membership coupons that you can offer potential clients. Using the coupons as a *gift* with the purchase of your product or service, you enhance your offer and attract people.

The gymnasium attracts 100 people to try out their facilities ... and from this number they would convert some into full paying members.

Further to this application, you could even add to the free membership coupon in a triune synergy. Perhaps a coupon from a video store for two free video rentals or even movie passes. Maybe a coupon to a sports store which gives discounts for their gymnasium clothing products.

One thing to know, you do not always have to share in sales and profits. Coupons and gift certificates could do wonders for your sales.

If packaging your products or service with other firm's coupons, gift certificates and invitations creates an *Irresistible Sales Offer (ISO)* for your customers, then you still have a viable synergistic venture. It

210

simply means no shared sales dollars, but a booster for your business. They too would benefit, with your coupons, certificates and invitations for their customers.

Money (shared sales and profits) does not always have to be involved in synergy businesses. Shared coupons, certificates, invitations, discounts and services could be the synergy tool.

Maximize your results by selling your competitor's products

(That sounds like an extreme move ...
must be Red Striped Zebra thinking!)

If you sent a letter to 1,000 people offering your product or service, and 20 responded, then out of that 20 you convert 5 into buyers, that could be considered close to *normal* performance.

If those 1,000 letters cost you $500 to print and mail, then each of those customers would have cost you $100 to buy. However, although you have 5 sales, *you have 15 who did not buy* for one reason or another. They were obviously interested enough to respond in the first place, yet they did not buy.

Many times it is because your product or service was not suitable for them. We see this every day. People go from one store to another, from one car dealer to another, from one service industry to another.

If you were able to capture some of those lost clients by offering them your *competitor's* product, you could not only lower your promotional costs but increase your earnings many times. If only three of the fifteen lost sales could be sold, with your *competitor's* product, you may share in enough profit to cover your original $500, or more.

The Radical Sale

Wow! That's radical! Selling the competitor's product or service? How absurd! ... Or is it?

A car dealership may spend $60,000 in a month's advertising to attract car buyers onto their lot. From the hundreds who respond and come to browse, they actually convert only a small percentage into buyers.

Let's say this figure is about 10%. This leaves 90% *unconverted*, but *obviously* interested enough to get in their car and drive to the car lot. In that 90% there would probably be another 10% or maybe as high as 30% who will still buy a car from another dealer.

How it Works

If the dealer had a *synergistic arrangement* with others, perhaps the Ford dealer with the GM dealer, or the Mazda dealer with the Toyota, they could offer those 'lost' customers the competitor's car.

Once the dealer knew, (without a doubt), the potential buyer would go elsewhere to buy, they could then tell them they could offer the competitor's car and complete the deal without any further hassle.

They could assure them they could get a good deal on a Ford, (Mazda, Toyota, Buick, etc.) because they have a 'special' relationship with the Ford dealer. They could offer them the car at $1,500 less, because of the 'special' arrangement, plus offer them some accessories as a gift for doing the deal.

Why lose a customer and a 'sale' if you could still make money by selling other people's products or services?

The *reciprocal* synergistic arrangement would have the other dealer also selling the competitor's cars to these potentially lost buyers.

This synergistic approach could extend to electrical goods, computers, clothing, furniture ... and even to services. If you sold a particular brand of computer and printer, you could approach your competitors and ask them to sell your product if the potential customer they originally attracted declines to buy their equipment. (The 'last resort' close!)

By explaining how they can increase the performance of their advertising and direct mail by having this back-up synergistic approach, they could capture those lost clients, and *take a share* of the sale of *your* equipment. In return, you could offer their equipment to those potential customers who say to you; *"I might go and check out other places."*

By offering the competitor's product, and the competitor offering your equipment, at 'special' bargain rates, the customer is *secured* and *both* businesses share in the sale.

Just another synergistic approach!

If the competitor does not want to take this path, you can still work in synergy by asking them to *give you the lost leads* generated from their promotions, and vise versa.

When you convert those lost leads into sales, you share some of your profit with the competitor.
This helps them recoup their advertising dollars and gives them a fresh source of revenue.

In Summary

There are many advantages with synergy:

- *One obvious advantage to joining in synergy is the reduction in your advertising budget. If two businesses share they can reduce promotional costs. And reduced promotional costs means more profit for your business.*

- *The second benefit is the wider market for you. Joining data bases and sharing customers provides a much larger pool of potential sales than would a costly advertising campaign.*

- *Add to this the performance benefit that comes from a combined synergistic venture, or ongoing relationship. (That's the performance benefit of similar magnitude to the 23 tons or 71%).*

- *Next is in out-maneuvering competition. When two businesses work together they can offer a totally unique package, product or service that is not available to your competitor. An accountant who teams with an insurance agent can offer a more attractive and unique package that is exponentially greater than the individual efforts ... and greater than what the competition can offer.*

- *Then there is the opportunity of capturing <u>potentially lost</u> customers or clients, by having the <u>radical</u> synergistic approach of selling competitor's products. Not only can the cost of advertising be lessened with this approach, but sharing in the profits of your competitor's sales can also glean many thousands of dollars. Sales that would have been lost previously to both businesses.*

Beyond this is the opportunity to increase your data base two ways.

- *By constantly asking for names during the general course of business.*

- *By combining your synergy partner's list with yours during promotions you secure new customers.*

The Red Striped Zebra business in synergy

*Synergy is NOT a common practice because
people do not readily join forces with others.*

Nor are they aware of the results it produces.

*Knowing this, you can stand your business apart by
approaching 'selected' businesses to join you in synergy.
If they are complimentary and forward-thinking, the
owners may well be very keen to expand their
sales and reach their fullest potential.*

If they are competitors, it will take some explaining!

*Nevertheless the synergy secret is one that can
skyrocket your Red Striped Zebra business.*

It takes an open mind and <u>opportunistic</u> thinking.

The thinking of a Red Striped Zebra!

The War
of
Attrition

*How to make sure you're not killing
your business by killing customers!*

Hemorrhage! That's what many businesses suffer from ... and the managers don't even realize it. The usual focus is on finding more customers. More, more more ... while simultaneously established customers are being lost ... thereby bleeding many businesses to death.

Here's how to plug the holes ...

In the movie; *Private Ryan*, we are left with a devastating image of carnage and attrition, as a large loss of life from the D-Day invasion was strewn along Normandy's beaches. Speilberg never mentions numbers, but the real invasion consisted of over 117,000 soldiers, with about 10,600 casualties, or about 9%.

Customer Attrition

In business, we focus on how to increase customers, sales and profits, but one of the most overlooked (and devastating) percentages is *Customer Attrition (CA)*, just as deadly on our business as a D-Day landing.

We do our best to find the leasing or finance company which offers the lowest percentage rate on equipment, cars, or buildings, simply to *save money* on those monthly payments, yet without knowing the percentage rate of our customer attrition we are *bleeding* money from our business *just as quickly as high finance charges*.

It's bad enough to ask a client how much their customer is worth over one year, three or even five years, and find that they do not know, but to also ask them what is the *percentage of lost customers and clients* over the same period ... and still get a negative response, is downright appalling and frightening.

Simply because those two numbers are portentous and crucial to business; knowing what the customer is worth in sales over time ... and knowing how many of those customers are lost each year.

> *It's crucial to know what the customer is worth in sales over time ... AND know how many of those customers are lost each year (in dollar terms) through attrition.*

Shock, stunned ... and totally amazed!

As an example, if you knew that you lose 50 customers each year, and you knew that a customer is worth $500 per year, (accumulated sales, i.e. the *Customer's Long-Term Value - CLTV*) then simple multiplication will show that you're losing $25,000 of lost revenue in year one, or $150,000 over three years (the spending *potential* of 150 lost customers).

Not convinced? Here's how it works over three years:

Year one you lose 50 customers @ $500 each:	$25,000
Year two you lose another 50	$25,000
Plus the second year's spending of the first 50:	$25,000
Year three you lose another 50 @	$25,000
Plus this years spending of the 50 lost last year:	$25,000
Plus the 3rd year earnings of the 50 lost in year 1:	$25,000

That's $150,000 of *potential* lost sales dollars if you were to keep those customers for three years. And for a larger customer base, it would be more shocking, stunning and amazing ... but that's *attrition!*

**Not
Knowing**

Webster defines attrition as: *decrease, reduction*. It means your business has been reduced by $150,000 - and you probably didn't even know it, because your sales and promotion efforts have simply been *topping up* the customer tank with new replacements. Nevertheless, if you could have kept those people in the first place, your business would have been $150,000 better off.

Those 50 customers translates to a percentage of your total customer base. By every 1% reduction you can make in your attrition rate, a substantial saving (or *increase* in sales) is made, for just one year, let alone three, five or ten. Wouldn't it be interesting, (if not a frightening exercise), to estimate how many customers you may have lost over 10 years ... along with their potential sales?

So, what is YOUR attrition rate?

If you discover it is between 15% and 25%, do not be discouraged, most businesses are in the same boat - and they simply do not know it. Many fail to keep records, ask for names and build data bases. If a customer becomes 'cold', starts to shop elsewhere, stops buying because of dissatisfaction, poor service ... or has moved to another town, how on earth would they know if they haven't kept comprehensive records? They don't ... and so they do not know what there *Customer Attrition Rate (CAR)* is, how much they're losing in dollar terms, how many times a customer buys, what offers they could give to keep the customer coming in ... and what to do to stop the customer from 'dying off' and going elsewhere.

But your task as an operator of a Red Striped Zebra business, is to 'know' it at all times ... and do something about it. Reduce it, eliminate it, develop programs to keep the customers buying from you and not let them defect to the other side!

Just as important to you as a monthly sales graph, your *CAR* percentage should also be mapped and followed. Your team should be totally aware of it and 'all' should be seeking out ways to drive that percentage down, so that new sales and profits are captured back into your business.

It takes a rare animal indeed to provide and develop the type of programs that *guarantee* customers are nurtured, delighted, spoiled and fussed over ... and a rarer one to make sure there is no such thing as a 'cold' customer ... one who has not bought, or even been contacted for a long

Wouldn't it be a lifesaver to have a system that warns you when customers haven't bought (or been in contact) for 60, 90 and 120 days? Let all the bells ring and whistles blow if; God forbid - a customer reaches the 90 day mark without a contact.

period of time. That rare animal is a Red Striped Zebra manager who is vigilant and passionate about customers.

Here's why businesses develop high *Customer Attrition Rates* and why they are hemorrhaging to death without even knowing it:

- *Poor attention to the customer's needs and desires. In other words, not supplying Awesome Customer Service.*

- *Failing to build a data base to 'keep track' of cold and old customers, or those who have not bought or been contacted for over two or three months.*

- *Failing to keep in contact with customers at least 12 times per year, via the normal buying process ... or via newsletters, promotions, special offers, invitations to exclusive club memberships, insider's offers and sales, educational evenings or seminars, greeting cards for birthdays or special events ... or phone calls that simply say: "We miss you" ...*

- *Not stocking the latest, innovative, cutting-edge product, services, fashions, quality food, etc. and allowing the competition to provide better than what you do.*

- *Employing people who lack gregarious, fun or pleasant attitudes and allowing those people to come in contact with customers, clients, patients or guests.*

- *Failing to provide education to customers on the value of your product or service, in relation to the price. i.e. a Perception of Value Education (POVE).*

And these are just a few that can cause customers to 'jump ship', defect to the enemy and stop buying from a business.

Do you recognize any in your business? Let's take a closer look at examples that can repel people from your business and increase your *CAR*. And keep in mind this next section is just on customer service alone, not on what 'innovative' or 'bland' products you may sell, or what pricing you offer, or what location you're in, that might also turn customers off.

Is YOUR Customer Service Offending Customers?

How many *Customer Offenders (CO)* are committed each day in your business? A what? What's a customer offender?

It's an 'offence' against the customer. You know, those specific things that *offend* customers, turn them off, cause them to never return to your business - or never to buy from you again ... and cause your attrition rate to go *sky high*.

Customer Offence

An offence is anything that *trespasses* or *violates* a customer. It is something that *irritates, angers, inflames, disgusts, wounds* ..... and worst of all, *repels* them (away) from your business.

Business Offence

An offence committed against a customer is also an offence committed *against your business*. Why? Because it hurts and violates your business ... and your sales, cash flow and profit. You can measure it in the examples given above in the loss of the *Customer's Long Term Value (CLTV)*, which as mentioned, is what your customer is worth to you in collective sales over one year, three years, five years. Once offended, that customer may either *reduce* their buying from you, or *never* return.

Sir Tom's Shocker

Sir Tom Farmer, the British legend who built the famed *KwikFit* auto repair chain, comprising over 1,000 service stores throughout the United Kingdom and Europe, personally told me during an audio recording session, that a young, first time customer may spend £100 ... but, they have calculated that the lifetime value *(CLTV)* of that customer could reach as far as £40,000.

Wow! Imagine offending that customer and never having them return. And imagine offending just 100 of those customers per year. That would be an abhorrence! But in a chain that services 20,000 customers every day, it would be easy to offend just 100, even though that 100 could provide £40,000 each to the business.

KwikFit bends over backwards to delight customers though and their telemarketing division make 5,000 calls every day just to check if people are happy. They are eradicating *Customer Offenders* daily by keeping score, checking by asking customers, using newsletters and every other customer building device ... thereby keeping the pulse of the customer.

Bye-Bye the
Buy Money

Worse still than just losing customers to attrition, is the further loss to the business in the money it cost you to first 'buy' that customer. (You do know that it costs money to buy a customer?). That's all that money you spend on advertising, promotion, salaries for sales people ... all gone via attrition! Simply gone down the drain because the customer was either (among other offenders) deliberately, or inadvertently, offended.

If customers buy from you and you lose them because
they receive an 'offence' and become offended,
then that's bye-bye the buy money!

Doesn't happen in your business?... Have a look first at a few classic offenders and then see if you can still say it:

1: The Permanent Scowl
Offender

I once heard a person complaining about a sales woman in a store. She was described as having this permanent, unfriendly scowl on her face. She never smiled and looked bitter. I asked if this was a turn-off and if it offended, and the answer was a resounding yes.

She said:

I simply do not like shopping in that store 'because' of that 'unfriendly' woman.

Does this store know it has an offender of customers who has actually increased the *CAR*? Who knows, but that store has suffered the loss of the *CLTV* of at least one person.

Shopping to a woman is a fun thing, yet when you have to be served by a frowning faced person, it *takes the fun out* of it. That, is a Customer Offender ... and the customer would 'never' tell the manager. They simply stop shopping there! Customer Attrition!

2: The In-Your-Face Offender

Customers have told me they are instantly offended by sales people who get 'in your face'. Pushy, in-your-face people trying to sell the customer on goods or services they may not want, or would prefer taking their time to 'think about'.

Gymnasiums are notorious for it. They want to 'sign you up' into long-term contracts. Push you into making decisions based on your poor body shape and how their membership contract will change all that. *High pressure* offences. The same applies in clothing stores, electrical stores, or wherever the store sales person is hovering - trying to make sales.

And the car sales person - wow, they're the big-time culprit for this CO. Over the last two months, I have literally walked out of five car showrooms because I was offended by the pushy, *non-listening*, in-your-face, brash car sales person. I also told them how they had just 'lost' business because of their attitudes.

If in-your-face, and pushy sales people offend customers, (which they do), then it's another Customer Offender!

But one day, I was pleasantly surprised by an easy-going, friendly, helpful person who wanted to listen, take interest and solve my leasing and car requirements. That guy will get further business from us!

3: The Sum-You-Up
Offender

One person told me that they, and their friends, are not the type to dress up, or wear expensive clothing. They told me, because when asked if they had ever been *offended* as a customer they said they've all experienced being 'summed up' immediately by sales people.

If they go into a music store, a car dealership, a clothing store or restaurant, they receive shoddy, indifferent service. They've been told 'not to touch' unless they are buying. They've asked questions and received offhanded, inattentive answers. They've been seated in the 'lower quality' section of restaurants ... and they've all been offended, (not surprisingly) because they feel they've been assumed to be 'not worthy' of proper and attentive service.

Even in affluent times like these, when people have far more spending power and resources than times past, those who choose not to 'dress the part' are ignored ... and offended. Once again, money lost!

4: The Don't-Come-Back
Offender

I know a person who bought a bicycle from a store, and although it was not a top-of-the-line, expensive machine, he was *assured* that if he bought the bike, the owner would do a free 'after sales service' in a couple of months. (Does this one sound familiar?). They promised to check the bike out, tighten up spokes, hubs, re-grease and make sure the cycle was doing fine.

What the Hell
Does He Want?

After two months, with a loose hub and cranks, the customer stopped by at the store and stood there for a lengthy time, waiting to be served. The owner's wife, who was busy eating a sandwich, simply didn't want to serve, as she new it was just a 'free' service customer.

Eventually, the owner looked up and said in an abrupt, nasty voice: *"What the hell does he want?"* He then proceeded to make all sorts of fuss over having to service the bike, saying he was too busy, the sale simply wasn't worth the hassle, not to bother him, etc.

The customer vowed never to come back (offended) and *told every friend he could* about the pathetic service.

5: The Rob-You-Blind Offender

While in Amsterdam airport, I always make a bee-line for a small coffee store that serves delicious cappuccino and fruit pies. Until my last trip!

Like most stores at Schippol airport, they take Sterling, US Dollars or Dutch Guilders. I was not too sure about the exchange rates and usually buy in US Dollars, but this time I decided to use the spare 20 Guilders I had in my wallet. When paying for the coffee and pie, I mentioned I had 20 Guilders, and was told by the owner; *"That's exactly how much it is!"* - so, I parted with the money.

Sitting down later and working out the cost, I found that this was not so, that I had been overcharged. (Just another ignorant 'tourist'). This was not very much money to be worried about for sure, but I found that attitude to be offensive. So, they will never see my money again.

Just another 'ol Customer Offender.

And yet, this happens every day in every town in the nation. Not just small offences, but large. People lose thousands to car dealers, furniture stores, real estate agencies, simply by being charged too high an interest rate for loans or leases, by buying inflated priced goods, by being cheated on trade-ins or by being forced into buying unnecessary, over-inflated extras. It's not just the cappuccino that's at stake here!

Another Customer Offender, committed by an unenlightened owner who simply doesn't understand the CLTV, or the power of negative advertising by an offended customer.

226

Watch out, if you're caught by today's customer
(a very sophisticated and educated species indeed),
then they will be highly offended ... and you'll
lose more than you bargained for!

6: The Go-Slow Offender

- *Ever waited in a line at the supermarket checkout, to watch a very slow moving person check out groceries at a snail's pace?*

- *Ever waited to be seated at a restaurant for what seems to be an eternity, or after being seated, waited for even slower and uninspiring service?*

- *Ever waited for some person to return your call, answer you fax, or simply get back to you with further information about what you want to buy, but it seemed to take for ages?*

People every day are being turned-off by slow, uninspiring service.

Theater lines, supermarkets, banks. Sluggish and slow moving people in dress stores, restaurants, retail stores of all sorts, they seem to be everywhere.

With less and less time to spare, customers require something more than the person who has no work ethic, no reason to move faster, no interest in providing speedy service. It is an offence that is tolerated by some, but many move on to businesses which provide much speedier service.

Those customers, after being turned-off and 'offended' because of slow and uninspiring snail's pace service, leave, never to return ... and they take their long-term value with them!

227

Customer Delighters

Remember this success formula mentioned in other chapters (It's a key to reducing the customer's attrition rate) ...

*The more ADVANTAGES you give customers,
the more VALUABLE you become to them.*

What is the opposite to offend? My dictionary says: *to charm, to delight.* If we can rid our businesses of Customer Offenders, which are either deliberate or inadvertent acts that offend customers, which in turn repel ... then the opposite of *Customer Offenders* must be *Customer Delighters. (Ah-ha! The penny drops!)*

Profound acts of service that do not just satisfy customers, but DELIGHTS them!

Customer Advantaging (CA)

It stands to reason that if the offenders *repel*, then the delighters must *attract*. That makes sense! But, it's simply not good enough to even just delight customers. We must become highly *pro-active* in today's business world and install *Customer Advantaging (CA).*

In essence, it means giving the customer the 'advantage'. Making sure they receive something that they would 'not' get elsewhere from competitors. Special or unique service that delights, special attention, exclusiveness ... 'more' than expected in products and service.

Make Customers the Winners

When you give customers the advantage, they then will adopt your business as a *valuable asset* into their lives. They then see your business as the *only* business to buy from. Why? Because it's more *advantageous* to buy from you rather than competitors. And because of that, they become the winners! The focus is on them to win ... not you! They know that they receive *more* from you. More value. More service. More durable products. Bigger, better and incomparable. It creates an exceptional proclivity and association with your business and them!

Therefore, they are *not* offended with your business. More importantly, they are *delighted*. There are no CO's, just heaps of 'extra' service, attention, value ... and *reasons to return*. They have more advantages from you than they would from your competitors ... they then *have the advantage!*

Your Winning Business

- *What can you do to give the advantage in your business?*

- *What matchless value can you add to your service?*

- *To your products?*

- *What 'advantage' does your Guarantee provide over others?*

- *Is your after-sales service inspiring and a delighter?*

- *Do your customers have identifiable reasons-to-return?*

Get it Right and You'll
Win the Attrition War

- *If you eradicate all CO's in your business, figure out and install Customer Delighters, and make certain you always give the advantage, (thereby becoming valuable) ... your business will spontaneously 'increase' profit, by experiencing increases in long-term repeat sales and the CLTV.*

- *And you will experience a 'return of investment' from the expense of 'buying' customers, because you reduced the Customer's Attrition Rate (CAR).*

Deputize the Posse

You and your people should immediately form a posse, to have a Customer Offender round-up. The offenders should be identified, listed and eradicated ... before any more *CLTV's* are lost for ever.

And do you realize who you should recruit for your posse? Your customers! Recruit a handful, make them deputies, invite them to your meetings, get their input, listen to them identify the CO's (as only *they* can) ... then start out on the eradication process and watch your business *boom!*

Pro-active or Re-active?

How do you reduce the *Customer Attrition Rate (CAR)?* Two ways:

- *Provide Awesome Customer Service, Extra-Mile Thinking (XMT), Customer Advantaging (CA) ... and by eradicating all the Customer Offenders.*
- *Become pro-active ... rather than re-active.*

The chapter called *ZebraServe* covers the customer service aspect. But, let's do something totally radical, (that's simply not done very often in business), let's focus on becoming *pro-active*, to lessen the impact of attrition.

Customers are lost for two reasons:

1. *The enemy outside*
2. *The enemy within.*

- *The outside enemy is your competitor, (better products, service, price etc.), influences, changed needs and desires.*
- *The enemy within is your poor service, lack of quality, inferior shipping, etc ... i.e. 'any' Customer Offender (CO).*

230

Customers, (as mentioned previously), are *human beings with needs, desires, wants* and *feelings.* They want to 'feel important' and they want someone to care about *them.* Being pro-active means to *take the lead-role* and to guide them, educate them, lead them, explain to them and show them what, in your opinion, is the most suitable solution for them.

I have a client firm which sells outdoor camping and hiking equipment. Rather than be re-active, trying to chase lost customers, or to fight competitors by price-slashing, they have established themselves as pro-active to the customer.

- *They have become the educators, the gurus, the ones you go to for advice and recommendations on the most suitable equipment.*

- *They run seminars, show videos, have specialists visit the store and educate the customer.*

- *They have created a data-base (they collect names) that contains not just the customer's name, but their outdoor activity interests, equipment preferences and sales records.*

- *They have created a customer's educational newsletter.*

- *They invite the public in for in-store demonstrations, special events, new product releases ... and their <u>attrition rate has decreased</u>, while sales have skyrocketed.*

Have you ever gone into a restaurant where the waiter explains the selections and makes a recommendation - and you act upon that? You feel *assured* that your choice is the best one to make, because of the guidance you have received.

That's it in a nutshell, a pro-active person, an educator, a friend of customers who uses his expertise and experience to guide the guest ... rather than just be a waiter.

Have you ever discussed with a friend or relative all the attributes of a new purchase, and sought input from others *before* making your buying decision?

- *The business person who guides the team to become advisors, friends, the 'helpers' of customers and clients, will be the one who will enjoy a lower attrition rate and higher sales.*

Customers must be nurtured, loved, cared for and cultivated. If you do *not* do it, your competitors *win!* (High attrition rate!). If you do it, *you* will win! (Low, or no attrition rate!). Do not wait until customers have been lost and then re-act ... it's too late then. Do it now. Take control and love your customers.

With all your might, win this war. Become pro-active. Become unstoppable at winning this battle ... whatever you do ...

... do not let attrition kill your business!

The 3 Simple Steps to Reduce Your Customer Attrition Rate - Now!

1. *Simply calculate your attrition rate - NOW!*

2. *Become Pro-active and lock customers in - NOW*

3. *Make your firm a customer lover/educator - NOW*

ZebraWrite©

How to write advertising copy that gets
immediate results ... time and time again!

Advertising is expensive.

For your Red Striped Zebra business, you must demand that your marketing dollar is 'maximized' and that every advertisement generates 100%, 500% or even 1,000% 'more' results than other businesses.

Presented here, is a unique copywriting strategy that can catapult your advertising results to new heights.

The whole world is driven by advertising! It is advertising that sells the world's products and services. Without it, every manufacturing plant would grind to a halt. We would have no modern world. Without a message being broadcast, we wouldn't know what was for sale. Without a sale taking place, no money would change hands. No business could keep going and no staff could be employed. The world would simply grind to a halt.

Advertising is the heart of our global marketplace. A huge engine that drives the world. It is far reaching and affects the lives of every person on this planet. The consumer who buys the product is *not* just the end result of advertising. The end result not only embraces the consumer, but also the financial welfare of the business which does the advertising. It simply keeps everything going. It affects the management, staff, their families, the outside suppliers to a business, and even the supplier's families. Whenever a business sells something, the money flowing from that sale is literally filtered in all directions. It reaches people who have no direct bearing on the actual product or service.

That same end result also supports the advertising agency, the whole newspaper industry, television, radio and magazines. Supporting these entities is an army of people who sell the advertising space and keep the whole show moving. And without advertising we would not have any of these 'media' businesses. They would simply cease to exist.

Yet, for all the expertise, experience and wealth of advertising genius that permeates our world, much advertising (and dollars) is literally wasted.

The 'theory' in modern advertising is to promote as loudly and as widely as possible.

He who has a thing to sell and goes and whispers in a well, is not so apt to get the dollars, as he who climbs a tree and hollers.

In a sense this 'holler' strategy is true. In a room full of noise we have to speak louder to be heard over the din ... and in this 'junk mail' world we have to advertise loudly to be heard. Yes, that's true ... but it can also be dead wrong. Why? Because the Red Striped Zebra business does not *blindly follow the 'norm'* in advertising, for there are many traps for the unwary. Black and white businesses do it that way ... you shouldn't!

Uniqueness is a Red Striped 'Advertising' Zebra

Being 'Unique as a Red Striped Zebra' takes on a very special importance in advertising. It is in this area that your true image and perception is exposed, promoted and established.

A shoddy advertisement will simply not do. Through advertising, you are broadcasting to your world that you have broken free from the crowd and you have an irresistible product or service to sell. This is where you raise your banner, your standard and your Red Striped Zebra image.

Advertising provides a powerful broadcasting tool that can establish you as the absolute leader in your field. It can also establish your service or product as the customer's favored choice.

However, to gain this elite and heady position, your Red Striped

Zebra business must adopt specific advertising strategies.

Big is Not
Always Beautiful

In the last few years there's been a number of gigantic explosions in the world. Advertising explosions. One of those explosions is billboards. If we take a drive along any main road in most modern cities we're assaulted with a plethora of huge billboards, all vying for our fullest attention. Why are they so big and so prolific? To grab our attention and create 'brand awareness' is the thinking. But do they get it? No! I've seen businesses waste huge amounts with *no measured results* for their investment.

And these signs seem to be growing overnight at an alarming rate. (I always wonder if the owners of these billboard firms live in the same cities as us ... or do they have special country retreats that they've not destroyed with their visual pollution?).

Huge Numbers Will
Read Your Advertisement

Billboard advertising is sold on the fact that many *thousands* of cars drive along a section of a road, so the billboard company *assures* the advertiser the message will be *read by a staggering amount* of people. It all sounds plausible when the high numbers are mentioned, the 'eye catching' big signs, the creation of brand awareness ... you just can't lose ... or can you?

We hear the same talk from the sales representatives of newspapers, magazines, mailing list people ... and others who deal in 'high volume' traffic. You've probably heard it many times:

"Do you realize that 51,000 people read this paper on a Thursday and 72,000 on Saturday, so you're sure to get a great response!" (Bet they don't offer a money back guarantee on the response claim!)

Let's explore the erroneous concepts of bigger, louder, brighter and more prolific in this chapter ... then compare it with the more potent Red Striped Zebra methods.

The Bigger, Louder
and Brighter Myth

Advertising generates only one thing; *money*. It produces sales true, but sales convert to money. However, to make those sales (and money) we must also *spend* money. As mentioned at the beginning, advertising is expensive! So, the first myth we must expose in advertising is that a big, loud and colorful advertisement, or promotional campaign, is not always effective.

The 'results' produced in advertising are not automatically increased by increasing the size ... or choosing more costlier advertisements.

A consultant with an international reputation was contracted by a firm to speak at a business development seminar in a large Californian city. The firm wanted the kudos and exposure with the small business community, being their natural market.

It had been decided the best way to promote the seminar, which was to also feature other guest speakers, was to take out *six full pages* in a business newspaper. Their thinking was to position this seminar as the city's *major business event* for the year.

They were prepared to spend many thousands on this space, and against our advice, decided to also charge an attendance fee that neared $2,000 per participant.

However, they did not take into account the fact that the city had been in a long and wearing recession. Small business owners found the fee too expensive and consequently only a small number registered to attend. Instead of the 300 expected attendees, the seminar was canceled due to the *lack of response*. The seminar was pronounced a dismal failure. Six full pages of advertising didn't work for them. Neither did the fact that many thousands read the paper.

It's not the size of the advertisements that matter. It's the *potency* of the words in the advertisement ... coupled with an *Irresistible Sales Offer (ISO)*. They had neither.

It's not the size of the advertisement that matters. It's the potency of the words used!

Big is not always beautiful, nor effective!

The Dismal
Travel Fair

Another business, (or would be business), was started by two enterprising people to promote a Travel Fair in their hometown in New South Wales, Australia.

With high hopes of a large attendance they put together a superb show, invited the leading travel companies, cruise ship lines, air carriers, and special tour people to display their products in the exhibition booths. They even featured swimsuit fashion parades, bands and food vendors.

To promote the show the media representatives sold a major newspaper spread to them ... and they also committed to a large volume of radio spots.

Great Show ...
But Nobody Came

The promotion was superb, the exhibits were great, but the two-day weekend fair only attracted 150 attendees. At just three dollars admission to the public they only earned $450. The rent space for the booths paid by the exhibitors didn't even cover the $9,500 advertising costs. The show was a disaster for the organizers ... and for the exhibitors.

What went wrong? Simply put, they staged their show in a beach resort town. A place where tourists travel 'to' for holidays. Not a cold, dismal factory town where people would love to *escape* from. Not a city where people would love to spend an hour at a show exploring the fantasy world of travel. They staged their event in a town where the inhabitants weren't interested in traveling away from. The people were already in paradise, why should they look to go elsewhere?

But, they presumed that by undertaking a *large advertising program*, success would be assured.

In both these examples there were contributing factors that caused the demise of the events and going big in advertising only compounded the problem. Big is not always best!

Even God's Sign
Couldn't Do It!

The third example is a church congregation in a major U.S. city. They had moved into a beautiful new facility and wanted to grow their church quickly. A billboard firm 'sold' them on the premise that 75,000 cars per day drove along the six lane highway. They were assured that the sign will definitely attract many people to their new church with this amount reading the sign. (Mistake #1 ... *Do not be fooled with numbers!*).

So, fully expecting a great response they arranged for their church, the minister's face and an invitation message to be artistically presented on a billboard. The design was approved by the church and then placed onto a huge, prominent billboard. It only cost $4,000 of 'God's money' for a two month rental period ... and that was to reach over 75,000 souls per day. This had to be a great bargain.

The only one to profit and get results from this advertising blitz (fiasco) was the billboard firm!

And the results? *No new visitors attracted!*

Results Driven or Corporate?

Choosing the biggest advertisement in the newspaper, or yellow pages, or even the biggest billboard on God's earth does not guarantee success. More importantly, is *what goes in the advertisement.* It's not the size of the advertisement that matters, but the potency of the message in the advertisement. For any given advertisement size and dollar amount, we could have 10%, 100%, 150% or 1,000% response. Size does not do it as much as content. Before exploring this further, we need to clarify what advertisements work, and what advertisements do not perform satisfactorily.

Every day of the year, in every format possible, we find two types of advertising. One is results driven and the other is corporate. The first is not as frequent as the latter, and yet it is the most successful of all.

The Dismal 'Corporate' Advertisement Myth

Arrogance is an interesting phenomenon If we harbor it, it presumes that we know best, that we have *all the answers*. It presumes that the feelings, desires, needs and wants of the other person do not matter.

Throughout the world, we see arrogance embodied in abundance. It's in every form of advertising. We see it demonstrated in the *name game*. Businesses splashing their corporate name across a page, or as a neon sign, across a billboard, or on a television screen. They are telling the world:

- *How good they are*
- *How long they have been in business*
- *How many square feet of showroom they have*
- *How huge their inventory is*
- *How they are 'leading the way'*
- *How their product is superior to others*
- *How their service is the best*

You get the picture. In all their corporate advertising and name positioning, they show no concern for the reader. They do not tell how we will *benefit* from buying their product or service. They only tell us about *their* business and *their* name. They tell us some nonsense about how great, cute, big, old, smart or caring they are, or some other foolishness. Simple arrogance!

Money Out ... Not In!

Corporate advertising at its best, produces *postponed* results. People may remember their name when it's time to buy shoes, or a burger, or a drink. At its worst it is ineffective, barren and wasteful to all but the agencies that handle the

Your advertising must produce immediate and measurable results. Do not fall for the brand name positioning trap ... unless you have millions of advertising dollars to burn through!

240

accounts. It is un-compelling, non-productive and highly extravagant. This type of advertising does not direct the reader to buy, or to make an inquiry, or to make any decision whatsoever. It does nothing more than waste time, space, money and productivity. It is money out, pure and simple. It does little to attract an *immediate* and *measurable* return on spent advertising dollars.

Are You
Compelled to Buy?

Next time you see an advertisement that promotes the name of the firm, or the product, take note and observe your reaction. Do you immediately make a decision to go and buy? Are you compelled to race out the door to go to their business and buy? If not, then that advertisement is not the type you should fashion your Red Striped Zebra advertising on. It 'must' summon a *response* from readers.

Don't Play
Follow the Leader

Large corporations have the money to spend on this type of advertising. Unfortunately, they set the *standard* for every other business to follow, right down to the Mom and Pop store. A small business manager believes that if it's fine for a large corporation to plaster the world with its corporate logo or name, it's also fine for them to copy this method. They know no better. They believe that's the way it's to be done ... just because the big boys do it that way. It's the *billboard thinking* syndrome. Big and large numbers. And it's a trap that you should avoid at all costs.

The Customer
Does Not Care

I repeat ... the customer simply does 'not' care about you! It is a *costly mistake* to believe your business name or logo, (or other business characteristic), should be featured in advertisements. And to have your name headlining any advertisement is pure folly. It only pleases the business owner ... not the reader. The customer cares little about you, your business name, how long you've been in business, how big your store is ... or any number of business features you put in front of their eyes with your advertisements.

They simply do 'not' care. They 'only' care about their needs, wants, desires, how it will benefit them, or their family ... that's it!

It is also folly to treat the reader as though we know what's best for them ... and being involved in non-sensible advertising is unproductive for a Red Striped Zebra business.

Reaping a harvest with 'results driven' advertising

An advertisement is supposed to do one thing only; make people buy! It is meant to attract customers, clients, guests or patients to your business or practice. So, why waste time promoting your name or any other feature. It is more important to show them how you can make their life *more* fulfilling when they buy your product or service. You must tell them why they will be 'better off' by buying from you.

With this in mind, how important is it to *boost* your advertising copy, so that you achieve that goal, and *maximize* the 'results' generated from every advertisement, direct-mail letter, yellow page advertisement or corporate brochure? It becomes crucial for the Red Striped Zebra business!

How Much to Buy a Customer?

If you were to pay $2,000 for a display advertisement or a direct-mail promotion and attracted 50 customers, your advertisement would cost you $40 per new person. That is actually the cost to 'buy' a customer. It would have cost you $40 to *buy* each customer from that advertisement. Then, whatever the price of your service or product, you would need to deduct that $40. (If you were to have that customer buy from you twice, five or twenty times more, that cost to buy becomes insignificant and the advertisement result becomes significant ... measured in the Customer's Long Term Value (CLTV).

Maximizing
Every Advertisement

What if though, you were to attract 500 new customers from that very same advertisement or direct-mail letter? The cost to buy would be much less. You would only be spending $4 to buy each customer.

If attracting more people were possible, our costs decrease, our sales and profits increase, all proportionate to the *drawing power* of the advertisement. Results driven advertising will do this for you. It will increase your sales and decrease your costs.

To do that though, means the advertisement or direct-mail letter would need to be *maximized*. In other words, *every* headline, word, phrase and offer would need to be the *most effective wording* that could be possibly devised.

Corporate advertising falls short of this, especially in the short term. Results driven advertising can, and will, bring in the money; immediately and measurably

---

Results driven advertising is maximized. It requires that 'every' advertisement compels people to respond.

To do this the copywriting must take first priority.

It must tell a motivating story, combined with an irresistible offer that adds 'real value' to people's lives ... then compels them to take immediate action!

Results,
Results, Results!

Results driven advertising is almost self-explanatory. It produces results! It generates a response! Is not this what advertising is meant to do? One would wonder!

243

The results type advertisement produces:

- *A response, a decision, an inquiry, a call or a buying decision.*
- *It tells a 'complete story' about the service or product*
- *It informs the reader how to go about making the purchase (A call to action)*
- *It relates a comprehensive story of 'why' or 'how' the product, or service will make a difference to customer's lives*
- *In an analytical and factual basis it presents the full story, unlike the corporate advertisement that relies on pompous name branding*

Mini-Sales Person

Results driven advertising is a mini-sales person. It is a sales person, in either printed or airwaves form. As a mini-sales person it delivers a *sales presentation* to the reader, in a *complete* form. It delivers the facts, it sells the benefits, it sells the 'sizzle' and then ... the steak. It delivers all the promises, establishes the performance standards, and relates the expected results the prospect will *experience* upon purchase.

It answers the questions and handles the objections. When it nears completion it directs the reader or listener what to do next. How to buy, who to call, when to do it. The response driven advertisement, or mini-sales person always offers a special guarantee, or *Risk-Transfer* offer to further compel the reader to act. It removes the fear of buying, it builds trust and rapport, it pre-educates the reader on the benefits, features, history, results and expectations.

It compels the reader, viewer or listener to visit your business, call you, drive way across town to buy from you ... and take action.

What's in it for Me?

Response driven advertising is far more beneficial than corporate, simply because your reader does not care about you, or your business. The only care they have is the one that says: *"What's in it for me?"*

This is what they care about. Whatever benefit, result, or performance they achieve from your product or service, that's what they care about. Not your business name, or your logo. Not how good, big, old, pretty or colorful your business may be. They simply do not care.

Understanding this gives immense insight into how to construct advertisements that appeal to *their* needs or desires. The results driven advertisement provides that criteria.

What concerns the customer is the <u>direct benefit</u> they achieve for their own, or their family's welfare, happiness, comfort, pleasure or satisfaction. That's it! Full stop!

The 37 Motivating Factors

It is not the product or service you are selling. It is what that product or service *can do for customers*. How it makes their lives better. If you understand this, the words you construct your advertising with will be far more effective than those that just describe your business ... or promotes your name.

People are human beings with feelings. They are motivated by desires, needs, concerns and pleasures. If you understand what these various human traits are, you can craft your advertisements to address these *motivating factors*. There are 37 you should concern yourself with.

People (customers) want to acquire:

1.	Fitness	8.	Contentment
2.	Time	9.	Relaxation
3.	Money	10.	Pride of Accomplishment
4.	Approval	11.	Enjoyment
5.	Improved Appearance	12.	Self-confidence
6.	Protection	13.	Position
7.	Praise from Others	14.	Promotion (business or social)

People want to:

15. Display their personalities
16. Resist control by others
17. Fulfill their interests
18. Savor beauty
19. Accumulate things
20. Win love and affection
21. Better themselves

People want to be:

22. Competent parents
23. Sociable
24. Up-to-date
25. Original
26. Proud of possessions
27. Influential
28. Convivial
29. First in things
30. Competent
31. Recognized as Authorities

People want to save:

32. Time
33. Money
34. Work
35. Humiliation
36. Risk
37. Pain

Craft Your Advertisement

Are your advertisements written in such a way that they relate to one of the aforementioned motivating factors from the list? If not, then you will never reach your potential customer.

People make decisions based on *whatever factor* in their mind motivates them. For instance, if a woman is to be married, she will have the factors of pride, prestige and one or two others present. If you are *selling* to brides, rather than just featuring a photograph and a name, (like most corporate advertisements), you would write your advertisement in such a way that it *taps* those motivating factors.

And your headline could read:

What every bride should know BEFORE she gets married ...

That would be an *immediate* attention getter ... and one that would make her read the copy. Copy that works on the *motivating factors.*

Measuring Results

Corporate type advertisement's results cannot be measured accurately. Ascertaining the direct results from a billboard is difficult to gauge. So too is a newspaper advertisement that implies a person can be happy if they drink a certain brand of beer, or drive a particular car.

In my city a bus has a well-known athletic shoe painted along the full side of the bus. How can measurements of the *results* of such a promotion be taken? Likewise, running an advertisement or series of advertisements in this corporate fashion may produce results, but they will be *deferred*.

Can YOU wait that long for people to get your message?

Open to Scrutiny

In the results driven advertisement, you have control. You can analyze the performance and profitability of any advertisement you run, because it *produces results that you can observe* and record. You will know:

- *'Exactly' how many inquiries, calls or visits are generated from the particular advertisement.*

- *You can divide your response rate into your costs and know exactly how much per inquiry your advertisement produces.*

- *You will be able to refer back to your past records and know what likely response all future promotions will be.*

- *You will then be able to discern what products to order, what will sell and what promotions to run.*

Kill the Big Numbers Thinking

Results driven advertising puts you in the driver's seat because an advertising representative can no longer sell you a wasteful, big campaign or a large newspaper spread on the pretext that it will attract buyers ... simply because the demographics may show it reaches thousands.

I have a client in the United Kingdom who fell for this trap. He called me and excitedly told me he was going to advertise in a card-pack that reaches 11,000 potential customers in his target market. It was a special multi-pack direct mail campaign that featured my client's firm ... and 19 other businesses. I told him to forget the numbers ... but asked him to concentrate solely on the cost to him for his entry into the pack. I also asked him to focus on the cost he was prepared to make in buying a customer, then divide that cost into the promotion cost. The result in new customers was the amount he should be looking for.

The results? Even with the beautiful glossy brochure and the 11,000 recipients, he ended up with just five new customers. (So much for demographics!).

The cost to him was around £800 for each new customer ... who in turn have become long-term clients, spending on average about £4,000 per year. At first it may seem like a failed promotion (and it would be if you focussed on 11,000 names), but in knowing what he was prepared to buy customers for ... and in maximizing his advertisements, he was not disappointed. His promotion was successful. The other 19 firms focussed on numbers and came up wanting.

How to generate 1,000% increase in responses from the same money

How can you multiply the *Magnetic Value (MV)* of an advertisement, so that it produces 100%, 500% or even 1,000% more results? Can you actually avoid 'increasing' your advertising budget, yet increase your results at the same time? Absolutely!

Constructing advertisements (or brochures, direct mail, yellow pages) that work, comprise seven identifiable components. These seven (each skillfully crafted) combined can generate exponential growth in the results.

It is not outside the scope of a Red Striped Zebra manager. You just have to keep in mind who will be reading the advertisement (your customer - the one with those motivating factors at work) and give them an offer *too good to refuse*. With a little practice you will be churning out 'killer copy' that works for you.

The Seven Elements

The seven elements or sections that make up an advertisement or brochure are easy to identify. More importantly though is the need to build potency into each element. But first, take a look at the seven:

1. *Headline (Attention grabbers)*

2. *Copy (Perception of Value Education)*

3. *Subheadings (Mini Sales Script)*

4. *Added Bonuses (Irresistible Sales Offer)*

5. *Risk-Transfer (Nothing to Lose)*

6. *Graphics (Words in Pictures)*

7. *Call to action. (Vital)*

1. The Attention Grabbing Headline

Every newspaper article has a headline. It is there to *flag* our attention and to create *immediate interest* in the story. That headline must be eye-catching and it must sizzle. And the key word here is 'flag'.

All our lives we have been reading newspapers. And we've been programed to read papers a certain way. First the headline, then the copy. So why then do we try to create advertisements with a different format, using different font types, sizes and other cute bits and pieces? As soon as our eyes hit the advertisement they glance away, looking for the *next juicy headline* in the paper. Stick to what works ... newspaper format!

Just a Nanosecond

So, from now on, make certain *all* your advertisements start with a headline. *Not* your firm's name. And make sure that headline is *juicy* and *interesting*. The word 'sale' or something glib like 'March Madness' is not what you're after. It has to *capture* a busy reader who is hit with thousands of messages every day. In fact, the headline of an advertisement *must* capture the full attention in a nanosecond. Only one chance is available, so it must capture them *instantly*.

Hot Headlines

Every advertisement in every media format is fighting to gain people's attention, but many fail, simply because they go for the cute graphics or an intriguing layout (produced by graphic artists no doubt ... not skilled copywriters) and many times they either have no headline, or at best, a very weak one.

The headline must be hot. It must wave that flag furiously and provide something of *strong interest* for the reader. Something personal that grabs their attention and stirs their motivating factors.

An insurance agent may run an advertisement that states:
Retirement Fund Guarantees Large Return, or he can add sizzle and personal interest by stating: *You Can Retire in Outrageous Luxury!* This headline plugs into motivating factor No. 6 ... gaining security.
A car dealer may advertise;
Used Car Sale or he could have a headline that says; *Your New, One Owner, Fastidiously Kept Car Awaits!* This plugs into factor No. 19 and 33 ... acquire things and save money.
The retail store may promote a *Suit Sale*, or they may state:
Your Invitation to a Business Class Image Awaits, at Great Prices!

Factors 14 (status) plus 19 (acquire things) and 33 (save money).

Observing this strategy, we promote our own seminars with a

heading that states: *Skyrocket YOUR Business Growth!* It creates attention and plugs into the motivating factors that affect business people..

Here's a few more headlines that create interest:

- *Suppose this happened to your home when you were out! (For insurance)*
- *12 reasons why it would have paid you to answer our ad a few months ago*
- *Check the kind of retirement you want (check list)*
- *Here's a quick way to reduce your costs - immediately! (Business)*

- *Now, any house improvement job can be a cinch*
- *New loan officer is out of control - but customers are thrilled*
- *Great new improvement - makes balancing check books easier*
- *Make this 1-minute test - of an amazing new investment plan*

- *Right and wrong business methods - and some ideas that will increase profits*
- *New 5-step home buying program gets you settled quick*
- *How much does ineffective time management cost your business?*
- *The 7 deadly mistakes to avoid when buying a house*
- *Do not buy that car - until you've spoken to us about this new plan*
- *Big costs that keep businesses struggling*
- *No more finance problems - life has become easier*

The Hidden
Sign Post

Notice with every one of those headlines there is a *hidden* signpost. The headlines not only *capture the attention* and *plug into the motivating factors* of the target group (home owners, business people, car buyers etc.) but they also point the reader to *read further*.

Take the first headline for example: *Suppose this happened to your home when you were out.* Suppose what happened? Could you, as a homeowner, not want to read more? Your curiosity *forces* you to read further. What about the new loan office who is *out of control?* If you wanted to secure a loan you couldn't resist reading more. The *big costs* that keep businesses struggling would certainly get the full attention and a full reading of a business owner.

Every advertisement, brochure, yellow page or
direct mail letter requires a powerful headline.
It must first capture the attention of the reader. Then, with
its hidden sign post or hook, force them to read further!

Only One
At a Time

Adding magic and attention getting potency to the headline can also be obtained with the words, 'you' or 'your'. Remember the mistake of the big and wide thinking ... thinking that huge numbers of people will read the advertisements. The classic mistake is in *not* realizing that with any billboard or advertisement *only one person at a time* reads the message.

The Magic
You Word

I noticed an advertisement in our city which says: *Great new gardening service for Memphians.* Who reads that advertisement. Does a Memphian? What's a Memphian anyway? (I'm being facetious here.).

What I'm driving at is the lack of *personalization*. If only one person at a time reads that advertisement, then why not touch the heart strings and say: *YOUR garden will be the talk of Memphis with our new service.*

The word 'your' makes the difference. It drives it home to the reader. It speaks *directly* to them. *You* and *Your* are the two most powerful words you can use to grab attention. It maximizes and personalizes every headline, thereby *commanding attention.*

Questions

In the same manner, the great advertising genius Ogilvy, found great success by constructing the headline as a question, preferably with a 'you' or 'your' inbuilt. His method would convert:

Suits dry cleaned for half price
into:
Would you like to have two suits dry cleaned for the same price most dry cleaners charge for one?

Try writing your headlines in question format. It may make a difference to your results because it forces people to participate in your message. Just start with a *Would you* .... or; *Are you* .... or; *Is your* .... or; *Do you* ..... or; *Does your* .... Then add the remainder of the words to make it apply to your product or service.

Your Headline Success Formula

- *Write a creative, eye-catching headline to your target group that taps their motivating factors.*
- *Make sure it has an open-end theme ... a hidden signpost or hook to force them to read further.*
- *Add a You or Yours to personalize it*
- *Try converting it into question format.*

Now, you now have the start of a potent advertisement.

---

2. The copy - informative and enthralling

A results driven advertisement is not short of copy. It tells a *whole* story. It is not concerned with cute design, but in *telling and selling* the complete story. In *Supercharging the Marketing Engine That Drives Your Business* I mention one of the most potent selling tools available. The *Perception of Value Education (POVE)*. The copy must be full of *POVE!*

The copy should tell the story of how the car that is for sale was fastidiously kept in a full word story, or the store selling suits should explain how their suits are constructed from fine New Zealand wool. How many stitches per inch make up the buttonholes, how they have cut and designed the garment, how the suits are fitted and adjusted until they arrive at a perfect fit.

The dentist should divulge his method of how he personally greets each new patient, how he takes the time to thoroughly inspect their teeth, and how he later sits with them in a relaxing office to discuss their future dental treatment. He should explain how a crown or filling is done, what the difference is in filling material, what the costs are, and how he is a kind, caring dentist who can administer his service without pain ... then demonstrate how this is done. (I'd be his first patient ... if I could find such a Dentist who understands the value of *POVE* in copywriting!)

The pizza store could tell the story in their advertisement of how they wanted to make a better pizza, how they have ordered, inspected and prepared the freshest ingredients daily. How the pizza dough is prepared from the finest flour. How they prepare the pizza so that in has more toppings and ingredients than any other. It should tell how they cook it, how long it stays in the oven, and how they speedily deliver it in a specially designed, heat-retaining carton.

The Field is
Wide Open

Do we see this type of copy in advertisements? Hardly ever! Yet it is *vital* for gaining a response. And because not many businesses advertise this way, the field is wide open for the Red Striped Zebra business.

Your product, or service should be written about in the same way as is you were writing to your friends, explaining in as much details as possible. It should be meaty, informative and enthralling. You should write it in an honest, straightforward, no nonsense approach, giving the reader, or listener the *full story*. It must demonstrate how you care ... and how your product or service will benefit them.

The inference that your suit, or pizza, or cars, or dental work is superior to all others is not stated, but is assimilated *automatically* into the copy, by the very fact that you are sharing everything about your product, or service. The comprehensive, expanded story sets your business apart from all others. Every other business you compete with may be similar, but the shared wealth of information given in your advertisement will establish your business, or product, as the customer's preferred choice.

The White
Space Myth

I've had flack from people. When working with clients there is always some person in a firm that utters the words: People are too busy to read all that copy. Advertisements need to be short and to the point!

I usually respond by holding up a piece of white paper and ask if they are motivated by it. White space does not sell. Words sell!

In fact, I could get you to read a full newspaper, with no graphics and in small type font size. (Much smaller than what you're reading now). Every single word of it! It would just have to have one headline too. It would state: *All About (Your Name) ...*

You would read everything, because it would be all about you. You would search every sentence, every paragraph to make sure it was factual, and that it told the most flattering story possible. One that painted you in a good light and didn't ridicule you or reveal things that you would prefer to keep secret. *You can't do that with white space thinking.*

What I find amusing is the complaint about wordy copywriting always comes in the same format. Every person who mentions it says exactly the same thing, with no facts to back up their argument. I believe that this *myth* has been propagated by graphic artists and ad agencies. They earn their money by creating artsy, slick productions that they can then charge their account clients a fortune for. If you were to ask them to *guarantee* the results of their advertisements ... or horror of horrors; only work on a commission based on actual results, they would refuse.

It's the words that sell product or services. Today's customer is a discerning person who wants to know the *full story*. If they are buying a car, renovating a house, buying a suit, investing, having dental work done ... or any number of things that interest them, they will read every word, every paragraph about the subject. *You can't do that with white space!*

You can read more about *Perception of Value (POVE)* in other chapters. This style is vital in your advertising, for it guarantees you will get results.

3. Sub-headings ... a separate 'selling' layer

Eyes are unusual organs. They seem to have a mind of their own. In newsprint, or in magazines, eyes can be manipulated to your advantage.

Having sub-headings in your copy, especially if you opt for the column format, (as does a newspaper article), will cause the eye to drop, or be drawn to each of those sub-headings. It is called *eye-gravity*. Pulling the eye toward these headings assists with keeping the person reading. (And you really want them to read everything!)

However, using the eye-gravity in your favor, you can craft those sub-headings into *selling statements*. Many people simply skim over an article. For these 'skimmers', those who do not read all the body copy, the sub-headings can take on the *selling role* of your advertisement.

An example is in the following brochure example we crafted for a leasing firm client.

The headline on the front of the brochure states:

You've found the leasing firm that is genuinely interested in helping your business!

Then, there are 12 sub-headings. They state:

- *You need a strong realtionship with a leasing firm*
- *You benefit from years of expertise and commitment*
- *You know exactly what you get*
- *Immediate, personalized attention*
- *You'll have a complete leasing resource ... at your fingertips*
- *A powerful marketing tool for you*
- *Here's 8 solid benefits you receive*
- *At last, you'll have the advantage*
- *A complete service*
- *Your peace of mind is our aim*
- *You need it, you've got it ... right now!*
- *Call now*

Without reading one word of copy, those sub-headings have explained to the reader what is on offer. They've sold the message to the *skimmer* ... and 'double sold' the comprehensive reader. It's a two-edged selling sword. A *separate layer of selling phrases* that add interest and convinces the reader to buy. And coupled to the actual copy, the brochure takes on a potent selling story. Also, many of the copy segments that follow each sub-heading start off with the words; *"This means ...."* A powerful way to further explain and sell your story.

Remember the story of the car dealer, or the pizza store, or the dentist? Imagine how 'alive' their POVE stories would

> *Bold sub-headings add power to advertisement copy. They pull the eye further into the advertisement, keeping the potential customer reading. They also add a secondary selling layer that motivates the reader to buy.*

become with sub-headings that pointed out the advantages.

You Get the Freshest Ingredients. More Toppings for Your Money ... or for the dentist; *All Processes Explained Fully. Pain Free. Experience Our Relaxing Treatment.*

4. Added Bonuses to Secure the Sale

Who gives away gifts or bonuses in advertisements these days? Not many do. And yet, giving something to the customer for free with the purchase of your product, or service, can almost guarantee sales.

The retail suit store who gives a fine crafted white shirt or tie with every suit will attract clients. The Pizza store supplying free drinks, or Pizza lunches at reduced prices for schools, will benefit. The car dealer who supplies accessories as a free gift with purchase, or the dentist who supplies a free teeth-care kit, all will excel.

People want to feel special! They want to feel as though someone or some business actually cares for them. (Remember the motivating factors?). In this world of greed and avarice, it is a pleasure to buy from a business that gives a bonus or free gift with the purchase.

People WANT to be pampered!

I remember receiving a beautiful leather document holder when I bought some interntional airline tickets from a travel agency. It had the firm's name stamped on the outside, tastefully done ... and ten years later I still use that holder for all my travel. The service I received from that agency was superb, but that added bonus of a free gift cemented my perception of them. Our firm purchased a number of tickets from them after that.

The Merry-go-round

In my country; Australia, we have a saying; *What you lose on the swings you pick up on the Merry-go-round*. It simply means that in this case of offering a free gift or bonus, what you may lose in costs to you will be more than made up in *increased* customers and sales. When you advertise, offer something extra to the reader ... to add power and entice them. It works! It costs you money, but it works!

HPV-LAC

In other parts of this book, you will have read the meaning in a formula format for *Added Bonuses*. I call it;

High Perceived Value - Low Acquisition Cost (HPV-LAC)

It simply means that what you offer as a free gift or bonus to entice people, should be perceived by them to have 'high' value ... but it should be a 'low' cost to purchase for you. And the cost of purchase becomes minimal when viewed over the long-term value of the customer. But let's look at the *HPV* first.

The Magic
Offer

Free can work like magic in any advertisement. A free gift or bonus can instantly boost your sales. But, using the magic offer to make 'free' really work for you means *making the gift or bonus into a 'high perceived' value*.

Here's an extract from a brochure that arrived in my mail. It was promoting a set of training tapes and in part, it read;

FREE Video Offer!
Buy all classic audio tapes
and you'll receive a great bonus ...
The Sales Leader Conference video!

The Secret
Formula

This attempt at a free gift offer and building high perceived value failed ... because the 'free' formula wasn't used. That formula must have three elements;

1. *It must have a 'dollar' value*

2. *It must be available for a 'limited' time*

3. *It must have a strong customer 'benefit'*

Now, using this formula, let's re-write the advertisement to create a High Perceived Value in the mind of the reader ... and clinch the sale.

Free Video!
Now, you can add real impact
to your next sales meeting!

Buy all twenty classic audio tapes before November 30 and you'll also own the potent Sales Leader's Conference Video!

Valued at $70, this powerful tape gives practical demonstrations of sales professionals in action. Your sales team will see *exactly* how to set appointments, use the proven S.M.A.R.T. sales strategy ... and ***bring home MORE sales!***

HURRY! Order before November 30 and get this $70 video - absolutely FREE!

See how the focus is on the free gift, how a dollar amount was applied (not the amount you paid for the video - just the retail value) and the huge benefit the gift would be for the recipients? That's the magic formula of 'free' at work. It creates a High Perceived Value!

Throw a Sprat
to Catch a Mackerel

It all comes back to; how much does it cost to 'buy' a customer ... and how much are you willing to spend for each new customer?

A *captured* customer should (for the Red Striped Zebra business) become a *long-term client*. That client, over time would give your

260

business many more dollars. Far more in fact than what the initial giveaway item was worth. If it costs you $12 to supply a video gift (your actual cost, not the $70 value in the advertisement) on a $300 sale audio tape program, that figure is minimal. If that client spends another $600 each year for three more years, the $12 pales into insignificance compared to the $1,800 generated. It's the *throw a Sprat to catch a Mackerel* strategy. You use a small fish as bait to catch a larger one.

The Low Acquisition Cost (LAC) is in the $12 to buy the video. The High Perceived Value (HPV) is part of the $70 retail value the video is shown to be, plus the benefit to the customer.

What Can You Offer?

Your business would have something free to offer if you gave it some thought. Something that can be supplied at a *low cost* to you, but a *high perceived value* by the reader.

Here's some examples of 'free' to help you:

Free gift (some part of your product or service)

Free consultation	*Free problem evaluation*
Free newsletter	*Free invitation (educational seminar)*
Free trial	*Free booklet*
Free information kit	*Free use of product*
Free sample	*Free gift certificate*
Free coupon	*Free meeting*
Free information	*Free survey*
Free demonstration	*Free analysis*
Free estimate	*Free video*
Free freight	*Free audio cassette*
Free catalogue	*Free gift for providing referrals*

As a Red Striped Zebra business, doing things *differently* from others is a key element to business-breakthrough success. By supplying a gift, or bonus in your advertisements, brochures or yellow pages ad, you will *immediately attract attention.*

My dentist advertises his *free consultation* exactly that way; in the yellow pages. I was attracted to him instead of the hundreds of other listings. He since has worked on all my family and most of my staff. All because of a free consultation offer that followed the *magic free formula* for success in advertising.

Choose an appropriate free gift to place in your next advertisement. By doing so you will set your business apart, leaving your competition way behind.

5. Risk Transfer

People are cautious and suspicious. They only will buy if there is *no risk* in doing so. They want to receive real value for money and they do 'not' want to be *ripped off.* This makes them cautious when it comes to making a buying decision.

Invisible Walls

They understandably, do not like taking the risk. And, they do not like taking the risk when buying 'your' product or service. Between you and every potential customer there exists an invisible wall. A wall built from the bricks of doubt, fear, anxiety, caution, concern and apprehension. In fact, it exists for every business.

Customers will buy if they truly believe they will be *better off* buying from you. If there is any doubt whatsoever, then there exists risk. A risk of parting with their money and not getting what they want.

You already know *everything* about your product or service and what it can do for people. They do not. They must go on their own judgement ... and many times they do not trust even that.

Problem is, when a person buys, 'all' the risk is on them.
Totally unacceptable for a Red Striped Zebra business.

Transferring
the Risk

You can transfer that risk from them and place it exactly where it should be in the first place. On you! This will make their buying decision to become a cinch! Why? Because there is no longer any risk ... they cannot lose. They only gain. It becomes a sure bet for them.

Most businesses do guarantee their products or services. They are the black and white businesses who do business the same way, year after year. (Decade after decade!). You know the type. They offer some version of the usual *30 day money-back guarantee.* These weak and 'done to death' guarantees simply do not excite ... nor do they attract customers or cause sales to spiral!

The Red Striped Zebra business always *out-performs* the black and whites. Especially in guarantees and *removing the risk* from buying. They are the businesses that place the risk on 'their' shoulders ... not the customers. They 'believe' in their product or service so much that they can offer a rock-solid guarantee that out-performs all others.

Risk Transfer
in Your Advertisements

Incorporating into your advertisement (brochures, newsletters, direct-mail too!) an 'ironclad' guarantee about your product or service will not only remove that risk from the reader's mind, but will generate more sales.

In establishing a solid guarantee in print takes a huge breath on your part, because you must be sure you 'do' provide a good service or product. But keep in mind one thing; people will *not* take advantage of you if you offer 'too much' in the risk-transfer guarantee. (People are basically honest ... and there are only six crooked people in the world ... and they just move around a lot!).

What you may lose in a return will be more than made up in increased sales. We've proven this over and over again with our own clients. Some of those were very reluctant to offer a risk-transfer, but nonetheless they tried it, liked it and experienced increased sales.

Building
the Guarantee

Perhaps you can offer a seven, fourteen or thirty days trial period, with payment coming due 'only' on the last trial day.

Even more 'gutsy' yet very powerful a guarantee is the *Pay only if you are totally thrilled with the performance of our product!* ... We have a client who tried this, stating that they will: *Uplift all stock and destroy the invoice if you're not totally satisfied within thirty days of delivery.*

It was a gutsy move, but they have never had to do this. However, they have gained new clients because they actually removed the risk. Their customers had nothing to lose and everything to gain!

If you supply a service, a free 'trial' period could be offered ... and once again, if there is any dissatisfaction *termination without obligation* could ensue. We have secured 'cautious clients' in this way in the past. They experience our services with absolutely no risk to them. I also know a colleague who secured a contract with Harley Davidson, simply on this risk-transfer strategy alone. They had nothing to lose by granting a free trial.

The Gift

One of the most powerful risk transfer offers provides the customer with a free bonus. This is in the form of a *gift* (Added Bonuses) that the customer is able to keep ... *even if they ask for their money back* on the main product, or service. Your risk transfer offer could state:

Here's your risk-free iron-clad guarantee

If for any reason within the next thirty days you are not 'totally thrilled' with your purchase, please return it to us for an immediate, no-questions-asked refund.
PLUS, keep the special gift, valued at $70, as a free gift from us, simply for trying our (twenty-set tape program, suit, consultancy, dental work, furniture etc.)

You alone will know what to offer, what you can afford to lose in a *worse case* scenario. One thing is certain though, you may lose on a few sales, but overall the response will *overwhelm*.

Honest Folk

People are inherently honest. They are more worried about 'you' being dishonest than you are of them. A small percentage do take advantage of risk transfer offers, but they are few. (As mentioned, those six crooked people just seem to move around a lot!)

Transferring the risk from buying is the quickest way to make your sales soar. Even in our seminars it works well. We offer a complete and immediate refund if participants are not *totally thrilled* with the material they are learning, by the halfway point on day one. Seldom are we asked to return any charge card slip or check, but that powerful offer certainly helps instill confidence and increase sales.

Added
Credibility

Not only does the Risk Transfer remove the risk of buying, but it gives a business credibility. Prospects will perceive your business as possessing *integrity* and *credibility* ... ready and willing to *back to the hilt* your product or service.

A Red Striped Zebra business removes *all the risk* from buying, resulting in the customer feeling at ease and ready to make what really matters in business. The bottom line ... *a happy risk-free buying decision.*

Offering a potent guarantee that is <u>over and above</u> what your competitors do, will give you immediate credibility.

6. Graphics

Photographs, drawings, and illustrations add more than just interest to any advertisement. They are meant for one thing only ... to explain in graphic detail *what your copy is telling them.* If your business was a duct cleaning service that specialized in cleaning all the air distribution ducts in houses, why waste your time with a pretty photograph of a house? If your headline screamed:

**_Do you realize there could be up to three tons of
dirt, fungus, spores and life threatening
disease lurking in your air ducts?_**

Then that headline *demands* a photograph of your cleaning team standing up to their waste in this horrible stuff. That would certainly add real impact and demand attention from the readers of your advertisement or brochure!

We have a client who supplies a cleansing chemical for water treatment in major hotels. He has taken photographs of some of the water tanks that sit on top of these hotels. They're full of pigeon waste, algae and all other nasties. (They look real bad by the way ... and some are on leading hotels!). These photographs underpin the headlines in the brochures, stating:

**_Don't let your guests have a nasty
experience when they drink your water._**

Action
Shots

Photographs of the real estate or travel agent, insurance or accountant cannot take on this dramatic approach ... but why do firms go for these boring (black and white Zebra businesses!) head and shoulders shots? Far better to undergird the notion of an accountant who comes on site with a photograph that shows that. A travel agent showing brochures to a client, or a real estate agent showing clients into a home tells a far stronger story. A head and shoulder's pose does not.

Even a suit of clothing displayed in an advertisement can be invigorated by having captioned arrows pointing to the stylish cut, or special lapels, or high-class fabric mentioned in the copy.

The object is to *sell* the product or service, *not design a pretty advertisement.* Pretty is out! Pretty is stupidity, because it wastes money. A well-designed results-driven advertisement is far more interesting and *results-effective* than its *artistic* counterpart.

Columns Work

Surveys also show that having the copy laid out in two, three, or four-column format, (very similar to newspaper articles), also assists in capturing readers.

For years we've been 'trained' into the newspaper and magazine reading format. Why then do we try to reinvent the wheel? Creating your advertisement in a similar fashion enhances the opportunity to capture prospects ... Prospects who are pre-disposed to reading that format laid out throughout the publication that your advertisement appears in.

Also, if you use a type-font similar to the newspaper or magazine the eye of the reader will not have to re-adjust. They will read your message much more easily. Columns and similar fonts work!

7. A call to action!

Last, and most important, is the *call to action*. Readers of a results driven advertisements are *led on a journey*. One that has taken them through the flagging down stage of the headline, through the eye-gravity sub-heading and into the copy. They have learned *everything* about your product or service and have been offered a generous gift. You have also transferred the risk from their buying decision. What now? They are interested, they want to buy, or simply to inquire. It is time to act.

What I find amazing with over 90% of advertising that I read is that there is no call to action. No instructions to call, to 'act now' or what to do to 'take advantage' of the offer.

Telling the reader (remember, you are only speaking to *one* person at a time) what to do, how to call, how to subscribe, how to order, where to go to, when to do it ... and who to ask for, is crucial.

The Sprat has been thrown and the Mackerel has taken the bait. The prospect is on the hook and needs to be reeled in. Some statement telling what to do next is needed, along with your address, telephone or fax number ... and other pertinent information.

To further speed up their response a cut-off date, (motivating factor 36 or 37 - risk of losing out or pain) ... or by offering a further discount or gift can be mentioned for the 'early' bird. It is a *response* you are after ... and when an advertisement motivates the reader *that is the time* for action. Telling them to make the call or do the required action increases the potential for results.

Hurry! Call Now! Every Moment Counts.

Call our TOLL-FREE number: ....
And remember; if you call *before* November 30 you will receive the tremendous video tape offer.

But hurry because supplies are strictly limited. They're only on a first-come, first-served basis. Get yours by calling NOW!

The Big Test

On nearing the end of this chapter, it must be stated that there is no rigid rule in gaining outstanding results in advertising. We must *test* all advertisements.

You may create an advertisement that has brilliant copy, graphics, sub-headings, risk transfer and bonus offers, but it may fail due to the poor headline. You may create a powerful, compelling headline but lose the reader in the weak copy.

I have observed advertisements that have had a headline change and then run a second time in the same newspaper, with outstanding new results.

Fine tuning advertisements, after we run and test them, guarantees success. If you know your copy says it all, but the headline is poor, change that headline until it screams out to be noticed, then run it again. Keep records of what works, and what results are generated from every advertisement. Doing this will assure you of success, and will broaden your expertise in creating results winning advertisements.

The *I Get!*
... or; *So What?* Test

On a blank sheet of paper, draw a line down the middle and write these words: **So what?** (on the left side) ... and **I get!** (on the right).

Then every headline, every statement and every sub-heading you have created for your advertisements or brochures should be tested against those two headings.

*If they fall in the **So what?** side, change them.*
*They must 'all' fall in the **I get!** column.*

When you make a statement about your business, such as: *We've been in business 70 years*, or *We have the largest showroom*, or *We have friendly staff* etc. people are simply not impressed. They are more apt to think; *So what? Who cares? ... I don't give a toss!*

Remember, customers (who are living human beings) only care about their needs, wants, desires, feelings ... and those of their family. They do *not* care about your claims or statements about your business. You can go broke tomorrow and they would simply move on to another business.

However, if you can say:

Because of our friendly staff you can be assured of a delightful experience in our store! ... or; With 70 years experience behind us we have the available expertise to guide you in making the exact choice that fits your needs perfectly.

*These statements fit the **I get!** column.*
They tell the reader exactly what they get! ... Get it?

269

So What?

Statements about
your business, product,
service etc.

I Get!

Statements that tell
the customer exactly
what they get!

In Summary

You can create advertising that will generate the results you desire, simply be incorporating the essential elements:

1. *Headline (Attention grabbers)*
2. *Copy (Perception of Value Education)*
3. *Subheadings (Mini Sales Script)*
4. *Added Bonuses (Irresistible Sales Offer)*
5. *Risk-Transfer (Nothing to Lose)*
6. *Graphics (Words in Pictures)*
7. *Call to action. (Vital)*

In addition, being attentive to:

- *The 37 Motivating Factors*
- *And the **So What?** ... **I Get!** test*

---

*Being **unique** in your advertising, will establish your business as a Red Striped Zebra. People **will** take notice! It will also result in higher performance levels from every advertisement you run, albeit television, radio or print.*

And the Magnetic Value (MV) will increase, as you incorporate every facet of results-style advertising. With this approach you can maximize your results without increasing your advertising budget.

Apply the results-driven advertising approach to your Red Striped Zebra business for outstanding success.

Need help? We have comprehensive audio tape programs available for you to learn more ... or we can undertake your copywriting for you.

The Battle of Rork's Drift ... or Custer's Last Stand?

How to beat your competition by building an unstoppable team!

Business is war! Every day there's a new battle, a new fight. The enemy is your competitor. The spoils of war are the customers, clients and sales.

Can a Red Striped Zebra business win in a battlefield filled with competing forces? Absolutely! How you fight the battle is the real secret. Here's the battle strategies you must know to win.

The year was 1846. Three hundred red-coated British soldiers lined up in rows of three deep as they nervously eyed the attacking Zulu nation. Fifteen thousand armed warriors stood along the ridges surrounding the British encampment at Rork's Drift in South Africa, on that hot and terrifying day.

Imbedded in the Zulu's shields were beads that rattled when shook ... and with 15,000 rattling shields it sounded like a freight train approaching.

The Zulus appearance was an awesome, terrifying sight as they teamed down the slopes toward the small group of British, intent on wiping them off the face of the earth.

The soldiers could see they were outnumbered 50 to 1, and so could their officers. Slaughter was imminent. Or was it?

The muzzle loading rifles were readied, and with the Zulus rapidly approaching the officers roared the order to fire to the first row of defense. A barrage of lead balls tore into the flesh of the native warriors, and immediately that first row of soldiers dropped to their knees to reload. Within seconds the officers shouted fire again, and the second row fired over the heads of the first kneeling group. As this second volley shattered the front Zulu runners, they too dropped to their knees to reload as the third row fired over their heads, upon the order.

Like a Well Oiled Machine

Like a well oiled, repeating machine, each row went through the process of firing, dropping to their knees, reloading, standing and firing, over and over again. Each cycle the officers roared commands to fire, drop, and reload. Each minute that went by the 300 soldiers were pouring volumes of lead balls into the sea of Zulus with high speed precision.

A well-orchestrated fight for life. Through the haze of black powder smoke and deafening roar the Zulus kept running, but each few steps they were met with a hail of lead as the British kept their highly creative and precision firing going.

The Sydney Art Gallery in the grounds of the Domain Park has on display one of the grandest paintings depicting this magnificent battle. A very large canvas, perhaps ten feet long by six or more feet high, the work is as impressive as is the story. How a tiny handful of men were able to beat the Zulu nation when they were totally outnumbered by the fierce competition. On that day, eleven Victoria Crosses were awarded for bravery, more than in any other British battle since!

Choose your battle plans

In a moment we will examine another famous battle from the nineteenth century that had a completely different outcome.

Vital
Lessons

Why we are examining these battles is to glean vital lessons. Lessons you can use in your Red Striped Zebra business today. Lessons that are learned from the observation of *human nature* ... and by learning how people react under inimical, hostile conditions.

The battles we face today are just as real. They are a challenge to our welfare, our family's welfare and our staff's welfare. They are the battles for business. They are those battles we fight simply for:

- *Keeping customers (holding your ground)*
- *Making sales (gaining ground)*
- *Fighting competitors (taking 'their' ground)*

And the battles we fight in business are just as frightening, sometimes just as fierce, always unrelenting ... and usually we're *outnumbered*.

If you break free like a Red Striped Zebra, you can choose to fight your battles as did those brave British troops ... with *creativity, uniqueness* and *precision* teamwork. If you are 'not' innovative, you fight by the rules of your competitors, which renders you totally at their mercy.

Price-Cutting Battles

Take price-cutting battles for instance. They cut, you have to follow, thereby suffering a reduction in your cash-flow. You're fighting by *their* rules ... and they can drive you out of business if they are stronger and more cashed-up then you. You soon can become overwhelmed. With the hit or miss approach in just trying to stay with them, (as do the 'black-stripers') ... you soon allow the enemy to take your hard-won ground.

So, choose your battle strategy
(Red Striped Zebra style suggested)

Brave George Custer

General George Custer was a very brave man. He had no qualms about facing his enemies, he had a job to do and he didn't hesitate to do it. He was like many business people today. Ready to fight, ready to face the enemy, (or competitors), and ready to square off, face to face.

But, brave though he (or we) may be, the enemy, or competitor, does not always fight on our terms. Custer found this out!

Custer's Successes

He was on the way to Little Big Horn in Montana with the 7th Cavalry, flushed with successes from previous skirmishes, and was going to do likewise at this next battle.

Arriving early on that fateful June 25th morning, in 1876, he immediately 'split' his 225 troops, sending a force across the river to attack the Sioux from the flanks, while he would ride directly into their camp to place fear into the enemies' hearts.

What he didn't know was that Sitting Bull and Crazy Horse had joined forces with these Sioux, swelling their ranks to 12,000. Custer's troops were outnumbered 53 to 1 ... not much different from the Rork's Drift odds!

The Sioux had expected an attack and were lying in wait for Custer's men, and so, the troops were caught in an unenviable position; being on horseback in the middle of a river, as they were fired upon by their enemy who were camouflaged in the long grass. A relentless one-sided battle ensued as the U.S. troopers were killed one by one.

A call to retreat caused further casualties as they clamored back through a small depression that lead out of the river, and were constantly fired upon by the Sioux lining both sides.

Eventually the remaining troopers, along with Custer, made it to higher ground for his famous 'last stand' as the vicious and relentless battle continued until most were dead, except for those soldiers who had previously split and were able to escape back to fort to recount the terrible loss.

What went wrong? How did a battle hardened battalion lose so dramatically ... and on another continent a totally outnumbered handful of soldiers win? And what lessons can our Red Striped Zebra business learn from these battles?

The battle plan

It's not how you 'fight' your battle,
but 'how' you fight your battle that matters!

Say again in clear language? ... I said it's not so much how *hard* you fight, how *brave* you are, how *forceful* you are in battle that matters. What really matters is how *creative, unique* and *innovative* in battle you can be! The British soldiers showed creativity, uniqueness, and innovation. The U.S. soldiers demonstrated sheer force, rushing headlong into the fight.

In business today you do not need *brute force* to win against your competition. What is required is a fresh, creative and innovative approach. You have to ascertain the strategies of your enemy; the competition, and decide NOT to fight by *their* battle plans, but *only* by yours.

The Battle for the Roses

'*Au Nom De La Rose*' is a flower boutique with a difference. In a city of some 8.7 million people, and thousands of flower stores, how does a business owner fight the competition battle, and come out victorious? Following Custer's example of 'rushing in headlong' with the most obvious approach, the owner could try three separate battle approaches:

1. *Attempt to undercut the competition and start a price war. However, that will not win the battle, because profits shrink. Why 'win' the battle and 'lose' all the spoils simultaneously?*

2. *Try to gain more customers through an advertising blitz. That may work, if the advertisements are well written ... and of course if the marketing budget (ammunition) is available.*

3. *Supply a 'better' range of flowers and creative arrangements. That would further enhance the offering, but not necessarily totally win a fierce competition battle.*

Or they could think like a Red Striped Zebra
and carry out a Rork's Drift innovative battle plan.

Here's how ...

Classy Red-stemmed or
Peach Colored Arrangements

Au Nom De La Rose is in Paris, France. The home of beauty, culture ... and florists! Lots and lots of florists. The owner of this boutique decided that his competition battle can be won by *re-inventing* the battle. His first job was to sell all his flowers already in stock. Clear them out and *never* restock them again. He then changed the name of his store to something 'special'. The new, beautiful appellation of *Au Nom De La Rose* ... a name that simply rolls off the tongue.

The next step was to restock his flower store. Not with the same varieties as all the other 'black and white' competing florists ... but with roses. Nothing but roses! All varieties, all colors, from the long-stemmed classical red roses to the beautiful pastel pink arrangements.

Do not ask for carnations, daffodils or marigolds, you will not get them. *Au Nom De La Rose* only sells roses!

The owner then developed new, fabulous arrangements to display his roses in the best way possible. From classy boxes containing red stems, tied with a bow tie, to the beautiful golds, and peach colors for weddings.

Roses, roses, roses, the boutique is brimming with beautiful roses.

Au Nom De La Rose has been featured in newspapers, and even on American national television news. Why? Because the owner decided to compete in a battle where 'he' set the rules of warfare.

Today, his business has outstanding and huge leaps of sales success, not to mention the brilliant media coverage that hasn't cost aFrench *franc*.

The competition is too fierce, too overwhelming and too well funded to meet head-on. The owner of Au Nom De La Rose knew this and discovered innovation, creativity and uniqueness as the weapons of war needed to position as a Red Striped Zebra leader.

There are better ways to fight competition battles. The old front-on charges are relics of bygone ages. Creative tactics can overwhelm your competitors. Not the direct, cut-price, cut-throat methods employed by many, but by establishing your 'own' battle plan. You name the terms, the way in which the battle is run, the length, the strategies. *Joining their battles is folly.* Leave it to those black and white Zebras who know no better.

Four Winning Battle Strategies

The British won the battle at Rork's Drift with four powerful strategies. These same strategies can be equally used today in business, with as much success.

They are:

1: Establish
Your Position
The British troops established their position. (And their U.M.P.) In the chapter; *The Good Guys Wear White Hats*, you learn how to establish a *Unique Marketing Perception.* This positions your business in the minds of customers as a unique, creative and 'worthy' business. It lets them know who you are, and what you do. It means *standing your ground, tall and proud* and letting the world *know* who you are

The British did this at Rork's Drift. They did not split into two as did Custer's men, they *stood true, on their ground, and did not budge.* They were the 'British' troops, representing the British crown ... and the Zulus knew it. There was no wild and scattered dash on horses, no charging headlong into an unknown force. They stood their ground and maintained their *Unique Marketing Perception.*

Our Rules
We do not win battles on the strength of weapons or by fighting by the competitor's rules, (Vietnam showed this), but from standing tall

and unstoppable ... demonstrating to everyone in sight how *unique, individualized* and *distinguishable* we are from all others. We must fight by 'our' rules - Red Striped Zebra rules! (Desert Storm proved this!)

> *It's not the size of the dog in the fight, but the size of the fight in the dog that matters.*

The British soldiers stood apart, stood their ground, and never flinched. They broadcast to the Zulu nation that they were there to stay, they were *formidable,* and they were *unstoppable.*

As a Red Striped Zebra, this strategy of *establishing your U.M.P.,* and standing tall will establish you apart from the rest. It will position you as a winner. Undivided, unstoppable and ready to take on the competitive forces around you.

2: Repetitious and Ongoing

The troopers worked to a systematic, ongoing and unstoppable cycle. They fired, dropped to their knees, reloaded and fired again. Custer's troops were firing wildly, unorganized and scattered. In business, it is the *repetitious, ongoing* and *organized* strategy that wins.

Rule of Seven

Jerry Crockford, Australia's copy-writing 'guru', told me during one of our audio program recording sessions that an advertising message to a customer has to be put in front of their eyes up to *seven* times. Seven *repetitious* promotions of the same message.

How often do people try a direct-mail letter, or an advertisement, and give up after one try ... when it is the third, fourth or even seventh message that finally makes a customer respond?

Even in the body-copy of an advertisement, this rule of seven should be attempted, repeating the message you want them to hear seven times. Over and over again, skillfully weaving into the copy the 'message'. Covering every angle to sell your sales message and to help customers make a decision to buy.

That's the Rork's Drift repetition strategy at work!

Creating your *'results-driven'* advertisement, brochure or direct-mail letter, embodying your *U.M.P.* ... then having it appear *regularly* and *repetitiously,* will beat any competitor who is *spasmodic* in their promotions.

If you throw enough (as in the Rule of 7) spaghetti against a wall, some of it will stick, but the wild 'one-hit', ill-planned Custer variety of promotion will not.

In a country town of Australia, an insurance agent once purchased an ongoing, small advertisement that comprised his picture, name and company. This advertisement has been running on the lower front page, in one corner, for over *ten years. Every issue, for ten years!*

Every person in that town *knows* this agent. Not knowing of him is impossible, with that type of systematic, ongoing exposure. He has created for himself an ongoing, repetitious message that is as familiar to readers as the newspaper's name. He wins by *repetition!*

3: Work
in Synergy

The British soldiers worked in synergy. They worked *together* to form an unstoppable army. Custer's troops were *divided*, and on horseback, which automatically placed them in an 'individualistic' mode.

If all your people worked in synergy, for the *common good* of the business, your marketing and business growth becomes unstoppable. However, the reverse is true if they do not. If any person in the business acts on Custer's individualistic or 'Maverick' approach, the business suffers.

Leading
the Troops

A client business in the United Kingdom which sells products in the building industry, had a manager who would go into the 'field' to act as a sales person. However, their clients did not like him, nor did they want him to come onto their building sites. He was inept at selling, and unfortunately the business was suffering.

We informed him of his bad choice of 'leaving the leadership position' to join the 'sales front-lines' ... which resulted in weakening the *synergy* of his troops. So, realizing his mistake, he resumed the skill he was good at, which was in managing the business and supporting his sales people ... and they started to win battles once again!

The Rork's Drift troops had officers who were leaders. Men who were tough minded and knew how to motivate, encourage, lead, inform and direct their troops efforts to success. *Tough love.* They *loved* their troops because they were in there with them, but *tough,* as demonstrated in their superb direction in the face of adversity.

Synergy
in Japan

The Japanese are synergistic people. They work for the company, full stop! No hidden agendas, no point scoring, just the welfare of the corporation. The lesson to be learned from the British troopers, the Japanese and even our man in the U.K., is to develop a synergistic approach to battling the competition. The officers (managers) need to be in synergy with the troops (staff), and the troops are to be in synergy with the officers. And *together*, they work for the firm - to win battles!

In a Red Striped Zebra business, management *must* work *with* their people, not *against* them, not dividing them (as did Custer) and not dominating them ... but in synergy with them.

4: Maximize
Your Weapons

The British troops maximized their weapons. Even though the old, muzzle loading rifles were nowhere as near as efficient as Custer's repeating, and very modern weapons. They were terrifyingly slow, especially when thousands of warriors are bearing down upon you, intent to kill you. Yet, in this battle, they proved far more efficient than their more modern counterpart. Why?

Simply because they maximized
their weapon's usage.

The hollering officers kept up the unrelenting pace of fire, drop, reload and fire again. Their skilled troops could fire and reload those old rifles three times per minute. The barrels were red-hot as volley after volley flew through the air. They worked those rifles faster and more efficiently then they had ever done before. This was a battle to the death ... and they knew it.

In business the same *maximizing* of weapons must be employed if sure victory is to be won. The sales force is one area that always needs maximizing ... and it is also one of the vital *Marketing Pillars* in your business.

Maximizing Your Sales Force

- *The sales person must know their weapons, their selling tools, product information and understand customer's psychology.*

- *They must know, emphasize and promote the U.M.P. of your business over and over ... and at a moment's notice, such as one premier hotel that requires 'every' staff member to know their U.M.P. in logo form, and to be able to repeat it to any guest who asks. It is: "We are Ladies and Gentlemen, serving Ladies and Gentlemen."*

- *They should maximize their selling kits, collect and use testimonials or endorsements and develop their visual aids.*

- *They must be 'trained' to the maximum. Highly skilled in prospecting, approaches, presentations, objections and closing.*

- *So must be the telephone operator who is the first line of defense, the one who answers the first calls. Does that operator provide over-the-top service as calls come in? Is the U.M.P. known and promoted by the operator ... or are calls handled in a sloppy Custer manner?*

If people synergize, and work together for the <u>common good</u> of the business, which is to <u>increase sales</u> and to <u>take market share</u>, then a Rork's Drift, 'unstoppable' synergy takes place!

Your advertising budget can be wasted, as was Custer's inefficient firing ... or maximized with response-driven messages.

Every square inch of an advertisement, brochure, direct-mail letter or yellow page advertisement *must* be maximized. And those square inches need to be *content-rich* with *benefits, benefits, benefits* ... and *more* benefits for the reader.

Maximizing every aspect of your selling/promotional weapons is a requirement for winning battles ... and a requirement for a Red Striped Zebra business!

This following example shows how.

Fried Chicken and Roses

The Results Corporation, an Australian business consultancy firm, relates a wonderful story about one of their clients who had a competition battle to win.

The owner of a new fried chicken fast food store asked them to help him launch the business. His problem, as he related it, told of fierce competition. (He was outnumbered - Zulu style!) An American chain had their chicken store nearby, and further along on the block was an Australian chain store. He was smack in the middle of fierce competitors and wanted to know how to stand apart and succeed.

How could he launch his business and gain market share? How could he battle these giants when he was out-positioned, out-numbered and out-skilled in marketing? It required a Rork's Drift strategy.

Imagine giving away flowers with chicken!

During the initial meeting one person mentioned giving away a gift or premium with every fried chicken order. They suggested flowers! Flowers, for goodness sake. No wonder the owner's reaction to that suggestion was rather negative ... *"That's the dumbest idea I've ever heard! Imagine giving away flowers with my chicken!"* he laughed!

In fact, the thought of giving away flowers with any fried chicken order, in any country or in any store, is certainly laughable. Or is it?

The possibility of 300 soldiers, firing muzzle loading rifles, beating 15,000 fierce warriors is also laughable. Or was it? The eleven Victoria Crosses won on that day certainly was an endorsement to that success.

After they all had a good laugh about the flower idea, the Results Corporation team then went on to convince the owner that this idea was not so 'flaky' after all. *"That could be your advertising headline."* they said, referring to his statement.

Rules of Engagement

They convinced him that it was a *creative* and very *innovative* concept that the 'black and white' businesses wouldn't consider and had the possibility of producing a result for him. It was simply not done this way by others. The competition would not promote 'flowers' because *that's not the way business (or a battle) is done.*

They convinced him that the best way to win competition battles is to engineer his own industry 'rules of engagement' ... and fight by nobody's rules but his own!

On the day of the launch, newspaper advertisements appeared, with headlines stating:

It costs money to buy advertising space ... just as those old rifles cost money. How you 'choose' to use it will determine your battle results. Maximizing your marketing material, (outlined in ZebraWrite), will help you win!

Imagine receiving flowers when you order chicken from us!

In the first two days of operation the owner gave away 3,000 long stemmed roses with the 3,000 orders of fried chicken. An outrageous amount of sales that far exceeded all expectations.

Long after the customers ate the chicken, the rose was still in the vase, being admired. And that rose eventually became the paragon that would help to build his loyal customer base.

This owner had won his Rork's Drift battle, and would go on to win many more through creativity. He could have chosen the head-on Custer approach, and be beaten by the better equipped competing forces, who would have fought by their own rules.

Unfortunately, too many businesses use the Custer approach, and many fail. It is the rare business indeed which adopts the cunning and creativity of the Rork's Drift battle. *Those which do have exceptional wins, and stand apart like Red Striped Zebras!*

The Battle for the Mexican Beer

Crown Distributors is a growing beer distributor, based in Memphis, Tennessee. It is not 'number one' (yet!) in the city as far as distributors go ... however, it performs like a number one!

Chuck Pierotti, a co-owner, is a highly creative manager who understands the philosophy of a Rork's Drift battle. He has many competition battles notched up, but one that significantly stands him apart though was the battle to gain the agency for the Mexican brand of beer; *Corona*.

Chuck had approached the Corona people to try to win the distribution rights, by the 'normal' (Custer) approach, but his letters and calls were without success in this fight.

He certainly didn't want the other local distributors to beat him in the battle to gain the rights, so he loaded his weapons with the creativity of a Rork's Drift officer.

It's creativity that wins battles. Force will not do it. Big, expensive advertising campaigns are not the solution to winning your battles. It's creativity.

Nothing else!

287

The Fortune
Cookie Idea

He launched one of these 'creative weapons' to get the attention of the Corona President in Mexico. It was a 'fortune cookie' ... a very large fortune cookie. When the President opened the cookie Chuck's proposal to distribute Corona through Crown Distributors was inside. (I told you he was creative!). Chuck had to capture the attention of a very busy man, and as his 'Custer' style (or black and white Zebra style) letters were not doing the job he decided to try this creative method. However, it still did not get a response ... more ammunition was needed!

Chuck was unstoppable by now, so he loaded up his weapons to fire a second and third volley attempt. He tried other creative ideas to get through, but no response was coming from Mexico.

The Winning Proposal
in the Sand Box

Chuck's next volley attempt called for far more innovative thinking (I simply love this story ... he moved right into the realm of Red Striped Zebra thinking by doing something that ordinary black and white businesses wouldn't do!) ... He decided to really *get noticed!*

The proposal was rolled up and placed inside a bottle. The bottle was then placed inside a wooden fruit box and then the box was filled with sand to the very brim. Once filled, they nailed a lid down tight to secure the contents. They addressed the box to the President of Corona and shipped it off to Mexico.

Could you imagine the look on the President's face when that lid was removed, to find sand spilling out all over his desk as they retrieved the bottle?

That volley certainly got his full attention! It was not too long before Chuck received a phone call from Corona. *It was time to talk business!*

Their Perception
Changed

Corona management had a change of perception about Crown

Distribution. (Remember, the Red Striped Zebra philosophy is about changing people's perceptions and being seen as *different* from all others). That change of perception resulted in Crown securing the distribution rights.

They must have been saying; *"If he could take on the local competitor, a much larger firm than his, using the same creativity, audacity and ingenuity as he's demonstrated to grab our attention, then he certainly must be able to build market share for our Corona beer."*

Chuck succeeded in winning this battle - Rork's Drift style! Crown Distributors won the Corona agency. In fact, they've now gained many other brewer's specialty products and are steadily working toward that number one position, establishing themselves as a Red Striped Zebra in the beer distribution industry.

Chuck Pierotti could have fought hard by the *normal* rules of engagement, (Custer's full charge ahead strategy). He could have sent letters, faxes and made calls, waiting in vain for a reply that may never have come. He could have allowed his competitors to overwhelm him due to their number one standing in the eyes of Corona. If you were the President, wouldn't you want your beer to be handled by the biggest and best? Absolutely! That would have been the thinking ... until Chuck launched his Rork's Drift battle plan and went into action.

> *The battle of Rork's Drift may be viewed as just old, faded history, but its strategies work today.*
>
> *Times change,*
> *people do not!*

The little guy, (the 300 soldier unit), won the battle against competing giants. Even though they were outnumbered. They didn't win with numbers and force, but by *creativity, uniqueness* and *innovation*. Chuck Pierotti and Crown Distributors; a unique manager in a Red Striped Zebra business, fighting with Rork's Drift battle strategies.

Creative marketing, sales and promotion strategies will give a surprise attack on competitors ... and winning victory for you on the business battlefield.

Pharmaceuticals and Representatives

Pfizer Pharmaceuticals in Australia have many competitors to fight. Over 130 companies vie for market-share in this high stakes battle.

What sharpens the edge in the pharmaceutical industry is the fact that sales representatives walk away from a prospective client, not really knowing if they had sold the product. That's tough! Not knowing if the physician, or hospital is definitely going to use and prescribe Pfizer's product, after the representative has made a great presentation.

What make matters worse is knowing that a representative from a competing firm will be 'hot on the heels' of the Pfizer representative, to sell the client on their company's products, and cast dispersions on Pfizer's product.

I singled Pfizer out, not because their battle plans are better, or worse ... no, it was because Pfizer first germinated the seed in my mind for the *Uniqueness is a Red Striped Zebra©* program, after they contracted me to deliver the keynote address for their 1991 annual conference, at the Sheraton Hotel, overlooking the beautiful Derwent Harbor in Hobart, Tasmania.

The primary concern of Pfizer's was the fact that competition was fierce, and representatives had a mammoth job to not only gain appointments with busy doctors, but also gain sales. They pointed out to me that they could only *gauge* sales through the rise in filled prescriptions at pharmacy stores within a representative's territory.

How to stand apart, gain more sales and gain the client's attention? That was their question and brief given to me.

Not only did I speak, but we divided over 150 representatives into brainstorming groups and worked at solving the problems and generating worthwhile marketing ideas.

Out of all this, and over the ensuing years, I've worked at this problem. How to stand apart, break free ... get noticed! A pharmaceutical representative or small business owner, a dentist or an accountant, the same story applies. The competition is fierce and battles need to be won for any business to thrive today ... and it's all about being 'different to' rather than trying to be 'better than' your competitors!

Engram
For Success

Although the pharmaceutical industry (as do many other industries) supplies clients with free giveaways, pens, mugs, writing pads, all with the corporation's name emblazoned upon, I now advise both the firm and the representatives to do much more than this.

To win a competition battle, Rork's Drift style, and to stand apart like a Red Striped Zebra, a business or a representative must make a *lasting impression* ... and *engram* the mind of the client doctor.

When it's time for a doctor to write a prescription, that representative, the corporation, and the product should come *immediately* to mind.

Lasting and
Immediate Impression

For the representative, learning to break free and fight this way may require dressing differently, perhaps upgrading to impeccably styled suits, or wearing a flower in the lapel as a trade mark. Perhaps it means having an outstanding presentation folder. Perhaps it's the pleasant and obliging manner of speaking, or adding humor.

It most certainly means providing *Awesome Service*, as outlined in; *ZebraServe*. Whatever it takes, it requires finding a way to be different, to fight differently, to stand apart from the crowd of other representatives, engram and excel.

To 'engram' means to make an immediate impact and a lasting impression; a *favorable* impression. In your business, do you or your representatives do that? Do they make an impression that makes an immediate impact, a statement, an influence on client's minds? The Rork's Drift soldiers did. Their British uniforms made that statement. In those days they wore red and white, not the camouflage of today. They stood out and made a statement. Make an *impression* and you'll *engram* for success ... just like the Red Striped Zebra in the black and

white herd! Even after you finish this book, you may forget much ...
but you'll never forget the Zebra image ... you've been engrammed!

Rork's Drift
Battle Strategies
Will Help You:

- *Establish your position with your UMP*
- *Promote repetitiously and ongoing for maximum effect*
- *Work in synergy to become unstoppable*
- *Maximize your weapons for greater sales power*
- *Provide awesome service*
- *Promote creatively to get noticed*
- *Secure contracts through innovative methods*
- *Advertise in an innovative and response-driven manner*
- *Stand apart by engramming on customer's minds.*

In Addition:

- *If you're not just 'satisfying' customers, but 'spoiling' and 'delighting' them, you are going to win more battles*
- *If you provide 'Irresistible Sales Offers' (ISO) you will win*
- *If your advertising delivers 'more' than promised, you will win*

Simply stated, you must provide your customers and clients with attention, offers, goods and services that exceeds their expectations ...

... and exceeds the expectation of competitors!

Stratagem Creative

Creativity won the battle of Rork's Drift, with strategies born out of necessity ... the necessity to stay alive when faced with imminent death by an oppressive number of enemies.

In this world born out of chaotic change and despotic competitors, allow the battle of Rork's Drift to inspire you and establish in your thinking the need for creativity in your stratagem.

As a Red Striped Zebra business, your goal is to break free, stand apart, get noticed ... and excel. To do that you do not need to fight dirty, or by your competitor's rules of engagement.

You choose to fight by YOUR rules of engagement; a creative and innovative battle strategy to guarantee outrageous success over tremendous odds.

The Quality Quirk

How to make your business irresistible to customers
with a philosophy of quality as your guide

Seventy percent of all United States businesses that undertake a structured 'quality' assurance program, fail at its inception within two years. Only thirty percent find success.

Here is an opportunity for your Red Striped Zebra business to reap the harvest by incorporating a no-nonsense, fail-safe approach to quality. The secret key you will discover here is in serving customers at a very real 'human' level ... rather than in a 'system' of regulation alone.

Kangaroos are lovable creatures! Instantly recognizable the world over as being synonymous with Australia; this unique animal baffled the first English explorers with its hopping motion, long tail and pouch. With 150 million throughout the country they still intrigue the world and have become a much loved inhabitant of Australia. Much loved until they are offered for *consumption* that is!

The Australian meat industry was in full swing during the late Seventies, sending container loads of product worldwide. Lamb and beef were selling well with a growing beef market in the United States. Then disaster struck! A U.S. meat inspector was examining the rectangular boxed beef packages, taking samples, making inspections, as is customary in maintaining a quality food import, when he noticed that something was 'not quite right' ... or not quite 'beef'.

Kangaroo Burgers
Anyone?

Horror of horrors, tests revealed that the United States beef import was padded with kangaroo meat. Was this just a prank by an Aussie packing company, or the dealings of an unscrupulous processor? The kangaroo is certainly a lovable animal, and the meat is now considered to be a delicacy. However, it was neither loved nor considered desirable in the United States food supply.

Examination later revealed that other shipments had actually passed through and had been used by a major fast food burger chain. Kangaroo burgers anyone?

296

An Industry
Almost Destroyed

The Australian meat industry went into a massive tailspin, for as expected, the United States froze the importation of Aussie beef ... and the headlines screamed worldwide. Global markets were on the precipice as Australia was faced with its most devastating export loss.

A massive investigation was immediately undertaken to not only find the source of this deception, but also to attempt to capture back the lost markets and the lost confidence, all caused through a lack of quality control in the out-going products.

From Major Crisis ...
to Staggering Success

Out of this calamity emerged AUS-MEAT, *(The Authority for Uniform Specification)* to represent the Australian Meat & Livestock Corporation. This new name was the start of a re-invention of a new industry ... one that was built on the solid foundation of *quality*. A new broom sweeps clean and a *new name* can perform like that new broom. It forms a rallying point for management, staff and customers. A beacon from which the new U.M.P. can be shone ... and to which the corporation could aspire to. AUS-MEAT was the start of something exciting.

Huddled together in corporate retreats, the *heads* of the meat industry toiled long and hard to:

- *Develop their new vision for AUS-MEAT.*
- *Create a fresh, new mission statement.*
- *Undertake the road of Quality Assurance.*
- *Develop training programs for those on the slaughterhouse floor through to supervisors, managers and packaging companies.*
- *And to satisfy the stringent Japanese market, (with their requirements for marbled-fat content in beef), a new software program was developed. This showed immediately on screen the correct image requirements, so inspectors had a 'benchmark' to work from.*

After a long and arduous process AUS-MEAT was able to represent and promote Australian meat worldwide with pride, placing it a long kangaroo-hop from its almost fatal collapse.

Today, The Australian Meat & Livestock corporation is the 'largest' meat and livestock exporter in the world.

From shipments of live sheep to the Middle East, to the vast United States market with its penchant for beef, people around the world are eating Aussie meat, thanks to the scare of kangaroo in the order.

Out of crisis came creativity and common purpose!

The side-effects, (in this case; 'good' side-effects), produced by the rigorous quality assurance program and new vision, has resulted in *lower* packaging costs due to better material, *higher quality* in the meat product, *very lean* beef, and most importantly, a *cheaper price* per pound.

In fact, Australian beef can be produced, landed and offered for sale on United States soil at *far cheaper prices* than the American counterpart, making the Australian product very desirable, especially to the large fast food chains.

In a world ruled by a more sophisticated and demanding customer, 'quality' rules supreme!

Kangaroos, Aussie Beef ... and Red Striped Zebras

What is the thread that binds these unique animals? It is the realization that we are light-years removed from the 'anything goes' attitudes of previous decades?

Somehow the customer has become *educated*. Perhaps it is

because of the vast sea of choices that has become available to the customer that Alvin Toffler forecast in his book: *Future Shock* over a decade ago.

When Henry Ford told people they could have any color they wanted, as long as it was black, they accepted his word ... and bought black. Today, if a car dealer told us the color we prefer is not in stock we can, (and do), make a bee-line to the next dealer who is sure to have our preferred choice. The customer is now 'demanding' *choice*, *quality* and immediate *attention*.

Red Striped Zebra businesses must be at the vanguard in providing quality in service, products, in attention to detail and immediate attention to customers.

Paradise ...
No Competitors

Henry Ford had it made. The competition was not on every street corner. Japan had not beaten him to the post with high quality vehicles and profound choices.

The Australian meat industry, along with New Zealand, also had it made. They had the 'old country' of England as a historical exporting market. She had not yet joined the European trading partners or closed its doors to the 'colonies' ... for life was good for Australia!

We could say the same for the electronic industries, clothing, footwear and sporting goods. Back in the good ol' days the raging tigers of Asia and India and many other countries were still sleeping. We had the whole game to ourselves. But now there is choice!

Choice Gives Freedom
... to Customers That Is!

Freedom to choose! Customers now have the option and they know it. The old days are gone. Global competition has entered the playing field and it's as if the customer has been led into a candy store with an *unlimited* offering to choose from.

To stand apart from the crowd, many corporations have introduced quality as the *factor* or *secret* to win the choice of customers.

It has worked for many, such as AUS-MEAT, Harley Davidson and Motorola ... but many others fail at its inception. One thing is for sure, whenever the customer has the *choice* of going elsewhere and finding the same, (or better) service or product than what you offer, you must be very, very sure that you provide the very best ... the *highest* quality available.

In Motorola's case, their success with quality has been reported to have shaved over $700 million from its manufacturing costs over the last few years.

The TQM Myth

Total Quality Management! After experiencing the Japanese invasion that overwhelmed the West with high quality products, corporations rushed headlong into TQM, believing this was the panacea that would heal their wounds. Just rub it in and all will be well!

Professor Edward W. Deming introduced TQM to a devastated Japan only after his teaching was rejected in the west, and specifically by his own land; the U.S.A. And yet the West has now embraced quality, knowing full well that it is one of the required ingredients in overcoming the problem of choice that customers are armed with.

Quality applied to the manufacturing process, or to a service industry can have some profound effects ... and it is thought that when China incorporates the process into their manufacturing of products we will have another *huge competing giant* to contend with.

With all the decades passing since Deming introduced quality, it could be thought that we had learned all the lessons and undergirded our businesses with the process. Not so!

Many firms simply 'cannot' get it right.

Incredible ...
a 70% Failure Rate

Arthur D. Little completed a survey of 500 American manufacturing and service companies. His results showed that only *one third* felt that total-quality programs had made a 'significant impact' on their competitiveness. In a more recent study by A.T. Kearney of over 100 British firms, only a *fifth* (even less) of those surveyed believed their quality programs had achieved tangible results.

With the reported assumption that 70% of all western corporations which undertake the quality road fail at its inception within two years, we must ask: *"Is embracing quality a dead-end street?"* And: *"If only 30% of the firms that undertake it get it right, is it really worthwhile?"*

The 3 Reasons Why 'Formal' Quality Programs Fail

1: Not a Short-term Approach

The answers to why quality programs fail are many and varied. But some of the leading experts blame the insistence of large corporations in expecting *short-term* results.

An example was Allen-Bradley, a Milwaukee based manufacturer of industrial automation equipment with sales of $1.4 billion back in 1991. Jim Weber, a manager on Allen-Bradley's quality council, reported that in the 1980's the success of its quality program was routinely measured against *short-term financial results* (i.e. *Has 'quality' improved profits this quarter?*), rather than against the customer's *expectations*.

2: Customer's Satisfaction Must Be Paramount

Florida Power & Light (FP&L) *embraced* quality with a vengeance. In the late 1980's it embarked on a journey to be the first non-Japanese winner of the Deming prize. It ended with an 85 strong quality department, 1,900 quality teams involving three quarters of their employees, and a very rigorous, highly statistical 'quality-review' system.

They did win their Deming prize in 1989. However, customers only noticed a *few small improvements* in the quality of its services, and these were *insignificant* when set against the mountain of quality effort. FP&L, to a large extent, were simply *going through the motions*.

FP&L have now reduced the quality department to a handful of employees, and most of the quality teams have disbanded. The whole process has become a lot less rigid as they now give *priority* to the customer. Going back to customers to find what *they* want is the lesson that has filtered out of this massive undertaking.

Allen-Bradley's views have changed too. The focus is also now on the customer. A Vice President of Operations stated that: *"Quality needed to be in the eye of the customer!"* The group now uses its sales people as a quality task force, continuously seeking *viewpoints* and *expectations* from customers, for measurement against Allen-Bradley's results.

What a huge waste of money for these and the other 70% of firms who attempt to install 'quality' programs. It all comes down to one thing, and one thing only;

Pleasing customers!

3: Empowering
the Powerless

Various corporations report the third hindrance to achieving success with quality, such as Xerox, is in the *empowering* of employees.

A Baldridge winner in 1989, Xerox has had success with quality but not without some problems. Richard Palermo stated in an article in *The Economist* that empowering workers means taking power from somewhere else.

Empowerment has become a big issue. Enabling the employee to *make decisions on the spot* adds *value* to the customer, and yet inside the corporation an employee making a decision without gaining permission from a superior can cause much friction.

If a hotel room-maid was empowered to make decisions, to perhaps be allowed to spend up to $500 or so to satisfy the request of a hotel room guest, this would cause a tremendous rise in the satisfaction of the guest, perhaps converting the guest to a long-term client ... but could cause friction from her immediate supervisor.

Steve Young, one of the authors of A.T. Kearney's study, stresses that although it is very difficult, empowering all of a firm's employees and making *each* responsible for quality can be very beneficial. Of the firms surveyed whose quality programs had succeeded, results showed that they were *twice* as likely to have *filtered* the responsibility for quality all the way down to the shop floor. Only by this *saturation* level was the *philosophy* of quality likely to be absorbed.

The three lessons to be learned from the experiences of others ... and without spending the enormous amounts those in the studies have, are:

1. *Building quality into your businesses, products and services is a long-term, 'continuous' effort.*

2. *The focus must be on what the 'customer' expects and experiences ... Nothing else!*

3. *The whole staff, from top management to lowest staff member, must be made 'responsible' for quality ... and 'empowered' to get the job done.*

End of story!

Here's a different approach.
A Red Striped Zebra business ...
empowered with quality

What of the millions of small businesses though, which cannot even afford to incorporate a fully blown *Total Quality Management* program? What do they do? How do they start to introduce quality into their service and products?

And what of your Red-Striped Zebra business? How important is it to build quality into your business if the odds of making it work are low?

We have discussed how choice rules. If the customer is *empowered with choice*, to counter this choice your business must be *empowered with quality* to meet their weapon of choice. The choice the customer is armed with can be used as a weapon against you, to force you to deliver what *they* want ... or you can use it as a *motivator* to induce you to build quality into your products and service, thereby negating their weapon.

It is not a matter of 'deciding' if quality is a process you must undertake. It is not your choice to make. Rather, it is imperative to fine-tune your business so you deliver <u>one thousand percent</u>.

Buying a super luxury car, such as a Bentley, in times past meant you didn't ask the price. If you asked the price you couldn't afford one. Even asking the showroom salesperson what the horsepower was would result in an answer such as; *"Sufficient!"* Nowadays, through our fine motor magazines we can find out that the price is over $350,000 and the horsepower around the 375 mark. Even Bentley realized that the customer today is *very demanding* ... and wants to know the facts.

The gem in this example though is that by building handcrafted 'high' quality into their vehicles, Bentley does not have to compete with a plethora of other car manufacturers, except of course for its sister ship; the *Rolls Royce* saloon.

Quality Means 'More' Money

It is estimated by *Bell South Business Systems* President, William Reddersen, that companies which do make continuous quality improvements can justify charging 9% and more than those which don't.

Bentley can charge more than 9% because they have developed a product that is synonymous with quality ... underpinning it with a *Unique Marketing Perception* that suggests snob appeal, class distinction, charisma and style. If you can do this with what you sell, then you can say: ...

Bye bye competition!

Vast
Opportunity

With 70% of major and medium sized corporations failing at incorporating quality into their businesses, and the vast numbers of small businesses who haven't a clue what quality is, this leaves the Red Striped Zebra business with an *immense opportunity* to break free and excel.

Like a Bentley, or a Rolex watch, a Federal Express package or Disneyland, you too can stand your businesses apart from the crowd by building quality into every aspect. When you do, the customer, client, patient or member will *beat a path* to your door.

Who Really is
Your Competitor?

In your hometown your competitors are those businesses which sell the same product or supply the same service ... Or are they?

If you own a dry-cleaning business, is every other dry-cleaner your competitor? What if one-third of those cleaners provided shoddy workmanship, were unable to get stains out, lost buttons, double creased trousers, faded garments. Would they still be your competition?

What if the other third were more expensive, or were discourteous to customers. Would they still be your competition?

You would have to say a 'big no' to all of those questions. If you truly establish as a Red Striped Zebra business you would have no competition to consider.

Let's examine further:

- *What would happen if your business provided a 'superior' cleaning service?*

- *What would be the result of being faster, i.e. having the clothing in by nine and finished by four, which included a solid money-back guarantee?*

- *What if you were to keep the customer's name and requirements on computer, so you would know exactly what they expected ... and were to send thank you, birthday and Christmas cards, gift certificates, coupons etc.?*

- *What if you were to provide a beautiful reception area which included free morning coffee and doughnuts?*

- *What if you gave special discounts for quantities, or provided a set annual fee for customers for a set amount of clothing?*

- *And what if you had created a strong Unique Marketing Perception that told customers how caring, courteous and proficient your business was ...* **who would be your competition then?**

Quality is not just boring hyperbole. It is not just the 'doing it right' attitude. The service and product should be first-class to begin with! What a terrible lesson we had to learn from Japan. To have them flood our western countries with their goods, simply because we did not care too much about the customer.

► *"You can have any color, as long as it's black!"* we told them.

► *"You're not worthy of the extra effort to apply quality and attention to detail."*

► *"We are not going to waste money on improving, or developing new designs. The designs we've got now are fine!"*

► *"These products and service are good enough for the likes of you ... take it or leave it!"*

The customers left it!

The Saturn Miracle - A Better Mousetrap (Stage 1 & 2)

Saturn Corp., the General Motors subsidiary in Spring Hill Tennessee has established itself as a Red Striped Zebra firm.

They recognized two primary opportunities that other

manufactures had overlooked. First the fact that quality was *lacking nationwide* and a gaping hole needed to be filled with a vehicle that was high quality, built in America, by Americans, for Americans, and owned by Americans.

Second was the need to *satisfy* the new breed of customer, one who had been reeducated by the Japanese manufacturers into believing they were *worthy* of high standards and modernistic design.

Saturn could have invested its nine billion dollars and nine years on its futuristic plant and then sat back with a smug grin, believing that it had revolutionized the industry, but not so. The job was only half done. Saturn executives believed that the focus of their quality program was NOT in just building a profound vehicle in a sparkling new Tennessee factory ... but in providing first-class quality service to a highly sophisticated and newly educated customer, who were now driving Mazdas, Toyotas and Hondas.

Researching
... Belly to Belly!

Saturn executives spent many countless hours talking with car buyers, asking them what they really wanted, what their desires and expectations were and how they would prefer to be treated.

The Saturn people found that customers really didn't want to haggle ... at least 95% of those researched didn't. They wanted a fixed price that the dealer would stick with. They also wanted the same sales person to handle the whole transaction. They disliked being passed from one to the other, whispering by the sales people about the 'deal' in the managers office, and being told that a decision has to be made immediately because 'some other customer' wants the car in question. (Read the *Tale of Two Emu's*).

Surprise ... surprise!
It turned out that people would prefer to go to have teeth pulled rather than visit a car showroom.
At least the dentist treated them with respect, didn't hassle them, pressure them, rip them off and haggle with them over price.

Saturn responded by establishing showrooms where haggling, pressure and rebating is banished. There is one sticker price that is applicable to all, and the customer is treated like a true friend.

This is quality in action! Quality vehicles being sold with a quality in service.

Quality 'conversion' ... an evangelist for the cause

And the response by the public? John Oslund, journalist for the *Minneapolis-St. Paul Star Tribune*, states in a story he wrote about Saturn that a typical customer is Charles Callaway, an optometrist. He hadn't bought an American car for 19 years. But, he had bought Japanese and German cars in that time.

Callaway is not just a Saturn buyer, he has gone through a *conversion of quality* and become a 'convert'. Because of Callaway's enthusiasm for the Saturn car, generated by the Saturn buying and driving experience, he is like many owners who have become *evangelists* for the 'cause'.

He volunteered to staff the Saturn booth at the Atlanta car show and drove some 88 miles from Dalton to Atlanta one Saturday. His only compensation was a ticket into the show. Callaway already has a color picked for his second Saturn and has been converting his relatives to become Saturn buyers.

Wow!
That's a convert!

Oslund also reported that Kris Carlson of Burnsville, Minnesota, bought a Saturn, loves it and swears by it. Carlson occasionally visits the Saturn dealership where she bought her car, just to help out. She talks to customers with enthusiasm, shows them the cars, rides along on test drives and basically helps out until an 'associate' is available.

Like Callaway, her compensation is minimal, just lunch and an occasional oil change. It's the pleasure they share in helping other people with the Saturn experience. Once again: *Wow!* Only over-the-top quality service, undergirded by high quality products can achieve these amazing results. To have customers and clients sing praises is no mean feat, nevertheless it is a feat that *can* be achieved.

What is amazing though, is that many dealers of other car manufacturers still don't get it. They blindly watch the Saturn experience, but still persist in their Neanderthal ways of *neglecting* the customer. It is almost abuse when the making of a few dollars for the dealership takes preeminence over the well-being of the customer. Willy Loman in Arthur Miller's Death of a Salesman states: *"Be liked, and you will never want."*

Saturn is liked! Well liked! And the corporation will never want. Many of the other dealerships are disliked. I actually detest one dealership because of sinister dealings ... and these 'dealings' actually reflect on the car manufacturer and on their product.

How many people in this nation dislike, or detest some of these dealers because of inferior service? The mind boggles!

Saturn re-launches

The story of Saturn has been told over and over. But, unfortunately, all stories come to an end. People's love affair with the car, the Tennessee barbecues for satisfied buyers and the celebration of polymer-paneled cars was starting to wane. It was time for a new car.

Saturn has introduced the 2000 L-Series sedan and wagon. Brand new medium sized cars that go toe-to-toe with the best selling Toyota Camry, Honda Accord and Ford Taurus.

And will they win? With its reputation of delivering high quality and safety at low cost, Saturn is poised for a re-launch of the firm that re-wrote the books on pleasing customers.

It is quality at a fair price, coupled to the philosophy of treating people well that will knock over the other guys - again!

Mom's the Word!

Quality means providing not just a superior product. It also means embodying the little things that go toward making awesome service.

The Little Things
That Please

A Red Striped Zebra business can in-build quality by paying special attention to the little things that please customers.

- *The dry-cleaner who supplies the special coat-hangers, the free coffee, the birthday cards, the caring attitude ... and makes it both convenient and fun to do business with.*

- *It's the Saturn dealer who rounds up the troops to cheer you with "I say, I say Saturn" as you take delivery and drive away.*

- *It's the business which gives you that little something extra ... something 'special' with your order.*

It is recognized by the *accolades* given by enthusiastic customers, who sing the praises of the business to their friends.

Quality is caring in <u>action</u>!

Quality service is the business owner who treats a customer as if they were serving their own *mother*. And how do we treat our own mom? With *caring* of course. We see to her needs, offer her refreshments, make sure she's seated in the best seat, satisfy her requirements and slip a little extra something into her handbag. We treat our moms well because we love them. We supply them with *quality service* ... and never knew it was called quality!

A full-blown Total Quality Management program has been under our noses all our lives and we hadn't recognized it. It's called; *loving our mom!* That's how we need to treat our customers and clients, just like loving our mom. TQM in action. (Better put: LOM in action). *Mom's the word!*

The tooth, the whole tooth ... and nothing but the tooth!

Paddy Lund conducts a successful dental practice in Brisbane, Queensland. In fact, it's not just successful, it's exceptionally successful! It's a Red Striped Zebra dental practice which stands apart from the competition.

You do not call up his practice and make an appointment; he has a silent number! Paddy can pick and choose whom he wants as clients, and many of those clients are *referrals* from existing clients. They fly from all over Australia just to have him work on their teeth. He is a highly sought after speaker at dental conferences in Australia and the United States ... and he charges far more than any other dentist.

So, what is it that stands Paddy apart, makes him a Red Striped Zebra in a field of black and whites?

Well, for one thing, he is not super-human. Paddy is a dentist, just like other dentists. Paddy works on teeth, just like others. He deals with the same problems every day, just like other dentists ... yet his practice is far more successful. Why? What's the secret?

Quality and a Happiness-Centered Business

Paddy was not always a happy man. In his eye-opening book; *Building a Happiness Centered Business*, (available from our office) he outlines how he was a highly stressed person. He mentions how dentists have a very high suicide rate ... and with this statement he paints a picture of a desperately unhappy man who just couldn't go on any more. He was unhappy, his staff was unhappy ... and many of his patients were not happy with the service they were receiving.

Paddy's
Happiness Meter

Paddy changed. He developed a happiness and stress meter. A monitoring tool that was used to measure (scores from 1 to 10) the stress and happiness levels in the practice, on a day by day basis. He and his staff had meetings at day's end to discuss all the issues that bothered them and caused low scores on the meter. They would score their individual stress and happiness levels on the meter as they 'felt' at the end of the day.

They learned to start saying simple things, like *please* and *thank you*, and not to criticize or utter sarcastic remarks during the course of high pressure moments. And the practice started to change. Little by little, they were installing quality ... not out of a need to serve the patient at this stage ... but from a need to survive and be *happy* in work.

Customer
Focus

Perhaps by accident, perhaps by design, this happiness and serving each other in a more gracious, pleasing manner started to flow towards the patients.

Paddy recalls working on a woman patient. A well dressed, successful business woman. During the procedure, Paddy had a lapse in his 'happiness' focus and was 'short' with his nurse. He could almost see in the eyes of the patient the loathing she had for Paddy, because of the way he verbally abused his nurse. It was though this patient had been on the receiving end of abuse (from a man?) before. In that very instant, like a flash, he realized how his practice was being seen and *perceived* from the patient's viewpoint ... and how 'low' he had sunk.

It was time to not only concentrate on quality 'inside' the practice, but to let in flow towards the customer. Happiness centered style!

Root Canal
in Style

Today, Paddy's practice is saturated with quality service. It's the *'mom's the word'* philosophy that makes the difference.

312

As mentioned, people do not like going to a dentist. It hurts! Paddy relates a funny story about two people sitting around one sunny day, deciding what to do. They go through the options; a drive in the country, a day at the beach ... or a visit to the dentist for some root canal work. Ouch!

However, a trip to Paddy's practice is very different. When you drive into the parking lot there is a reserved space ... with the patient's name on it. From that start, they know they are going to be treated well. They then walk into a beautifully decorated reception area and office, where they are attended to. Then, the patient is ushered into a plush interview room and served hot tea and home made cakes on fine English bone china.

Paddy sits and has a friendly discussion in the interview room, discussing the patient's dental needs. Together they plan out the visits, procedures, costs and payments. He wins over the full confidence of the patient, and subsequent visits are reinforced with his caring, very gentle and highly proficient work.

A Change
of Name

Paddy had found that the best way to give quality service in the practice, was to alleviate the fear patients suffered from. He discovered that many of the tools dentists used had names that could strike fear into a nervous patient. Tools like an excavator or a carver. He changed them to spoon and plastic ... along with many other 'scary' sounding names, such as a probe. So when he asks the nurse to pass him a spoon, it doesn't incite fear as would an excavator. (Sometimes, it's the little things that make the difference!).

He added a pain meter. A device that is held in the hand of the patient that when pressed, alerts Paddy if the patient is feeling any pain or nervousness.

Add to all this the precise records, birthday cards and over-the-top service he and his staff are constantly now plying on patients and you have a profound example of quality service in action.

This quality approach has established his practice as the absolute leader in his city, and probably the remainder of the country. He is often asked to reveal his methods ... especially on the question of customers *paying their fees in advance*!

Standing your business apart like a Red Striped Zebra means adding the *extra dimension* of quality service ... service made up with a host of extras, presented with a *caring* attitude.

In the Long Run
... it's Consistency

John Gilbody is my coaching partner. He is an acclaimed British business consultant who migrated to Australia in the seventies, earning his living by installing quality assurance programs into corporations. He was one of the main players in the AUS-MEAT metamorphosis. Today, he works with our clients in installing the Red Striped Zebra program.

John has a special way of explaining what the concept of quality is, and how it can make a huge difference in a business's performance. A simple example is performed as he asks the potential client to sign their name on a sheet of paper. After they have done this he then asks them to sign their name again, and keep doing so for about thirty times, one under the other. Together, they then examine the first and last signatures.

I have never seen this done without noting a *large* discrepancy from the first signature to the last. The signatures are not consistent.

Consistency Wins

The concept of quality is to build in consistency. The very first product or service, must be identical to the last. A production line must produce a finished product that is consistent, whether it is number one, one hundred or twenty thousand and one.

In the application of quality in your Red Striped Zebra business, you must undertake to supply quality on a consistent basis ... 'every day' of the working year.

One
Fatal Slip

One slip can lose you business. If a business supplies shoddy service just once, say perhaps on one particular evening in a restaurant, the table of customers who receive that poor service may mentally bar the restaurant from their minds. Worse still, they may tell their friends of the bad experience, even though normally the restaurant performs well.

I have read food critics who have blasted the food or service of *favorite* restaurants of mine in their newspaper columns. And yet these restaurants have *consistently* delivered good food, coupled with very friendly, quality service. Discussions with the owners have shown that the food critics have shown up on extremely busy nights, where staffing had become a problem in both the kitchen and table service. They convinced me ... but what of the many thousands who read the scathing remarks?

A Red Striped Zebra business must present quality *consistently,* from the first to the last. If mistakes are made, then all is not lost. A caring letter sent to the client or customer, with a sincere apology and a small gift will sometimes do more than win back a confidence. It can cement a long-lasting relationship. If a slip is made it sometimes can be caught on-the-spot ... with remedies immediately undertaken.

Staying with the restaurant example, how often have you eaten at a restaurant and have been kept waiting for service, or your order was not quite right? A restaurant with its quality service well in place will *catch* the slip, and supply another product, adjust the bill, supply an apology, and perhaps give a gift certificate to *guarantee the return* of the customer.

If they understood the long-term *value* (CLTV) of a customer, these small adjustments that might result in a loss, will be *inconsequential* to the final result of converting a customer into a long-term client.

Glaring Gaps

Look around today and what do you see. Do you see any *glaring* gaps in service in businesses you frequent? Do you notice any inferior or uncaring service? Are all products superior, or do you see inferior products, lacking quality? I do not have to tell you. You can see for yourself. The gaps are wide in promised service and quality products ... and what you actually receive.

- *As mentioned at the beginning, the research shows that a 'majority' of large corporations have failed at incorporating quality and in making it 'felt' at the customer's end.*

And ......

- *Small businesses are not geared toward the 'structured' approach of a quality assurance program.*

That leaves the field wide open ... *A real gold mine for the astute Red Striped Zebra business person who decides to install quality and increase results.*

How
to Start

▸ Start with discussions and agreements with your staff and like-minded colleagues.

▸ Interview customers and ask them what 'they' would like to receive from your business.

▸ Plan, generate and implement ideas that can be used on an ongoing, everyday basis. (Such as the stress and happiness meter).

▸ Adopt creative and innovative strategies and procedures for quality service.

▸ Work towards having every person in your firm agree and to 'sign on' to *saturate* the business with quality and over-the-top service.

▸ And meet regularly to monitor what is being done and what results (from the customer's viewpoint) are being achieved.

316

We provide awesome service

Beck's Hardware of Launceston Tasmania, a huge hardware complex, asked us to provide specialized training for their people. Quality in customer service was one of the areas we focussed on, and the *philosophy* of 'awesome service' was undertaken.

After a few weeks, I was walking through the store and found it amusing (and satisfying) to discover a newly painted and erected sign that read; ***We provide awesome service!*** It was positioned *behind* the counter, away from customer's eyes, but in the *full view* of the staff. It was their reminder of the *type* of quality service to supply on an ongoing, daily basis ... and a reminder to them that they had gotten the message.

You and your Red Striped Zebra business has new knowledge. You now know that customers care little about you, your business, your business name, how big you are, how much stock you have, how long you've been in business. They only care about their own needs, desires, wants and feelings ... and they are now armed with the new weapon called; *choice*. Choice means *alternative* or *preference*. They use it at will and will buy from your business if you give them what they want ... or *immediately* go to an *alternative* if you don't.

It is now deemed necessary that quality must be 'in the blood' or in the philosophy of a firm, from management to the front-line staff... rather than a formal rule book.

You also now realize that customers are better educated, discerning and sophisticated. They do *not* want to be pressured, cheated, haggled with or treated without care. They *do* want to be treated exactly same way in which you would choose to treat your mother ... with quality!

Realize the field is wide open for establishing your business as the leader. Simply start by introducing over-the-top quality into your service, products and business. Then, your business will be as Unique as a Red Striped Zebra!

Open the Temple Doors - it's WAR!

How to tap your creative genius within to generate business-breakthrough solutions for your business

We're in an age of revolutionary change. And in a world in chaos. Chaotic change means uncertainty. It's a time that calls for creativity and innovation in our thinking in order to thrive in business.

Is there better ways for a Red Striped Zebra business manager to think and act? The ancients had a method that was superb and has been adopted by corporate Japan. Learn this new thinking style that will open many creative doors of opportunity for you.

Janus was an interesting god of ancient Rome! Two-faced actually! And yet what we 20th Century sojourners think as a character flaw, the Romans considered this a vital *asset* to their nation's welfare. So too do the Japanese!

Janus had his own temple with two opposing doors, and these doors were only opened in times of war. He was the Roman god of war who was crafted with two faces, each looking the opposite way through the opened doors. The concept provided the Romans with a *symbolic reminder* that in any dangerous situation, such as war when the country is at risk, *all* viewpoints had to be considered and weighed accordingly, before reaching any decision. No opinionated war generals here, no self-serving politicians, no power hungry dictators ... and no loud-mouths with all the answers were tolerated.

Two-faced
January

The first month of the year is our January. Named after Janus, it is the month that looks *back* on the old year, and *forward* to the new.

What a concept, what an eye-opener for the release of creative thought to difficult decisions in life and business. To take on the attributes of January and *look both ways* in decision making or problem solving. To weigh *every possibility*, *every opportunity*, and not unleash rapid opinions or judgements until all the facts are considered.

Seeking *everyone's* information, viewpoint or input *before* reaching a decision. It's almost a foreign concept in our world, and yet, to become a Red Striped Zebra we 'must' be open to every idea, notion, concept, thought and opinion.

Compare this to our highly competitive world of today. If we have an idea we race to register it, or trademark it. Sitting at a conference table we may break out in a sweat if we do not get our opinion heard, and many times we have to listen to the loud-talking opinionated manager, department head, general or power hungry dictator who may command and overpower a meeting. Any person come to mind? I know plenty ... and they are the ones who seem to be the very obstacles to incorporating Red Striped Zebra principles into a business. Bring on Janus!

The role of Janus prevailed to facilitate the making of difficult decisions!

Are the principles of pagan gods any use to us in business today? You be the judge!

Japan and Janus

Japan, as usual, has snatched an amazing thinking strategy from under our noses, using it to the fullest. We still wander around in a daze wondering how they have come so far with so little. We cannot understand how 70% of all U.S. businesses which undertake *Total Quality Management* fail at its inception within two years, while Japan sails merrily along with its Quality Assurance programs well in place. Why?

It's all to do with good old Janus!

Before we explore this further, let's leave Rome for a moment and visit war-torn Japan in the late Forties. An emperor had run this country. *No Janusian thinking allowed!* Power from the *top*, no exceptions! That power contributed to destroying this great nation.

A Broken Land
and People

Japan has a land mass that covers about the same area as

Tennessee, broken into islands and only half habitable, yet it now supports 110 million people. The outlook was grim at that time for a defeated people. They had no natural resources, were occupied by a foreign force, (the United States), for the next nine years since war's end. Even the women weren't allowed to possess kitchen knives in their homes, such being the rules of defeat.

Two atomic bombs had devastated the land, along with conventional bombing, and many of its young men had died during the long war. How could it possible break free and become a Red Striped Zebra and position itself in years to come as a world leader?

In business today, many people declare bankruptcy when things go bad, or cry foul when a large aggressive competitor moves into their town. When customers cease buying, or the economy falters, some business people have terrible times just trying to stay afloat. Yet Japan rose from the ashes to become *a world power in only forty years.*

We can point the finger to identify certain clues to their metamorphosis, such as:

- *The rejection of W. Edward Deming's principles of 'quality' by the U.S. and the ready acceptance of him by Japan.*

That was a catalyst, for sure.

- *Then there was the 'copying' of western products and technology by Japan. That gave them a start ... but somehow I believe they would have made it anyway. (It was the SONY corporation which lead the way into miniaturization and advanced creativity in electronics ... not by copying but by being innovative leaders.).*

But, a copy, (or even quality assurance), doesn't necessarily produce a world leader. The answer is found in the very way Japanese people differ to western people ... and their acceptance of *Janusian* thinking.

People ...
the True Resource

True, Japan had no resources, except one; its people! A lot of them! And a visit to a Japanese corporate meeting, or an office, reveals much about these people, their style and how true Janusian thinking operates.

In a business meeting we complain if the meeting goes over time. Japanese meetings go on for endless hours, with *every* person giving their *input* of information, *not* opinions. Participants could be from the factory floor through to the plant's or firm's management, yet *each* person is asked for information on the subject being discussed.

Gleaning
From All

After this plethora of information flows, what finally filters out of the meeting is the direction and strategies they undertake. No 'one' person gives opinions, tries to point score, acts aggressively to force decisions ... *it's every person's input and it's true Janusian thinking at work.*

So too are their office spaces fine examples of Janusian thinking at work. No walled offices, no shut doors, no partition screens. Just a *sea of desks* in large open spaces. And constant communication or exchange of information taking place throughout.

How very different in our world. We must 'make appointments' to meet each other, even on the same office floor. Many doors are kept closed, exchanges of information can be hindered if *private agendas* are present, and many people are only told details or news if their superiors deem it fit to share.

The 'global picture' of many businesses is understood, viewed and shared solely by the top echelon. (Power from the top) The 'minnows' are kept in the dark with tied hands.

How the west was lost

During a recent consultancy with a very large corporation, I was told that although the firm had installed Total Quality Management into the firm, some *700 middle managers hadn't thoroughly embraced the concept*. This caused a breakdown in the desired results.

It is a known fact that if a business wants to succeed at installing quality, 'management' must adopt it wholeheartedly ... This is so true! However, any business the west has *lost* to foreign competition can many times be directly attributed to being inflexible. Not being open, creative nor unable to release the reigns to give the business horse its head.

Seven hundred managers may have 700 fixed opinions, (*"We've always done it this way before!"*), 700 private agendas and 700 egos fueled by the western world's culture of climbing the corporate ladder to success ... and many times it's dog eat dog. These 700 problematic thinkers can hinder the growth of the business - as it did in this firm's experience.

Colonel Sanders launched an empire with his *secret ingredient*! (And it wasn't just his 11 herbs and spices!). The Japanese have it; and that secret is *Janusian Thinking!* But many western businesses fail at installing either Total Quality Management, or in making sales and growing, simply because they do not have the *Janusian Thinking ingredient* that melds *thought processes* and *corporate goals* into one.

---

*The lesson to be learned as an open-minded Red Striped
Zebra manager is to Janusianize your thinking
to gain maximum results in your business.*

The quality gurus state that the embracing of long-term, continuous improvement toward an end result, along with *total loyalty to the firm*, does not sit well with our western psyche. Japanese place their corporations *first* in importance, not their ego's, opinions or ladder climbing. They work as a *united* force of people in *full agreement*, wading through a sea of information and input toward a goal of corporate success.

Janusian Thinking for a Red Striped Zebra

The very essence of Janusianism excites me! Why? Simply because it does wonders for a business. It releases the brakes, opens the mind and allows Red Striped Zebra strategies and philosophy to flourish.

- *It opens the door to <u>possibility</u> thinking. (It prevents the negative; "Always done it this way" or "That won't work" statements from being made. It stops the 'old' dinosaur thinking in its tracks.*

- *It means that if there is one face, one viewpoint, perhaps one belief about a business problem, then there 'must' be an opposing face, opposing viewpoint, or an <u>opposing answer</u> to that problem. It forces people to 'look' for that answer.*

- *It breaks the <u>mind-set of limitations</u>. All things become possible. New sales goals and records, new products, new services and new heights become possible. (Even taking on the 'giants' of competition and beating them ... every time. That worked for Japan, didn't it?)*

- *It <u>overcomes obstacles</u> by forcing you to search for the opposing view. From raising finances to finding great staff, finding new customers to finding new ways to promote, advertise and market ... it makes you look in 'unconventional' areas to find a way around, over or through your obstacles.*

- *It makes you look through doors you never would have thought about before. Janus has two doors to look through, not just one. There are <u>many ways</u> to look and travel through, not just one fixed, old and worn-out doorway.*

A Red Striped Zebra by nature *must* embrace Janusian thinking. It is the thinking that helps you to survive and thrive. It provides new directions and opportunities to magically present themselves.

Look
Out!

Take an example of a company that wasn't practicing Janusian thinking; *National Cash Register.* They controlled 70% of its market at one stage - but management wasn't looking 'both' ways ... as good Janusian managers should.

If they had done so they would have understood that the industry was changing rapidly, from metal strongboxes to electronic inventory devices. The new technology swept through and swamped them. In four years flat, old-style registers went from 90% to 10% of the market. NCR laid off 20,000 workers! Ouch!

The Janusian thinking company looks *both* ways ... because of the rapid changes taking place and fierce emerging competition they do *not* want to be blind-sided like NCR. These are the businesses which want to *create* and *cause* change ... not be beaten by it!

As Rome did - so must you!

As Rome used Janus in times of war, you must also use Janusian thinking in this war of rapid change and fierce competition.

Use it to know what the enemy is doing, to see both ways, to see what is happening in your industry, to discover what the customer wants, to view every problem from every angle, to listen to every person's input ... and to finally become leader of the pack!

Japan followed Rome's example - so should you!

326

Who is
in Control?

Applied to everyday business, Janusianism will *force* change. Today's businesses are forced into change by the current *circumstances* that are upon them. People have had to learn to use computers, facsimile machines, cellular phones, the Internet and high technology, whether they like it or not. Because of the unrelenting competition they've had to learn to advertize all over again, learn to serve the customer better, and learn to provide better quality products.

> *Janusian thinking replaces the*
> *'circumstances of change' with its own*
> *'rule book', and its own methodology.*

By 'pro-actively' adopting its concepts, you gain control of your business, because Janus *forces* you to use two faces ... and take the time to look at opposing views. Far better than being *forced* to change by change itself!

It's WAR!

Business is war! Your enemies are your competing forces of competition. The grounds you capture are customers, sales and profit.

With the temple doors wide open, and Janus looking out through each door, you have a new thinking tool to look at every aspect of your battle plan. You can weigh each idea and strategy without prejudice or influence. You can break the restraints of 'tunnel vision', simply because for every viewpoint you have, you *must* find an opposing view to balance your thinking. That's the main rule;

> *You 'must' find an opposite viewpoint*
> *to balance your original view.*

What If?

It's the 'what if' principle. *"What if we did this instead of that?"* *"What if we tried (advertising, selling, promoting, hiring, firing, financing, acquiring etc.) this way ... instead of that?"*

As you address every problem and opportunity, these two opposing viewpoints pre-empt future change. You become your own vehicle for rapid and radical change. No longer would you look at an opportunity and immediately say; *"That will not work because ...."*

You would no longer allow yourself (or your team) the luxury of a fixed opinion, or an ego. The game is too serious now for that. You are building a Red Striped Zebra business and you should now demand change on your terms ... through Janusian Thinking.

> *Janusian Thinking*
> *It's the art of*
> *weighing all the*
> *pros and cons to*
> *any given situation.*

Seeds of Imagination

Imagination is very important to business development, as is solving problems and generating ideas. A Red Striped Zebra by nature has to become very *imaginative*. And imagination is magic, for it manufactures a seed of an idea that can grow to become a mighty tree of success.

A Dumb Idea ...
or a Seed of Imagination?

Federal Express of Memphis was such a seed of imagination. Frederick Smith imagined a business that flew overnight packages across the length and breadth of the country. And as I write this passage the corporation has recently secured routes in Asia and is now working on South America. *The World on Time!*

> *What tiny a seed of imagination*
> *grew such a mighty giant!*

Smith asked Frank Maguire, who was later to become Senior Vice President of Industrial Relations, to come to Memphis and talk about a position with Federal Express.

Maguire asked what was the idea. Smith told him he wanted to bring a plane full of packages to Memphis, load them on other planes and fly them off again to other places. Frank told me that he thought that sounded like a dumb idea ... at first!

Find
a Sucker

Howard Putnam, whom at the time was Group VP Marketing for United Airlines, told me they had been trying to sell their old fleet of Boeing 727-100 convertible (from cargo to passenger) aircraft without success. Then along came some 'sucker' from Memphis, Tennessee, named Fred Smith, with his 'dumb idea' package company ... and he bought all of those planes!

His 'dumb idea' corporation has not only become the major player, but its name has become a verb. We now *Fedex* our packages. Not bad for an imaginative seed.

Every time I'm in my hometown of Sydney, Australia, I marvel at the finest piece of architecture I've ever seen; the Sydney Opera House. What is more amazing is that they built the building back in the Sixties, and with its shiny, white sail-shaped roof it looks as though it sailed back in time from somewhere out of the third millennium. A seed of imagination that has grown to endow Sydney harbor with a world-class logo of beauty.

Seeds of imagination, seeds of creative thought,
an open mind to go where no others dare.

That's your role as a Red Striped Zebra business.

Inside
Stripes

Who said a Red Striped Zebra business must be just 'outward' in its appearance? You must be red striped on the *inside* too!

A mind as sharp as a razor, generating creative seeds of imagination is as *necessary* to you as the outward appearance of your business. As the *architect* of your business future, you should release your mind to design thoughts as big as Federal Express, or the Sydney

Opera House. The size, direction and scope of your business should have *no imposed limits*. It should be *limitless*. It should be endowed with the most creative thought processes possible.

As the third millennium takes shape your seeds of imagination should help you design a business ... the likes of which has never been seen before! No more rules, no more 'norms', no set standards to follow. You forge your *own* industry breakthroughs!

> *You are the Red Striped Zebra business person.*
> *You set your OWN standard, direction and pace.*

Is it
There Yet?

The Results Corporation, an Australia consulting firm, is awash with imaginative seeds.

One of these seeds germinated in the form of desiring to make an impression on clients who order audio-cassette programs. They box the programs in a distinctive packaging material to make an impression, then overnight the package. The following day at 3.00pm a staff member calls to ask; *"Is it there yet?"* Wow, that makes an impression of over-the-top service and it is a simple strategy that arose from a *seed of imagination*.

Pyramex, a client of ours, developed a mailing tube to house samples of their products they send to their distributors. This tube is covered in a wrapper resembling money (dollar notes), with the words imprinted as a headline; *Make More Profit With Pyramex*. It grabs attention and helps them enhance their U.M.P. to their distributors. Just another *imaginative seed* germinated in a marketing meeting that sets them apart from the crowd. (The 'brown' cardboard box - black and white Zebra crowd.).

Imaginative seed, creative thinking, and innovation should drive your Red Striped Zebra business!

Whether you're designing world-class business operations, opera houses or a better way to impress and wow customers, they all come from *creative seeds of imagination*.

A simple spark of thought has designed *everything* on the face of this earth. You too can let imagination rule in your business and generate ideas, (great ideas), that will make you look 'different' from the crowd. Perhaps your imaginative seeds can grow as big as Fedex's ... but even if it was only a small seed that addressed the color or design on your packaging, or an imaginative seed that helped your customers pay their bills quicker - if it makes an impression and adds to the value of your U.M.P. ... then you've done well!

The Intuitive Red Striped Zebra

Professor Weston Agor, of the University of El Paso, is one of the leading researchers on *intuitive processes* in business today.

Each year many researchers, academics and business people attend a conference on 'intuition'. *The Global Intuition Network (G.I.N.)* is an organization that stands at the cutting-edge in researching and presenting this amazing power ... and yet the very thought, or mention of 'intuition' in business makes people uneasy with a feeling that they're not on *stable* ground.

As we are rapidly learning to tap the genius-mind within, various areas of research are honing in on their specialities, giving us discoveries of our awesome potential.

We are finding that *intuition, perception, gut-feelings* and *hunches* in business are indeed real, and should be acknowledged.

Business Hunches,
Gut-feeling, Perception
... and Intuition

Research demonstrates that an *intuitive* thought about a particular business problem is formed from a 'package' of information. If listened to and acted upon, this intuitive thought will usually give true answers. As crazy as it may seem, over our entire life, *every* piece of

331

information, every daily event we have been exposed to, has been stored in vivid detail for *all* time in the mind, according to the neuroscientists.

This wealth of information is combined with the present situation we are involved in. All the sounds, color, numbers, problems, opportunities, people, ideas and comments presented to us combine with our past wealth of knowledge and experience. We then 'experience' an answer, presented to us as a hunch, gut-feeling, perception ... or an intuitive thought.

Acted upon, this information is usually the correct path for us to take action on.

In standing apart from the crowd we need *all* our senses to be finely tuned. A Red Striped Zebra would need to ... and so should you! The prowling Lions of competition are out there, watching!

Intuitive process is one of those necessary senses. The research is now demonstrating that we can learn to develop our intuition. Simple exercises such as guessing what letters, and how many, will arrive in the mail each day ... or who may be calling when the telephone rings, help develop this skill. Visualizing situations before sleeping and then expecting an answer to a tricky problem upon waking is another method.

Learning to listen to that deep *inner voice,* that deep feeling in the gut, that little quiet thought in the back of your mind ... these are all intuitive processes at work. The biggest problem we face though is in separating these intuitive insights from the hurley-burley of life. The fast-paced, noisy world tends to block our reception to intuitive processes. Learning to be quiet, to be still, to meditate and allow your genius within to generate answers, takes practice, and discipline. But, when you take the time, tune in to what your mind is advising you ... and learn to act upon that advise. Why? Because ...

Intuition is your helpmate in times of tough decision making!

Creative and Lateral Thinking at Work

Edward DeBono leads the field in Lateral Thinking. The highly esoteric thinking process that either leaves us confused, or opens the door to new fields of opportunity in business. But, creative thinking doesn't have to be difficult. It simply means finding an unusual answer to a problem that looks difficult or unsolvable.

We marvel at men like Donald Trump, who construct breathtaking buildings, then end in a sea of unmeasurable debt. When we think he's 'finished' he rises again like a Phoenix to build more stupendous buildings and projects. That's creative (and unstoppable) genius at work!

He uses it to either design fabulous apartments or hotels, or uses creativity to solve the debt crisis he was faced with. It's the *same* creative thinking process, but applied to either *generate amazing projects*, or *overcome horrendous problems*.

A business which stands apart like a Red Striped Zebra must exist on creative thinking every day. It cannot survive on processes, or on half-hearted programs. It must be *constantly* changing, adjusting and trying new strategies and ideas ... all generated by creative thought.

Creative
Helicopters

Some years back I was contracted by a helicopter business to assist with growth. The business was operating two large Sikorsky Sea Kings, doing tourist sight seeing on the Gold Coast in Australia. Business had not been brisk and their competition was operating smaller craft in choice locations at lower costs. They needed to go *outside the box* in their thinking. Applied creativity was the order for this business.

Blanch, from the *Golden Girls* TV show states; *"If you want to find a man, you go to where the men are. At the hardware store!"*

That makes sense ... (Blanch always does!). In this case, if the helicopter business wanted to find the people (customers) to ride the big birds they needed to go where the people were.

Champagne
Flights

The first 'creative' strategy we developed was to offer a *champagne flight* from the city of Brisbane, 40 minutes away, and land in the middle of the Gold Coast horse race track for the *Magic Million* race day. This would be similar to taking a helicopter into the grounds on the day of the Kentucky Derby.

That was where the people were. Why just try to 'copy' the other guys, offering the 'norm' ... i.e. sightseeing trips along the beach. No, to thrive in business the Red Striped Zebra firm must operate away from the herd of black and whites.

Next Trick -
Promote Creatively

So, here is this fabulous way to travel to the grand races in style. But, how do you reach the people and make them an offer they can't refuse? In the newspaper *racing form* of course. People who attend races read racing forms don't they?

We placed a response-driven style display advertisement right in the middle of the form, (where it couldn't be missed) showing the big Sikorsky and offering an impressive luxury flight to the races.

Response was great and those helicopters were full of race fans who were showered with champagne. And not only did they ride to the races in style, but the *feelings of importance* they had when they disembarked in the middle of the race track in sight of sixty thousand people was the *real winner* for them.

The helicopter firm won by giving the people what they wanted ... a pride trip in style! It was no longer a joy ride firm, but a supplier of image and prestige! And an added bonus was the television coverage of the impressive turbine powered 'copters landing and disembarking passengers. All because of some creative or lateral thinking in action.

What creative idea could you do to
bring joy, pride, prestige and the feeling
of winning, to your customers?

The next 'creative' strategy was to take the helicopters to the holiday makers ... right at their hotel and resorts. We arranged for a craft to hover just above the water in front of a resort where people were relaxing, while ground crew distributed brochures offering special luxury tours. I must admit, that was impressive and a little scary! Sea Kings are not like normal helicopters. They are big! And they make a lot of noise. A large crowd gathered just to watch this spectacle ... but the concept worked. These escapades brought the awareness of luxury 'copter flights to the forefront in people's minds.

Turning the problem around, i.e. taking the helicopter to the people rather than expecting the people to come to the helicopter pad was the creative twist. Its a little bit of Janusian thinking (seeing both sides) and a little lateral thinking.

Double Glazing
With Creativity

This same creative twist was incorporated in the marketing strategy of Roxburgh Windows, a Scottish client. They faced the dilemma of trying to grow their business in an industry suffering from bad press. An industry that has many high-pressured tele-marketers calling prospects at every hour of the day to sell double-glazing.

To give potential customers a Perception of Value Education (POVE) about Roxburgh, its products and people, we *took the business to the people*, rather than try to get the people to come to Roxburgh.

Through a 'you get' style newsletter we built into the pages the *full story* of the firm. We included photographs of workers in the factory, the sales staff, even the receptionist. We pulled out all the stops to 'personalize', 'individualize' and 'humanize' the business.

We showed the manufacturing process, the quality of products and even the installation team. *Trust* had to be *built* (to overcome the damage done by all those crooked tele-marketers and unscrupulous double-glazing firms) and the firm needed to present itself as a caring, quality business supplying the finest in Scottish craftsmanship.

While all the other window firms play by the 'industry' rules, Roxburgh forged their own rule book, and since gained an increase in acceptance, customers and sales.

Speed-of-light
Change

Many business people think of Creative or Lateral thinking as a gimmick. Something not to be taken too seriously, or to be tried for a little while then discarded when the next book, seminar or idea comes along. For the number crunching, hard-nosed accountant type personality, it is even more of an anathema ... because it can't be measured ... or it interferes with 'old and tried' business practices. It should *not* be so! Why, because the ages have changed.

The world has undergone a number of revolutionary periods or ages that have changed the thinking processes of every group of people on the planet who went through those times. And the business world is also transforming and changing rapidly. In fact, today's method of doing business is not so very old. Just decades! Since the end of the Second World War we've developed the 'modern' marketing, advertising and promotional techniques that mold our lives daily. Prior to that time, business was done at a more relaxed and subdued pace. Certainly not an 'in-your-face' way as we see today.

But, even though today's business seems to be 'set' in concrete, the way we do business is about to once again go through revolutionary and radical change. Will you be ready? If your business is a Red Striped Zebra, underpinned with Creative, Lateral and Janusian Thinking, you will be!

- *The agricultural age has come and gone.*
- *The industrial revolution changed the world, but it's over.*
- *The electronic age turned our lives around for a time.*
- *Then came the information age. (Many think we're still in it).*

Now, we're in the age of the mind!

A time when all is ruled by speed-of-light change!

This age *demands* creativity to stay ahead. Business will *not* be the same in two, three or five years time ... and in ten years we will hardly recognize anything.

Soaring young populations South of the Equator, aging populations North of it, (every 7 seconds someone turns 50 in the United States), an explosion of the World Wide Web in doing business, the forming of the European Economic Community, the rising of the Asian tiger nations, the forming of N.A.F.T.A., the privatising and selling of education ... and a host of new business practices will change this world forever. There is no room for the fixed minded manager. There is only room for the creative thinker. Will you be one?

One thing is sure,
Spaceship Earth
has no more room
for passengers
... only crew!

Obsolete
Business Practices

Dr. Robert Kriegel, author of *If It Ain't Broke, Break It!* states that 40% of all *current* business practices and knowledge are forecast to be *obsolete* within the decade.

Other reports have indicated that the knowledge of the world *doubles* every two years, but I have just heard that this is now down to every *nine* months. Wow! Where on earth are we headed?

The only way you can stay ahead is to *create afresh* every day. It requires creative thinking and idea generation every day, applied to every area of your business, from the mail room to the boardroom. It certainly means creative re-invention of your business - daily!

Stimulate, Activate and Arouse
YOUR Creative Genius

How do you awaken your creative genius? And do you have a creative genius within? The answers to these questions are simple. You do have creativity on board. Dr. Richard Bergland's book; *The Fabric of the Mind*, and many other writings from the world's leading Neuroscientists attest to the fact that the human brain is capable of genius levels of operation. While ever your right hemisphere of your brain exists, you have a powerful laboratory that can produce the most magnificent ideas, solutions and goals. That's what it's there for. Your creative, genius side.

Increase Your Genius Level
by Balancing the Hemispheres

Our western world is basically left-brain trained and rewarded. We pay the most rewards to the lawyer, accountant, financial advisor and banker, and the lowest rewards to the artist, sculptor, poet and musician.

We give priority in schools and college to those subjects that are *left* hemisphere, such as mathematics and science, and low priority to the art or music classes ... the right hemisphere. This *de-educating of the mind* has led us to a nation that functions with a small portion of our true potential.

However, research scientists have found that children who are given a well-balanced program of both left and right hemisphere classes have an *overall rise* is scholastic improvement. And in fact, the great geniuses of old, such as Einstein, Galileo, Marconi etc. were very accomplished in not just their left, but also in their right hemisphere activities, leading to the belief that true genius can be tapped by having a *balanced usage* of both hemispheres of the brain. Einstein as an example was an accomplished violin player and artist.

This all means that if we truly want to be creative, we must learn to play more. Use the right hemisphere more, not just the 'business' left. We need to paint, roller-blade, go fishing ... or whatever captures your interest. Doing so, will enable your brain to work better ... and help you generate ideas faster. It works!

Mind Charting
Your Way to Success

In seminar I have taught many methods to arouse and awaken creative thought processes. I teach visualization as one. Learning to deeply relax and visualize in vivid detail the situation at hand usually produces amazing new ideas and strategies.

Mind charting is another!

Using large sheets of whiteboard paper fastened to the walls, and writing your plans, ideas, goals and analysis of problems with *colored* (not just black) felt tip pens, electrifies the right hemisphere. It responds to color, sight, shapes, objects and the abstract. It puts you into the realm of the artist as you paint your problems or information onto those sheets. The right hemisphere responds and lets ideas flow as you map your way around the sheets. Having the added participation of other people power-boosts the session and very creative ideas soon flow.

This method is really profound, for it allows coffee breaks to be taken ... and when you return the ideas are *still* on paper in vivid detail. (Unlike a normal meeting where most things are forgotten!). New ideas that come to mind during or after the coffee breaks, or even the next day, can be added or expanded upon. And in the end your creative thinking processes will give you some powerful and potent strategies and answers for your business. From there, summary sheets can be typed and distributed to participating members.

We've used this idea generating tool for years. Why, because it works! And it should become a *thinking tool* for your Red Striped Zebra business.

If this is the age of the mind (and it is!), then to make you business a Red Striper requires much mind usage.

Creative ideas, innovation, uniqueness are all thought processes from within. You can take the field if you realize this and let your ideas flow!

Janusian Thinking, Seeds of Imagination, Intuition, Lateral and Creative Thinking

These thinking processes will give you a 'kit of tools' to use in your business. They'll give you:

- *The ability to look at different perspectives in business, as would Janus.*

- *The ability to grow tiny seeds of vivid imagination into mighty business trees.*

- *The ability to develop your intuitive processes, gut feelings, hunches and perception.*

- *And the ability to develop creative thinking processes to apply to your business everyday.*

These are the thinking tools you should use as you Red Stripe Zebraize your business.

... And the tools you use to break free from those who choose to remain behind with the herd.

In Full Gallop

Remember R.P. Adam Ltd., the Scottish chemical firm? As at the writing of this book this firm had just completed a trade show exhibit in Birmingham, England. With apprehension the management had initially booked space, designed the booth, assigned staff, printed brochures and undertook a direct-mail support campaign. They were not convinced that trade shows were fruitful ... because past experience had proven to be both costly and unfruitful.

But that was before the Red Striped Zebra program.

Now, they had moved into phase two. For some time they had been going through their *metamorphosis*. Becoming a Red Striped Zebra business. The trade show was the emergence, the 'showing the world' how different they now really were. A Century old firm that had totally transformed!

At the show they were to compete with literal 'giants' in their industry. The 'big boys' ... the corporate giants. Firms that had vast resources of money to spend on trade shows. Neon and laser type exhibits. But, as they soon found, even bright colored lights does not, a Red Striped Zebra make!

Getting
in the Spirit

We allowed them to use our Zebra herd logo as the back drop of the exhibit ... enlarged to seven meters long. (That's big!). The staff wore waistcoats with red stripes to get 'in the spirit' for the event. (See the photograph featured on the inside flap of this book's jacket cover.). The brochures featured Zebras ... and the whole theme was to tell potential new distributors how 'different' they really were from the other guys ... and what the firm could literally *do for them* to help make their businesses grow. A far cry from the 'we are great' crowd!

The Results
Came In

For three days they were inundated. Thousands attended this humongous trade show ... and thousands stopped by to talk ... attracted by all this Red Striped Zebraism. Attendees were taking photographs of the booth everyday ... and at show's end the firm had captured over *one hundred potential new distributors* to carry the R.P. Adam torch!

Icing to
the Cake

But, to add icing to the cake, the show organizing committee stopped by and awarded the firm a huge trophy for being the best exhibitor. Photographs were taken of the presentation, hands shaken ... and the comment was; *"It's firms like yours that make this annual show so successful!"* Bloody brilliant!

Now, of course, I insisted that we receive copies of these presentation photographs, plus photographs of the booth, for our newsletters and seminar coaching, but what made this roaring success an example worthy for inclusion in this end section, was this: ...

- *Proof positive that the Red Striped Zebra program gets great results ... as witnessed in this exhibition.*

- *Further ongoing results as we expose and expand the firm to a wider audience via Zebra marketing.*

- *But, more importantly; the Zebra thinking 'attracts' people! In this case, thousands ... with over a hundred potential new distributors ... and many new customers!*

It was not always the case. Many trade shows in the past were dismal and costly. The results were not there. But the Red Striped Zebra program helped them become 'attractive' to people.

So, do you 'get' it? The key word here is *attract*. The whole zebra program is to attract ... making **your** business a Red Striped Zebra firm will cause it to **attract more** customers, clients, patients, guests ... people!

- *Once attracted, if you put in place all that you've read, they'll reach the inescapable conclusion that your business is their 'preferred' choice ... and the only one worth buying from.*

Other clients also 'get in the spirit' with the Zebra program, in that they too *dress* the part. The folk at *Pyramex Safety Products,* (from the President down), all dress in red and white striped t-shirts that feature the company name and zebra logo, every Thursday. Just a simple, but truly effective reminder on a selected day of the week that they are *different* from all others ... and a reminder to 'do' things *differently.*

You do not have to dress in stripes, wear red striped waistcoats or take this program and *go the full zebra*. What you are encouraged to do is to undergo a perceptive mind-shift. To make *your* business different. Make it unique. Make it innovative and creative. And in essence ...

Dare to break your business free
and break the success barrier

... like a Red Striped Zebra

About the Author

Neill Newton is Australian.

He is an acclaimed speaker, coach, author and writer.

He presents his zebra message to hundreds of business people, on three continents. And leads a team of high profile business development specialists in coaching clients in seminars, consultancies, boot camps ... and via printed or taped programs.

For over two decades he has pioneered business-innovation strategies to help people attract customers, make more sales and profit. This has culminated in the launching of the *Uniqueness is a Red Striped Zebra*© program.

Want to know more?

Here's a sample of our audio tape programs:

The Magic of Metamorphosis©

At last, a tape program that gives you 'proven' success strategies, rather than just theory!

Here's a powerful four-tape program featuring Neill Newton and Howard Putnam, showing how to transform your business for success.

Howard was the acclaimed CEO of Southwest Airlines who tripled revenue and profits, in just three years.

Neill and Howard spent many hours in studio for you. Now, you'll be able to learn step-by-step breakthrough strategies, such as building a winning image ... to building a winning team by 'hiring attitudes and teaching skills' on this potent four-full-hours of coaching.

It's a definite 'must have' tape program, handsomely finished in a beautiful plastic case, with brilliant artwork by the renowned illustrator; Jeff Lewis. You'll be proud to display this one on your office bookshelf!

© 2000 Newton World Training Inc.

Z e b r a W r i t e ©

Now, at your fingertips you'll have a step-by-step advertising tool to help you make MORE sales!

Here's something entirely different. An audio tape and training manual program to will help you write advertisements that will attract more customers and sales ... every time!

Jerry Crockford, Australia's guru copywriter joins Neill Newton on this program to share all the strategies needed to write potent advertising copy.

Suddenly, after listening to this tape program and studying the manual, you'll be transformed into a powerful copywriter. Jerry is paid many thousands to produce advertising, direct-mail letters, yellow page advertisements and brochures that work. But you can learn all the tricks of the trade for one very low price.

Everything from hot headlines to the close is outlined ... so you will never have to be disappointed by advertising that costs you plenty but just not work.

This program is a must!

Another beautifully illustrated program, to enhance your office.

PlanetZebra ©

A potent program featuring business-boosting strategies from 6 business legends!

Here's a powerful six-tape, six-full-hours of coaching from Neill Newton and these legends:

- *Sir Tom Farmer,* founder and Chairman of Kwikfit fame, the United Kingdom auto repair chain. He started with one small store in 1971 and now has over 1,000 units turning over £500 million per year. Learn from him what it takes to totally delight customers.

- *Jane Pierotti,* the acclaimed national speaker and IBM's first female representative who later became National Product Marketing Director, then Vice President of Marketing for Holiday Inns. Learn how to develop a powerful vision in your business.

- *John Spoelstra,* the nation's top sports marketer and celebrated author of: 'How to Sell Ice to Eskimos'. As President of the New Jersey Nets, he multiplied their worth by 250% in just three years. You'll learn potent concepts to jump-start your business.

- *Howard Putnam.* Once again, this acclaimed CEO of Southwest Airlines has joined Neill on this program to show you how to engineer a new image for your business.

- *Jeff Slutsky,* the famed author of 'Street Fighter Marketing' and highly sought after speaker, shows you how to be creatively successful with a low marketing budget.

- *Dr. Robert Kreigel Ph.D.,* best selling author of 'If It Ain't Broke Break It!' and 'Sacred Cows Make the Best Burgers'. Neill and Robert share with you strategies to eliminate time and money wasters.

Having six legends on one tape program is normally unheard of ... unless of course it's from the Red Striped Zebra collection. Once again, this is a 'must have' ... handsomely finished tape program.

More importantly, it will give you nuggets of gold to use in your business and make more profit.

Newsletters

If you've never before subscribed to a newsletter, here's the ultimate business growth letter you should not miss out on ...

ZebraBrief©

Here's a potent newsletter that focusses on just one thing; business-boosting, Red Striped Zebra style.

- *Each issue is crammed-full of customer attracting strategies, sales increasing formulas, ideas, tips and success case studies.*

Neill Newton shares his potent Red Striped Zebra strategies, along with proven business 'legends' (business owners, marketing wizards, renowned speakers, acclaimed consultants, authors etc.) so you can be assured of a constant source of business-breakthrough tools, arriving in your mail.

High quality and content-rich, you'll be able to build a wealth of information that will give you a winning edge.

And it's a small price for a brief that could be worth thousands to your bottom line. (Call for details as price is subject to change.)

© 2000 Newton World Training Inc.

Seminars and Boot Camps

Here's your opportunity to 'be there in the flesh' ... and to learn first-hand how to make your business boom!

URSZ Program ©

A one-day program, budget priced and time restrained, to suit owners and managers of small to medium sized businesses.

The *Uniqueness is a Red Striped Zebra* concept, philosophy and strategies are introduced and participants are coached by Neill Newton, in an intensive, sleeves-rolled up day.

Break-out sessions, group discussions and the *MindStorm Seat*© are all part of this mind-shifting program that will open up new and exciting sales growth avenues for you.

© 2000 Newton World Training Inc.

CampZebra ©

Prefer more 'intensive', 'personalized' and 'step-by-step' coaching? *CampZebra* is staged at a conference facility over an intensive period (2 ½ days - 20 hours), where participants learn how to transform their businesses for success.

CampZebra also features the *ZebraForce Team*© who work closely with participants, in developing vision, strategic planning, Zebra marketing strategies, idea generation and a plethora of innovative success strategies.

© 1999 Newton World Training Inc.

The RSZ Metamorphosis Camp

The ultimate! Twenty exclusive businesses only in each *Metamorphosis Camp*. Participants are usually familiar with the Zebra program, and immediately move into a full transformation of their businesses.

Creating strategic plans, visions, UMP's, and hands-on business-boosting processes. A complete 'make-over' of artwork, advertising and image is also undertaken during this profound 5 day - 60 hour intensive period, held at a resort complex.

ClubZebra ©

An 'exclusive' membership to *ClubZebra* provides an attractive range of business-building advantages for an annual fee. (paid yearly or monthly debit). For this you receive:

- *A number of hours consultancy via telephone*
- *Free audio tape program of your choosing*
- *A tape per month of an interview or training session*
- *Free subscription to **ZebraBrief** magazine*
- *A 50% discount on any of the above seminars*
- *A 'member's only' seminar once per year*
- *Discounted items from corporate sponsors*
- *A 25% discount on any business-boosting product*

To find out more about these potent business-boosting tools, seminars, private consultancy, tape programs, speaking engagements, or catalogue, etc. please contact:

Newton World Training Inc.
Post Office Box 242023
Memphis 38124 TN

Toll-Free 1-888-683 4244

WWW.PlanetZebra.com

GIFT CERTIFICATE
Worth thousands in new business growth

This certificate entitles you to three (3) full issues of *ZebraBrief*. At your fingertips you'll find each issue crammed-full of customer attracting strategies, sales increasing formulas, ideas, tips and success case studies. So now, you'll be able to apply proven, potent and up-to-the-minute business boosting strategies to your business. A priceless source of business-breakthrough tools, arriving in your mail.

Simply photocopy this page, then mail it attached to a cover letterhead, with your name, title, business, your industry and of course, your mailing address.

Absolutely FREE - but worth thousands in new business